ANNALS

OF THE

Boston Primary School Committee,

FROM ITS

FIRST ESTABLISHMENT IN 1818,

TO ITS

DISSOLUTION IN 1855.

COMPILED BY

JOSEPH M. WIGHTMAN.

BOSTON:
GEO. C. RAND & AVERY, CITY PRINTERS,
1860.

TO

HON. JAMES SAVAGE, LL.D.,

ONE OF THE PRINCIPAL AND MOST ACTIVE ORIGINATORS, AND THE

ONLY SURVIVOR OF THE ORIGINAL OFFICERS OF

THE PRIMARY SCHOOL COMMITTEE,

This Volume is Inscribed,

AS AN EXPRESSION OF THE RESPECT, ESTEEM,

AND VENERATION OF

THE COMPILER.

PRELIMINARY CORRESPONDENCE.

Boston, August 27th, 1859.

Hon. Frederic W. Lincoln, Jr., Mayor :

Dear Sir, — At the final meeting of the Primary School Committee, held on the evening of January 2d, 1855, at which time it ceased to exist as an organized body of the City Government, I presented a brief historical sketch of some of the leading incidents connected with this branch of the Boston Public Schools.

By a vote of the Board, I was requested to have it printed for the use of the members, *if,* in the opinion of the President, Secretary and author, it was deemed expedient. The proviso was added, at my request, as, from the imperfect manner in which the sketch had been prepared, I was unwilling to have it go forth in that form ; and, as nearly all the records and papers relating to the first seven years of the organization had been destroyed, in the office of the Secretary, (James Savage, Esq.,) by a fire in Court street in 1825, I felt apprehensive that to obtain the materials for a correct history would be difficult, if not impossible.

I have, however, been more fortunate in this respect than I anticipated ; and penetrated with a sense of duty to endeavor to correct some of the erroneous views and statements which have been made from time to time in the printed reports and other city documents, in reference to the Primary School Committee, — animated with an increasing interest during the investigation, and a desire to perpetuate the records and acts of an organization so eminently worthy of the respect of the community, I have continued to persevere in my efforts to comply with the vote of my late associates.

The time required to obtain information and verify important facts, without encroaching too much on the avocations of business, and the absorbing cares of public office during the last three years, have combined to delay the final preparation of the work until the present time.

The manuscript is now complete; and if, in your opinion and that of the City Council, it is desirable that these Annals of the Primary School Committee should be printed, in conformity with the vote of the late Primary Board, I shall be most happy to tender it to the City Government as an humble contribution to the history of our Public School system, which, originating in our own city of Boston, has been instrumental in extending the blessings of free education throughout our common country.

With sentiments of respect,

I remain yours truly,

JOSEPH M. WIGHTMAN.

CITY OF BOSTON.

IN BOARD OF ALDERMEN,
August 29th, 1859.

The foregoing communication, from JOSEPH M. WIGHTMAN, having been read to the Board by His Honor the Mayor, it was voted that five hundred copies of the Annals of the Boston Primary Schools be printed.

Attest :

S. F. McCLEARY, CITY CLERK.

PREFACE.

THE object and motives of the compiler in the preparation of these "Annals," are generally set forth in the letter to His Honor the Mayor, tendering the manuscript to the City Government.

A few words, however, appear to be proper, if not necessary, in relation to the origin of the work, and some of the circumstances connected with it.

The compiler was elected a member of the Grammar School Committee for 1847, at which time the agitation in regard to the organization and management of the Public Schools was at its height. Aware of his want of knowledge, it was his endeavor, during the four years he was honored with a seat at the Board, to obtain such information in relation to the operation of the school system as would justify the conservative course he desired to adopt in reference to the changes which were proposed.

Surrounded with experienced and learned associates, and receiving from them a degree of courtesy and attention which deserves the most grateful acknowledgments, it was from no feeling but that of an imperative sense of duty, that any difference of opinion existed between some of them and the compiler, as to the value and expediency of some of the important changes which were proposed to be made in the administration of the schools.

Actuated by a sincere desire to avoid all rash changes in a system of education which had stood the test of time and experience, and having been frequently required to draw up the reports of sub-committees, on important questions, an investigation into the elementary history of our Public Schools became a necessary duty.

The connection of the compiler with the Primary School Committee, at the same time, placed him in the position of a defender of that organization, against the various attacks to which it was subjected, from time to time, for several years previous to its dissolution.

Under these circumstances, was commenced the collection of those facts in relation to the history of the Primary Schools, which are herewith presented. As a historical record for reference, the compiler has endeavored to give the documents and votes in the language of those by whom they were prepared, — particularly in those cases in which accurate information was desirable, for a correct understanding of the condition of the schools at particular times.

Valuable aid and encouragement have been received from numerous friends in obtaining authentic information, and the free use of many original papers and rare printed documents, by means of which the early history of the Primary Schools is rendered comparatively complete.

Since the fire in 1825, the records of the Board have been regularly and correctly kept, and are now in the possession of the Grammar School Committee. These, with the various printed reports and other documents on the city files, being accessible to any interested person, it has been deemed inexpedient to enlarge the present work by extended extracts from those sources, the main object of the compiler having been to preserve those papers upon important subjects, which are in manuscript, or if printed, copies of which are only to be found in the possession of private persons. In the selection of these papers a due regard has been had to the historical facts which they embodied ; and when they have been presented entire, it was because no digest, however carefully made, could do justice to the original.

Those portions relating to the early history of the schools, have been submitted to Hon. James Savage, to whose kindness the compiler is under deep obligations ; and it is to him that he has presumed to dedicate this work, which, however imperfect it may be as a literary production, will at least possess the more important merit — a truthful record.

Boston, *September 27th*, 1859.

ANNALS

OF THE

PRIMARY SCHOOLS.

INTRODUCTORY HISTORY.

In writing the history of the Primary Schools, their connection as a branch of our school system will render a brief historical sketch of the origin and progress of the Public Schools of Boston a proper and interesting introduction.

The Public Schools date their origin almost as far back as the settlement of the town. So early as the "13th of ye 2nd moneth (April), 1635," we find, among other proceedings of " a generall meeting upon publique notice," that "Likewise it was then generally agreed upon yt our brother Philemon Purmont shall be intreated to become scholemaster for the teaching and nourtering of children wth us." A tract of land "thirtie acres" was allotted to him " att a generall meeting ye 14th of ye 10th moneth, 1635, at Muddy River," (now, it is supposed, a part of Brookline), and the grant was confirmed " att a meeting ye 8th of ye 11th moneth, called January, 1637."

Mr. Purmont, however, was not the only " schoolemaster" residing in the town, as it appears, from the record, that "att a meeting ye 17th day of ye 2nd month (April), 1637, it is agreed yt Mr. Danyell Maude, schoolemaster, shall have a garden plott next unto Stephen Kinsley's house plott, upon the condition of building thereon, if neede bee." This "plott" was on the "Neck." Still as there is an incidental mention made, ten years later, of "The Schoolemaster," it may be supposed that Mr. Purmont was alone in the office supported by the town, and that Mr. Maude, if he exercised his profession at all, did it either in the neighborhood or on his own account. According to Snow's History of Boston, Maude lived next south of Mr. Cotton's, in Common Street, afterwards the mansion of Lieut.-Governor Phillips.

Several of the islands in the harbor of Boston having been granted to the town by the General Court of Massachusetts, we find it recorded on the "10th day of ye 11th month, 1641." "It is ordered, that Deare Island shall be improoved for the maintanance of a Free Schoole for the Towne, & such other occasions as ye Townsmen for the time being shall think meet, the sayd Schoole being sufficiently Provided for." The island was soon after entrusted to the care of Capt. Edward Gibbon, "until the Towne doe lett the same." In 1644, it was let for three years, at the rent of £7 per annum, for the use of the school; and again, in 1647, the former lease having expired, it was let for seven years at a rent of £14 per annum, "for the Schoole's use in provision and clothing." In the next year, 1648, this lease was extended to twenty years at the same rent. In 1649, Long and Spectacle Islands were assigned to the use of the school; and the Selectmen were directed to take order that they be leased for the use of the school, at a yearly rent of sixpence on every acre.

This school seems to have been a favorite with the inhabitants from its commencement; and bequests were made for its use in the wills of several individuals. William Phillips, in 1649, " agreed to give 13s. 4d. per annum forever to the use of the Schoole, for the land that Christopher Stanley gave in his will to the Schoole's use." Five hundred acres of land in Braintree were leased at forty shillings per annum for the same use; and about the same time other lands belonging to the town were leased for the same purpose. In 1654, " It is ordered, that the ten pounds left by legacy to ye schoole of Boston by Mis Hudson, deceased, shall be lett to Capt. James Olliver, for 16s. per annum, so long as hee pleases to improve itt." The rents on " Deare Island, Long Island and Spectacle Island, due to ye use of ye schoole," were ordered to be collected, and the " renters " were required to appear yearly and pay their dues. Deer Island was in 1662, leased to Sir Thomas Temple, Knight and " Barronight," for 31 years, at a rent of £14 a year, " to be paid yearly, every first day of March, to the Towne Treasurer for the use of the Free Schoole."

We do not learn from the records when Mr. Purmont ceased his labors here; but in 1650, we find the following record:—" It is also agreed on, that Mr. Woodmansey, ye Schoolemaster, shall have fiftye pounds p. ann. for his Teaching ye Schollers, & his proportion to be made up by ratte." Mr. Woodmansey, whose name appears to have been Robert, is again named, in 1652, on occasion of a sale of land by the town, with reservation to the inhabitants of a right to " enlarge the Skoolehouse ; " and it appears that the house in which he lived was the property of the town, and situated near the school, with only one lot between, which belonged to the schoolhouse. In 1657, the rent of this lot was assigned to him. In 1656, " It is ordered yt ye Selectmen shal have liberty to lay outt a piece of ground outt of ye Towne's land, wch they give to ye building of a house for instruction of ye youth of ye Towne." In the same year, we find an order respecting " building ye Schoolehouse chimney." At this time (1656), it appears that there was but one school supported by the town.

In 1666, the town " agreed with Mr. Dannell Hincheman for £40 per ann. to assist Mr. Woodmansey in the Grammar Schoole, & teach Children to wright, the Yeare to begine the 4th of March, $\frac{6 5}{6}$." Soon after this appointment, Mr. Jones was sent for by the Selectmen, " for keeping a Schoole, & required to perform his promise to the Towne in the Winter, to remove himselfe & familye in the Springe, & forbiden to keep Schoole any longer." From this it would appear that he had opened a school on his own account, which may have interfered with the town school, and consequently was not allowed by the Selectmen.

In 1667, from sickness or some other cause, Mr. Woodmansey appears to have been unable to attend to his duties, and Mr. Benjamin Tompson was " made choice of by the Select Men for to officiate in the place of the Schoolemaster for one Yeare, Mr. Hall being appointed to agree, for tearmes, what to allow hime per annum."

In December, 1669, it was " Ordered, Mr. Raynsford to give notice to Mrs. Woodmansey that the Towne occasions need the use of the Schoole house [probably schoolmaster's house], & to desire her to provide otherwise for her selfe." From this it would appear that Mr. Woodmansey died previously to December, 1669. In March, 1670, " upon the request of Mrs. Margaret Woodmansye, Widdowe, to provide her a house to live in, if she removeth from the Schoole house; it was granted to allow her eight pounds per ann. for that end, dureinge her Widdowhood."

December 22, 1670, we find the first mention in the records of the famous " Master Cheever," who for thirty-eight years after this, exercised so important an influence upon the education of the people of Boston. He died August 21, 1708, " venerable," says Gov. Hutchinson, " not merely for his great age, 94, but for having been the schoolmaster of most of the principal gentlemen in Boston, who were then upon the stage. He is not the only master," adds the governor, " who kept his lamp longer lighted, than otherwise it would have been, by a supply of oil from his scholars." Previous to the death of Mr. Cheever, the increase of the town required more schools; and in 1682, two new ones were established. Mr. Cheever was succeeded by Mr. Nathaniel Williams in 1710, and he in 1734 by the celebrated " Master Lovell."

In March, 1710, five inspectors of schools were appointed, but little is known of their object or duties.

In 1741, the population of the town was 16,382;

and on the 23d of June, a committee appointed to examine the schools reported the number of pupils, and their distribution, as follows:

At the South Writing School, . . .	73
" " Queen Street* " . . .	73
" " North Grammar " . . .	230
" " South Latin " . . .	94
" " North " " . . .	65
	535

Showing a total of 535 scholars in all the public schools at that time.

June 24th, 1758, the Selectmen having been appointed a committee to visit the schools, reported that "they had attended to that service, accompanied by a number of distinguished gentlemen, and found in the

South Grammar School, . .	115 scholars.
" Writing " . .	240 "
Queen Street Writing School, .	230 "
North Grammar " .	36 "
" Writing " .	220 "

Being 841 in all, and which were found in very good order."

At the visitation of the committee, July 1, 1772, there were 823 scholars reported as present, which, for some reason, shows a less number than in 1758.

In March, 1785, a new writing school was established at the south end of the town (Pleasant Street), over which Mr. Cheney was installed as master April 26. During the revolution the schools were much disturbed,

* Now Court Street.

and the number of scholars decreased to such an extent that many years elapsed before they recovered from the effect. In May, 1785, the number reported in both the Latin Schools was only 64; in Queen Street School, 150; North Writing School, 150; School on the Common (Mason Street), 119; Mr. Cheney's, 81; making but 564 in all the schools. At this time a rule was adopted by the School Committee to admit no children to the Writing Schools under seven years of age.

It appears from the records, that originally the schools were under the supervision of the Selectmen of the town, in whose care they continued until 1789. In September of that year, a committee of one from each ward was appointed, at a town meeting, to draft a new system for the organization and government of the schools. This committee made their report Oct. 16, in which they recommended that the number of schools should be seven, and that they be placed under the direction of a school committee, composed of the Selectmen, and one from each ward, to be chosen annually by the town. Up to this time there had been no provision made, in Boston, for the education of females at the public expense, and therefore all their instruction was derived from private schools. In view of this, the committee proposed, that in the new system the girls should be admitted to the Grammar Schools, and instructed in the same studies as the boys, but at different hours, and only from April to October in each year. This report was adopted in town meeting, and the first school committee was chosen October 20, 1789.

From the "Hist. Collections," 1794, we learn that "a handsome two-story brick building was erected in

1792 in Bennet Street, where the North Latin School formerly stood. In one apartment, Writing and Arithmetic is taught; in another, Spelling, Reading, English Grammar, and Geography. In the centre of the Town, on the N. side of School Street [now Court Square], is a building with two handsome school-rooms, erected in 1790, in which boys are instructed in Latin and Greek. Another is a new house, lately built of wood, and used in the same manner and for the same purposes as the North School [Bennet Street]. There are two wooden buildings in the South part of the Town for the same purpose. All the free schools are supported by the Town; and youth of both sexes are admitted at different hours. In the month of July, annually, the Selectmen and gentlemen of science chosen by the Town as a School Committee, with other gentlemen, visit these schools and examine them. The visiters dine together at Faneuil Hall at the expense of the Town."

The bequest of Dr. Franklin, for the purpose of providing medals to be distributed to the most deserving scholars, became available in 1792; and in that year the inscription and device were agreed upon, and twenty-one medals ordered to be prepared for distribution in the schools. They were first distributed to the pupils to whom they were awarded, in February, 1793, though they bore the date of 1792.

In 1800, there were in the town, seven free schools, containing 900 scholars, of whom about 160 were taught Latin. There were besides a number of private schools, at which there were about 500 pupils. At this time the salary of a master was $666 66, with a gratuity or allowance of $200 in addition; the salary of an usher was $333 33, with an allowance of $100. The town tax of this year was $61,489 25, of which the school expenses were $11,100 85.

In the spring of 1804, a new school-house was built in Chardon Street; and in 1806 the whole number of pupils in the schools was 1760, of which 1030 were boys and 730 were girls. From this time the number of scholars did not increase in so great a ratio, inasmuch as it appears that at the visits of the committee, in August, 1816, there were only eight schools and 2,000 children, being an increase of only 340 for ten years. The great increase from 1800 to 1806 should, however, be attributed, in a degree, to the admission of the girls to the schools.

In December, 1817, the bells of the schools were ordered to be rung at the hour of beginning, and tolled till the master be present. They were also to be tolled at the hour of dismission. The school hours for commencing in the morning were, from April to October, 7½ o'clock; and from October to April, 8½. At this period the schools were regarded with increased interest by the citizens; the advantages of public schools as the means of education were self-evident; and their extension had begun to receive considerable attention, for there were those who felt that, in some respects, our educational system was defective, since it rendered *private* schools a necessary auxiliary to those which were *public* and free. To understand this, it will be proper to state that, by the laws of the Commonwealth, it was provided that, " No youth shall be sent to the Grammar Schools, unless they shall have learned in some other

2

school, or in some other way, to read the English language, by spelling the same." The laws likewise provided for the establishment of preparatory schools, where grammar is not taught; but to this time there were no public schools in Boston where children could be qualified for admission to the Grammar Schools. The age at which they were eligible was fixed at seven years, and but few were ever admitted under that age. It was consequently necessary for parents to send their children to *private* schools, where they could be taught the first rudiments of reading, before they could receive admission to the Grammar Schools.

Having thus briefly and imperfectly sketched the historical incidents connected with the Boston Schools, previous to the establishment of the Primary Board, we will now proceed to our main subject, the history of that organization.

ORIGIN OF THE PRIMARY SCHOOLS.

In tracing the history of an organization, its origin is justly regarded as one of its most interesting features; but after the lapse of years, when most of the active men by whom it was fostered and cherished into life, have passed away, and age made the record of the past dim and obscure on the minds of the survivors, it is extremely difficult, if not impossible, to go behind the written record and trace with any degree of satisfaction the primary cause or impulse

from which its origin may be dated. The first impulse
may have been given by a simple remark or an acci-
dental occurrence, which, striking a chord in harmony
with the views entertained by others in regard to the
wants or interests of a community, is responded to in
such a manner as to render it eventually beneficial
and successful. In its progress and development, however, it often becomes so modified and changed by
various influences and circumstances, that the original
idea can scarcely be traced or recognized among the
numerous elements which, though blended together,
have each been more or less instrumental in produc-
ing the result.

As all of these difficulties exist in the present case,
it may be deemed unnecessary by some, and presump-
tion by others, to attempt an analysis of this nature,
or seek for the original germ with any hope of success. But though the germ may not be discovered,
there are those who first watered and cherished it,
and it is right that we should endeavor to give "honor
to whom honor is due," and render the proper meed
of justice to those worthy, philanthropic, and self-de-
voted men through whose persevering exertions the
Primary Schools were projected and established.

From a careful investigation of all available evidence, it appears, that one of the most prominent
impulses which resulted in the establishment of the
Primary Schools of Boston, was undoubtedly derived
from the introduction of Sunday Schools. These
schools had been instituted in England by Robert
Raikes, in 1781–82, and had spread with great rapid-
ity, and been attended with eminent success through

all parts of Great Britain. The original objects of these schools was to gather the poor, degraded and neglected children from the streets, who were left to grow up in ignorance and vice, without any salutary home influences or regard for the Sabbath, and by kindness and persuasion interest them sufficiently to draw them together on the Sabbath, and by teaching them to read, lay a foundation for imparting to them a knowledge of their moral and religious duties. In Great Britain, with no system of public education, the Sunday Schools were soon thronged with thousands of children whose social condition was such as to preclude them from obtaining the most simple elements of education, except by this means. Ignorant as they were, the idea of being taught to read gave a charm to the Sunday Schools, and a success that probably no efforts, based on religious or moral instruction alone, would have accomplished.

The first Sunday School in the United States was instituted in the year 1791. Its object was to instruct, gratuitously, children to read and write, who were unable to attend school on other days. The teachers were paid a salary, and the design did not extend to the religious instruction of the scholars. In 1811 the present plan was adopted in Pittsburg, Pennsylvania, but it was not until about 1816, that Sunday Schools were successfully introduced into Boston. Previous to this time many of the most eminent of the clergy and members of the various religious societies were deeply impressed with the importance of Sunday Schools as a check to vice and pauperism, and engaged most earnestly in their establishment.

As a means of promoting the object, a society was formed under the name of " The Society for the Moral and Religious Instruction of the Poor," and it was probably under the influence and auspices of this society that the first Sunday Schools were gathered.*

* In corroboration of this, is the following letter from the Town files for 1818. Mr. Thurston was one of the earliest friends in the establishment of Primary Schools, and was as eminent for his high legal attainments as for his active and disinterested benevolence.

"Boston, *March* 18, 1818.

" *Turner Phillips, Esq., Chairman of the Honorable Board of Selectmen:*

" Sir :—Since I called on you, I have been to Mr. Webb's school in Mason street, to know if it would be convenient to have the rooms occupied by the school under his care for a Sunday school; he replied that the writing books, &c., are all locked up, and that no inconvenience would be sustained by the Sunday school, which he believed was productive of much good. Permit me, therefore, to request that you would lay our application for a second room in Mason street school-house, if you think it necessary, having already obtained a general consent of it for the use of that school-house last May.

" Our objects in attending to Sunday schools, are, to reclaim the vicious, to instruct the ignorant, to secure the observance of the Sabbath, to induce the children to attend public worship, and to raise the standard of morals among the lower classes of society. We are encouraged in obtaining these, by the experience which other places have declared to result from Sunday schools, and upon the little good which we hope has been done by them in this town.

" We believe in this way we strike at the foundation of the evils incidental to society, and with greater prospect of success than to reform the hardened offenders, — and yet through the children, not unfrequently the parent is reclaimed.

" I have thought this explanation of our motives and objects would not be unacceptable. Whether we shall succeed, time must determine. The society feel grateful for the accommodation of school-rooms already granted, and shall duly appreciate such further ones as the number of scholars in the vicinity seem in our view to require. These are, Mr. Webb's school-rooms in Mason street, and one of the rooms in the school-house in North School street. A compliance with our requests will greatly facilitate our efforts, and oblige

" Respectfully yours,

" WILLIAM THURSTON,

" *In behalf of the Committee of Boston Society for the Moral and Religious Instruction of the Poor.*"

Although the teaching of reading was one of the principal characteristics of the Sunday Schools, it was not anticipated by its friends, that, in Boston, which from its first settlement had been preëminent for its free schools and other means of general education, this kind of instruction would be required to any considerable extent; they were therefore surprised and disappointed, when, at the gathering of these schools, they became aware how large a proportion of the children were unable to read, or even had any knowledge of the alphabet. The extent to which this ignorance prevailed appears in a report of the society, (just mentioned,) made in November, 1817, in which it is stated, "that of 336 children admitted into the Mason Street Sunday School, none of whom were under five years of age, not one quarter part could read words of one syllable, and most of them did not know their letters." A knowledge of this fact brought with it a conviction of the insufficiency of the education, which could be imparted by an attendance of the scholars but once a week, and the great detriment, the giving of so much elementary instruction would be, to the religious element of their undertaking. This led them to regard the omission of the means, for the *public* education of children under seven years of age as a great evil, and a radical defect in our otherwise exemplary system of education.

Under these circumstances, it is reasonable, that the efforts and appeals emanating from those who regarded education as essential, but, in a degree subsidiary, to the religious instruction and moral elevation of the poor, should be deeply imbued with a union of these principles; and we are not surprised, that in the agitation which ensued upon the subject of Primary Schools, these elements, of an eleemosynary character, should be prominently brought forward in some of the plans proposed. Of the views entertained by those who advocated this peculiar organization, the following "Plan," which was published in February, 1818, will furnish a good illustration:

"I. Let schools be established for the instruction of all the children from four to seven years of age, at the town's expense.

"II. Let the present system of Sunday Schools go fully into operation.

"III. Let three discreet, judicious, prudent, industrious, pious men be appointed in each ward, whose duty it shall be —

"1st. To inquire into the state and circumstances of each poor family several times in the course of the year, and note them down, and at the same time encourage them to industry, cleanliness, and good morals; and by their advice and friendship, to assist them in contriving ways and means by which to gain a comfortable subsistence for themselves and children.

"2d. To persuade them to send their children to the Public and Sunday Schools, and to go to meeting or to church themselves with their children on the Sabbath, and show them what will be the result of laudable, useful, and pious practices like these.

"3d. To ascertain the number of the poor in each ward, male and female, where they live, and where they were born, and to what meeting, church or parish, if any, they belong, and report their names to the minister of the parish, &c., and request him to visit and show them the use and necessity of public worship, and the advantage it will be to them; and

" 4th. As fast as they discover an inclination in any one to attend public worship, and having ascertained the name of the minister under whose preaching *he* or *she* inclines to sit, it shall be their duty, by the permission of the church and parish over which he presides as pastor, to furnish *him* or *her* with a seat, and direct each where to find it.

" 5th. That it be recommended to the Board of Overseers that no money be given to, or expended by them, arising or growing out of the public funds, grants of the town, private donations, or public charities, upon any poor person out of the Alms House, except to such as shall be pointed out and recommended by this committee as suitable persons for charity.

" 6th. It shall be the duty of this committee, also, to take up all vagrants and street beggars, and deliver them to the Overseers of the Poor, to be committed to the Work House or Alms House, as the case may be.

" 7th. It is recommended that the above committee of thirty-six gentlemen shall form a Board, called the Board of Primary Schools, for the purpose of putting into operation the above plan, except so much of it as relates to Sunday Schools."

These views were probably entertained by many of the most earnest friends of Primary Schools, and particularly by those who were actively engaged in the religious and philanthropic associations of the day.

It is, therefore, to this cause we may attribute the idea, which has prevailed to some extent, that when the Primary Schools were established by the town, the number and qualifications of the committee, and the manner of its organization, were based upon this union of a religious and secular education.

That this is an error, is evident from the fact, that when, in the course of events, the subject of Primary Schools was formally presented for consideration at the Town-meetings, the idea of combining Sunday Schools and church attendance with our system of Public Schools, does not appear in the petitions for the schools,— the reports of the committees,— nor in the plan subsequently adopted by the town.

It is true, that at the beginning, and through the whole career of the Primary Board as an organization, we find the spirit of moral care and Christian benevolence which was originally breathed around it, continually exhibiting its benign influence in the action of the Board, and in the self-devotion of the committee.

It is with pride, therefore, that we acknowledge this salutary influence; and we regret that it is not in our power to do justice to all those revered and eloquent divines who stood foremost in the ranks as firm advocates and tried friends of this cause, while they contributed largely to the infusion of this spirit into it. Of these, many have passed away without our knowledge of their participation; but we gladly record the names of BALDWIN, CHANNING, DEAN, WINCHELL, FREEMAN, SHARP, DWIGHT and WARE, as prominent among those which should be registered with grateful remembrance as pioneers in this extension of popular education.

3

But with all proper regard to the influence we have been describing, it is manifest, that the ultimate success of the agitation for Primary Schools is due, in no less degree, to the judicious perseverance of those, who, taking a different view of the subject, felt the necessity, and advocated the establishment of these schools on the broad ground of public expediency; that without them, our boasted system of public instruction was defective, incomplete, and inefficient. Of those who urged the importance of Primary Schools on these grounds, none were more indefatigable in their efforts than ELISHA TICKNOR and JAMES SAVAGE. These gentlemen had long been united in forwarding various projects for the amelioration and improvement of the condition of the poor. It was mainly through their exertions that the "Provident Institution for Savings" had been put into operation, and its success had encouraged them to further efforts in the same direction. Mr. Ticknor had been a teacher in the Grammar Schools, and had seen and felt the deficiency in the system of instruction, by which a large class of the population were prevented from deriving any advantage from the Public Schools. It is true that by the laws of 1790, the schools were apparently free to all; but the conditions were such, as to limit the advantages to those who had the ability to qualify their children for admission. The law required, that the pupil should be seven years of age, and able to read in plain English lessons; but there were many parents who were incompetent to impart even this elementary instruction themselves, and whose means were too limited to pay, even the small compensation required, to send their children to to the Dames' Schools. Others were too illiterate to appreciate the advantages of education, sufficiently, to apply a part of their earnings to the instruction of their children; consequently, as the preliminary instruction was in all cases a *private* charge, except to those who were admitted to the Charity Schools, it was plain, that without some public provision, a considerable portion of the children were, and must be, debarred from entering the schools, while the constantly increasing foreign immigration was swelling the number of this class of children to an alarming extent. "It cannot be doubted," says Mr. Savage, in one of his letters, "that the true construction of the laws required the opening of schools, at the public expense, for children under the age of seven years, inasmuch as the laws passed by the Legislature in 1790 provided for the establishment of *preparatory* schools."

But the law in relation to this class of schools was not acted upon by the authorities in Boston, although it appears to have been by those in several other towns in the Commonwealth. That this neglect was not in accordance with the sentiment of the citizens generally, is evident from the prompt response, in favor of these schools, which was given by them whenever the subject was brought forward at the town meetings.

By the continued agitation and discussions on the subject, the inhabitants became more and more interested, although no definite action appears to have taken place in relation to it until 1817. On the 26th of May in that year, a petition, signed by 160 inhabitants, mostly residing at the north part of the town, was read at a town meeting in Faneuil Hall. The last paragraph in this petition, which was dated May 1, and addressed to the Selectmen, is as follows:—"It appears to us, also, important that Schools should be provided at the expense of the Town for the instruction of children under the age of seven years. Therefore we request that a meeting of the inhabitants of the town may be called, to take the above subject into consideration, and to adopt such measures thereon as the importance of the subject demands, and they may think most for the general good."

A town meeting was called, and the subject referred by the town to the School Committee, with the addition of one person from each of the twelve wards, to be appointed by the Selectmen. The following is from the records of the Selectmen, May 29, 1817:—" The Town having, at the late meeting, directed the Selectmen to appoint a committee, to consist of one person from each of the Wards, on the subject of schools, the following names were now selected from the lists offered by the petitioners, and from others nominated by the Board:—

Ward 1. HENRY J. OLIVER.   Ward 2. REDFORD WEBSTER.
3. JACOB HALL.   4. JAMES W. BURDITT.
5. JONA. P. HALL.   6. ISAAC WINSLOW.
7. GIDEON SNOW.   8. JOHN DORR.
9. SAMUEL MAY.   10. DAVID W. CHILD.
11. ISAAC STEVENS.   12. JOSEPH FIELD."

These committees met on the 18th of June, and the members of the several Ward committees were requested to visit every family in the Wards, and ascertain the number of children who did not attend any school; also the number of Women's or " Dames' Schools," and the number of their pupils; they were also requested, at the same time, to ascertain the number of deaf and dumb and blind persons in each Ward. In consideration of the labor involved, a number of gentlemen were appointed to assist the Ward committees in their duties. On the 17th of July the returns were handed in to the School Committee, who appointed a sub-committee, consisting of CHARLES BULFINCH, Chairman of the Selectmen, PETER O. THACHER and HENRY J. OLIVER, to arrange the returns, and report upon them. On the 30th of October, this sub-committee presented their report, adverse to the petition, which was read, accepted by the School Committee, and ordered to be printed for the information of the inhabitants.

The views which were then entertained by the authorities upon the subject of schools, and the interesting statement in relation to the town, at that time, joined to the fact, that but very few copies of this report now remain, will be a sufficient reason for inserting a copy of the entire document in this place:—

PRIMARY SCHOOLS.

BOSTON, *November* 3, 1817.

At a meeting of the Inhabitants of this town on 26th May last, a petition was presented from a number of the inhabitants for additional Schools, and was referred to the School Committee, which consists of the Selectmen and twelve other citizens, to which was added one person from each ward, thirty-three in all. The body, so formed, appointed committees for each of the wards, to ascertain by inquiry the actual state of education in the town. The reports of the several ward committees were referred to a sub-committee, consisting of CHARLES BULFINCH and P. O. THACHER, Esquires, and

Mr. Henry J. Oliver: The following report was presented by them, and will, we think, be regarded as a valuable historical document, and read with pleasure by all who take an interest in the welfare of the rising generation.

REPORT.

The Sub-Committee, to whom were referred the returns of the Committees of the several Wards, and who were instructed to consider the expediency and necessity of establishing within the town, at the public expense, primary schools for children under the age of seven years, and also of increasing the number of the public reading and writing schools for children above that age; having examined the several returns, and collected all information upon the subject, ask leave to report —

The duty of the town to provide the means of instruction for all the children is both a civil and religious obligation upon the citizens; but it is a reasonable duty, and has its limits. If, on inquiry, it is found that the existing schools are not sufficient to accommodate the public wants, their number ought to be encreased. But, although the sub-committee does not apprehend any unwillingness in the towns to provide liberally for the public instruction; yet, in deciding upon the obligation to increase the number of schools, it cannot be improper to have reference to the ability of the town to make further appropriations for their support.

	Pupils.
The Sub-Committee find that the Latin Grammar school consists of	147
The North public schools of 309 boys and 140 girls,	449
The West schools of 339 boys and 234 girls,	573
The Centre schools of 240 boys and 36 girls,	326
The South schools of 370 boys and 283 girls,	653
The school at South Boston of 100 boys and girls,	100
The African school of 30 boys and 20 girls,	50
The school at Alms House of 44 boys and 23 girls,	67
	2,365

These schools, containing in all 2,365 pupils of both sexes, are maintained at the public expense, and are, excepting a part of those at the Alms House, for children above the age of seven years.

The several Ward Committees were instructed to visit each house, to ascertain the name of every child from the age of four to fourteen years, who from any cause failed to attend any school; and to obtain full and accurate information of the state of education within their respective limits. The Committees appear to have performed their task with fidelity; and the result of their returns in a digested form, is added to this report, and is offered as part of the same.

It appears that there are in the town one hundred and sixty-two private schools of various descriptions, in which 4,132 children attend, who are between the ages of four and fourteen years. These scholars are supported at the expense of the parents, excepting eight,* which are maintained by the charity of individuals, organizing themselves into different religious societies in the town, and superintended by associations of young ladies, in the respective churches, who devote their personal attention to advance the progress of the children in manners and learning. The whole expense of these private schools amounts annually to forty-nine thousand one hundred and fifty-four dollars, furnishing employment and support to a very useful and respectable class of citizens of both sexes. Of the above sums, the expense of the earliest or primary schools for children between the ages of four and seven years, is eighteen thousand nine hundred and eleven dollars. It is found that two hundred and eighty-three children, between the ages of four and seven years, do not attend any school: Considering the population of the town, which now amounts to about forty thousand inhabitants,

---

* These Charity Schools were for girls only, and their organization and means of support may be understood from the " Final and Seventh Annual Report of the School of Industry No. I.," which is printed entire in the Appendix, from probably the only copy now preserved, and for which the Editor is indebted to Rowland Ellis, Esq.

together with the influx of foreigners and strangers, who are ignorant of our institutions, or who have not learned to value them, this is deemed to be a very small number. But the Overseers of the Poor are found not to be inattentive to the wants of the community in this respect. They distribute annually in their respective Wards, a sum, which upon an average amounts to five hundred and fifty dollars, to enable poor children of this class to attend the primary schools, which are kept in various parts of the town.

From the returns of the Ward Committees it appears, that two hundred and forty-three children above the age of seven years do not, either from the inattention of their parents, from indifference to the subject, or from inability, make any use of the means of education, public or private, which are afforded by the town. Of this number it may be presumed that two-thirds are females, who might be easily accommodated in the public Schools. Nor does there appear to be any difficulty in disposing of the boys, who are about eighty in number, in the existing public schools, especially as the females attend there from the month of April to October only, and the boys are then divided between them in succession, which gives ample room for even a much larger number than are usually found to attend.

Considering the importance of education to the present and future well-being of the individual, it is to be deeply lamented, that any child should be suffered to grow up in ignorance. Next to giving lessons of vice, the neglect of parents to attend to the education of their children is the greatest injury which they can inflict upon their offspring. In a country where schools are provided at the public expense, it is a debt which parents owe to the community, and an indispensable part of their office, to send their children regularly to School. Our laws have not provided penalties for parents, who neglect this duty. Perhaps it is best that its performance should be left to the influence of feeling and conscience, and to the dread which is felt of that indignation which will inevitably arise in the mind of a child, who, having arrived at the age of manhood, finds that his education has been neglected by those, to whom he is unhappily indebted for his existence. But in every society, individuals will be found, who are wholly regardless of their own improvement and happiness, and who equally disregard the best moral and religious interests of their children. Let the system of public instruction be ever so complete and extensive, some will always be found to neglect its advantages.

In no country is the system of free Schools established on more liberal principles than in this Commonwealth. The fathers of New-England well knew, that ignorance is the parent of superstition and vice, and that it is equally hostile to civil and religious freedom. They incorporated into our civil constitutions the principle, that provision should be made in each town, at the public expense, for instructing the children in the elements of knowledge. In the public Schools in this town, the children are taught the principles of the English language, and likewise the elements of Writing, Arithmetic and Geography. They are permitted to continue there from the age of seven to fourteen years, and in that time they become qualified to engage in mercantile and mechanical professions, are disciplined in the principles of moral and religious truth, and are formed to make valuable members of the community. The only qualification for admission to the public Schools is, that the child should know his letters and be able to combine syllables, and the instances are rare indeed where children have been refused admission from the want of this qualification. The instructors of the Grammar Schools are gentlemen of liberal education. All the Schools are under the care and inspection of a large committee, consisting of twenty-one citizens,* to whom are delegated all the powers of the town for the support and encouragement of public instruction.

For children under the age of seven years, it is true, no

---

* The School Committee was composed of nine Selectmen, and *ex-officio*, one member elected from each Ward.

4

schools are maintained at the public expense. But experience has proved in times past, and it has been demonstrated by the present inquiry to the satisfaction of the sub-committee, that this class of children with us is not neglected. Perhaps as large proportion of them enjoy the advantages of instruction as would avail themselves of it if schools were maintained in sufficient number by the public treasury. The system of small private schools for pupils of this description, supported by the parents, operates upon them as a tax, which, however, is not very unequal or burdensome. They send their children to such schools as are convenient, and at such rate of expense as they can afford, and the tax is paid cheerfully, because it is for an object which carries with it the reward both of feeling and duty. If public schools were established for this class, they must, to be of general utility, be very numerous, which would create a very great expense to the town. If they should be few in number, they would not be attended, for it would be inconvenient and dangerous to send small children to schools distant from their homes, and to allow them to assemble together in multitudes. Few parents would wish to send their children to a school of this description. Most parents naturally take a strong interest in the first development of the tender faculties of their infant children, and are willing to devote more attention to the business of education, where a small weekly stipend is paid by them for this object, than where the whole expense is defrayed by the public treasury. The sub-committee believe that most parents have some leisure, and that with us few are unequal to the task of teaching the elements of letters. It ought never to be forgotten that the office of instruction belongs to parents, and that to the schoolmaster is delegated a portion only of the parental character and rights. In the retirement of domestic life, parents have opportunities to impart instruction, and to gain an influence over their children which the public teacher does not possess.

It is not to be expected that free schools should be furnished with so many instructors, and be conducted on so liberal principles as to embrace the circle of a polite and finished education. They have reference to a limited degree of improvement, and from their public character there must arise some disadvantages which are not felt in private schools, under tutors to whom is assigned a small limited number of pupils. But, considering the great number and flourishing state of the public and private schools in this town, the universal attention which is paid by its citizens to their support and encouragement, the very small proportion of children who do not avail themselves of these institutions, together with the heavy tax which is already assessed for the support of the public education; the sub-committee report as the result of their inquiries, that the establishment at the public expense of primary schools for children under the age of seven years, is not in their opinion expedient, and that an increase of the number of the reading and writing schools is not required by any evident public necessity.

By order of the Sub-Committee,

CHARLES BULFINCH, *Chairman.*

Boston, Oct. 30, 1817.—At a meeting of the School Committee, in conjunction with the committee from the wards of the town, the above report having been read and fully considered,—Voted, that the same be accepted, and that it be printed for general information.

WM. WELLS, *Sec. to S. C.*

The following is one of the tables referred to in the above report. In another, the committee exhibited particularly the numbers in each school, with the various prices of tuition, which, from its length, it has been thought advisable to omit:—

RESULT OF THE RETURNS MADE FROM THE SEVERAL WARDS BY THE COMMITTEE ON THE SUBJECT OF SCHOOLS.

Wards.	No. of Children who go to no School.		No of Private Schools.		No. of Private Pupils.		Annual Expense.	Charity Free Schools	
	Under 7.	Above 7.	Men's.	Women's.	Boys	Girls	$ cents.	Schools.	Pupils.
1	57	46	2	19	232	275	5,638 00	....	....
2	52	53	1	12	128	169	2,846 00	1	60
3	26	28	..	16	161	259	3,175 00	....	....
4	9	14	1	1	70	24	1,249 00	....	....
5	8	8	1	10	162	231	7,346 00	....	....
6	20	23	..	13	100	190	2,879 00	....	....
7	7	4	1	12	100	232	6,425 50	1	32
8	6	5	1	5	15	119	2,285 00	...	....
9	13	20	3	6	89	133	2,300 00	1	35
10	6	3	5	10	125	212	8,162 50	1	65
11	23	23	1	14	112	164	2,020 00	4	173
12	56	16	3	17	185	280	4,828 50	....	....
	283	243	19	135	1,479	2,288	49,154 50	8	365

Number of Pupils—Boys, 1,479; Girls, 2,288; Charity Scholars, 365; total, 4132.

ANNUAL EXPENSE OF PRIMARY SCHOOLS FOR CHILDREN UNDER SEVEN YEARS OF AGE.

Ward 1	2,962	Ward 8	105
2	1,870	9	1,820
3	2,775	10	602
4	225	11	3,020
5	1,710	12	2,340
6	1,695		
7	787	Amount	$18,911*

This report was printed and distributed, but was not submitted to the action of the citizens at a town meeting, as the School Committee apparently regarded the vote of the town as placing the whole matter in their hands. Elaborate and carefully prepared as it was, it was not satisfactory to the petitioners, but was opposed in the newspapers by Mr. James Savage and others

---

* This amount was paid by the parents of the pupils, in the Dawes and other private schools.

with eloquence and effect. From one of these articles, in the *Daily Advertiser* of April 21, 1818, over the signature of " MANY,"* we make the following extracts:—The author commences by laying down this proposition — " All should·be taught to read; the poor and the rich should have an equal chance to understand the nature and principles of our Republican government;" and adds, " Many parents in this town send their children to private schools kept by women, while those who are unable to pay for their tuition, are obliged to leave them to traverse the streets, or shut them up at home. Of this class, there are hundreds among us already growing up to all kinds of iniquity. In the report of the School Committee of the 3d of November last, we are told that the number of children between the ages of four and fourteen is 526, ' *who go to no school.*' What are those children doing? Who has charge of them? Where do they live? Why are they not at school? The Committee have not informed us. Have *they* not a *right* to a good bringing up, and to a common school education? and have they not a *right* to a common share of the friendship of the community? If their parents neglect to provide them a school, is it not the duty of the town to do it? and if the town takes no interest in their welfare, is it not the duty of the Legislature to enact laws for the purpose of saving these dependents, these sufferers?"

" All children have an equal right to the schools, we know, on the following conditions, *and on no other*, viz.: 1st. The child must be seven years old. 2d. He must be able to read in the Bible sufficiently well to keep

* Written by Mr. Savage.

his place in a class. 3d. He cannot be admitted after the age of fourteen, however well he can read, or however deficient he may be in writing or arithmetic. Take, then, the case of a parent, (and there are hundreds in town,) whose circumstances are such as to prevent him from qualifying his children for enjoying the benefits of our Free Schools, under and after the age of seven. Can it be said that the doors of our schools are open to these children? We say that they are not; yet we are told, " they *are* open, *freely* open to their reception, but these children are as much deprived of the benefits of our schools as they would be of running, after their legs were broken, or their eyes were put out."

The School Committee having decided unfavorably to the wishes of the petitioners, another petition for the same object was presented to the town at a town meeting in Faneuil Hall, May 25, 1818. This petition, the most important from its success, was drawn up by ELISHA TICKNOR and JAMES SAVAGE, as we are informed by the latter; and as the original paper, now on the town files, is in the hand-writing of Mr. Ticknor, with several interlineations by Mr. Savage, there is no doubt of their action, or that the signatures were principally obtained by their efforts. The list contains the names of so many of the eminent and influential men of that time that we cannot refrain from recording the entire list, as a memento, alike honorable to them and to the cause.

The document is addressed,

To the Selectmen of the Town of Boston:

GENTLEMEN: — The undersigned, inhabitants of Boston, impressed with the deepest sense of the value of our institutions and laws, for the education of children in public

town schools, respectfully represent, that an extension of the
benefits of such establishments, appears in their view highly
desirable and necessary, that inquiry has satisfied them, that
many hundred children in this town grow up to manhood,
unable to read or write; that the admission to the present
public schools of those over seven years of age, requiring
a previous acquaintance with easy lessons, and many parents,
being themselves incompetent to give such lessons, and not
able to obtain such instruction for their children at private
schools, it seems expedient that such previous education
should be freely provided for by the town, no less than the
instruction at our established schools; that such schools
might be taught by females, and rooms provided in several
parts of the town, at a small expense, or the cheap Lancas-
trian system may be adopted; that the duty of providing
such schools and instructors need not necessarily be added
to the labors of our present School Committee, but might be
performed by a Committee of three in each ward, to be
named by the Overseers of the Poor, annually, which Committee might also, much alleviate the labors of the regular
officers.   Wherefore, they request that a meeting of the inhabitants of the town may be called to take the above mentioned subjects into consideration, and thereon to adopt such
measures as the importance of the matter deserves, and the
public good requires.

(Judge) Thomas Dawes,	James Savage,	Thomas L. Winthrop,
(Rev.) Thos. Baldwin,	Wm. Thurston,	Henry Gray,
" James Freeman,	Barzilla Homes,	Elisha Ticknor,
" Wm. E. Channing,	Jere. Gore,	Wm. Brown,
" Paul Dean,	John D. Williams,	Robert Fennelly,
" Daniel Sharp,	Daniel Weld,	Geo. Darracott,
" Sereno E. Dwight,	Elijah Williams,	Josiah Vinton, Jr.,
" Henry Ware,	Elisha Preston,	Moses Grant,
" Jas. M. Winchell,	Jesse Mayo,	Thomas Wallcut,
Isaac Vose,	Pliny Cutler,	Henry J. Oliver,
Josiah Stedman,	Samuel Bradlee,	N. S. Snelling,
Benj. West,	Uriah Cotting,	John C. Brown,
Daniel Ingalls,	Daniel Messenger,	Wm. Dall,
John Knapp,	Samuel Coverly,	Augustus Peabody,

Samuel T. Armstrong,
Oliver Fisher,
Thomas Brewer,
Lemuel Hayward,
Joseph Head,
Charles Barnard,
Isaac Stevens,
Ferdinand E. White,
Thaddeus Robinson,
Elijah Davenport,
Jno. H. Bacon,
Eben. Chadwick,
Henry Williams,
Ephraim Lock,
James Clap,
Timothy Merritt,
Robert H. Thayer,
David Andrews,
C. D. Coolidge,
B. P Tilden,
Thos. Thompson,
Thomas Wigglesworth,
Benj. Pollard,
Benj. Austin,
Benj. Shurtleff,
Nathan Hales,
William Cochran,
Samuel May,
Jechonias Thayer,
Samuel Snelling,
Charles Guild,
Jno. F. Loring,
Ignatius Sargent,
William Sturgis,
Benj. Howard,
Jeffrey Richardson,
James Means,
Geo. H. Hodges,
J. W. C. Baxter,
Jno. Borland,
R. P. Tolman,
Calvin Haven,
Josiah Salisbury,
Charles Hood,
Wm. Ladd,
Joshua Child,
Elias Haskell,
Francis Stanton,

David Dudley,
Edward Gray,
James Mann,
Charles Hayward,
William Ropes,
Ebenezer Parker,
Wm. Worthington,
Lewis Leland,
Edmund Munro,
Isaac McLellan,
John Tyler,
E. Brigham,
Isaac Parker,
John E. Tyler,
Robert G. Shaw,
John Baxter,
Lemuel Packard, Jr.,
John Peters,
John French,
Geo. Hayward,
Sam'l Clarke,
Wm. S. Shaw,
Aa. Hill,
Josiah Bradlee,
Nathan Davis,
John Bellows,
Edward Reynolds,
William Mackay,
Joseph Callender,
Samuel Gore,
J. Putnam,
Thomas J. Prince,
James Dennie,
Benj. Rich,
Jno. M. Marston,
Henry D. Gray,
Wm. Masters,
George Pratt,
Samuel Bates,
Samuel Blake,
Elisha G. Scudder,
Asa Whitney,
Thomas H. Ward,
Thomas West,
Nathan Rice,
James Allen,
Abel Adams,
Horatio H. Fiske,

John Chandler,
John Osborn,
Josiah Knapp,
J. W. Hayward,
Israel Munson,
Charles Thacher,
John Bryant,
William Eager,
Isaac Hall,
Lemuel Crackbon,
J. and S. Jenney,
Wm. Tucker,
H. Blanchard,
Calvin Bailey,
Henry Hovey,
R. Elwell,
Perrin May,
Enoch Clap,
Peter Coffin,
D. D. Rogers,
Jno. Baker,
Joshua Huntington
N. Joy,
Geo. Homer,
John Brazer,
Wm. Foster, Jr.,
J. Prince,
Redford Webster,
Thomas B. Wales,
Tristram Barnard,
Thomas Curtis,
Nehemiah Parsons,
Thomas Cordis,
Joseph Moseley,
John F. Priest,
Edward D. Peters,
Philip Curtis,
Prince Hawes,
Samuel L. Abbot,
John Tappan,
Howland Cowing, Jr.,
A. P. Cleaveland,
Joseph H. Dow,
Henry Chapman,
Isaac Jenney,
Samuel Billings,
John Dodd,
Charles A. Dennet.

This petition was referred by the town to a Special Committee, consisting of Messrs. REDFORD WEBSTER, THOMAS L. WINTHROP, ELISHA TICKNOR, JAMES PRINCE, SAMUEL MAY, JOHN D. WILLIAMS, JAMES SAVAGE, BENJAMIN WEST, and THOMAS JACKSON. On the 3d of June this committee made their report as follows:

The Committee appointed at the Town meeting on the 25th of May, to consider the subject of the petition of a number of the inhabitants, for the establishment by the town of schools for children under seven years of age, having attentively considered the same, ask leave respectfully to report.

That, in their opinion, the opening of such schools for children under the age of seven years, is highly expedient and necessary; that several hundred children of that age do not attend any school, because the Charity Schools are, in most instances, provided only for *female* children, being under the inspection of ladies, their founders; and the private schools are so expensive that many parents find it difficult to defray that expense; that the examination of the circumstances of the several parts of the town in this respect, made last July, presented a return by which it is found that two hundred and eighty-three, between the ages of four and seven years, did not attend any school; but from inquiry of some of the gentlemen who made the returns, the Committee are satisfied that many children of that age were omitted, their parents or guardians being unwilling to acknowledge that they were sent to no school. That the Committee, with greater confidence, recommend the adoption of such a course, because most of the towns in this Commonwealth provide schools for children four years old equally with others, and particularly is this adhered to in the large towns of Salem, Newburyport, and Portland; that the best mode of providing such schools, seems to them

5

to be by the guidance and direction of three gentlemen from each ward, of sufficient activity, firmness, discretion and energy, to be nominated by the School Committee.

The Committee also submitted the following votes as expressive of the action to be taken by the town :

Voted, That the School Committee be instructed, in the month of June, annually, to nominate and appoint three gentlemen in each Ward, whose duty collectively shall be to provide instruction for children between four and seven years of age, and apportion the expenses among the several schools.

Voted, That $5,000 be appropriated out of the Town treasury for the purpose in the foregoing vote expressed, to be paid by the Treasurer on warrants drawn on him in the same manner as warrants are for the expenses of the other town schools.

This report was presented June 3d, and postponed to an adjourned meeting held on the 11th of the same month, at which time its acceptance was opposed by Hon. HARRISON G. OTIS, Judge PETER O. THACHER, and several other gentlemen, and was supported with eloquent earnestness by Messrs. ELISHA TICKNOR, LEWIS TAPPAN, JAMES SAVAGE and THOMAS B. WAIT; the latter was a practical printer, and had never before spoken in public, but on this occasion he expressed his views with such clearness and effect as to render the eloquent opposition of Mr. Otis unavailing, and the report and votes were adopted almost unanimously. By another vote, " $5,000 was added to the estimate of the expenses of the ensuing year to carry the same into effect."

The whole measure was thus triumphantly carried by the people, in opposition to the Selectmen and School Committee, who, with one or two exceptions, were entirely hostile to the project; for some reason, they were most singularly sensitive in regard to it, and it was believed to have been from their solicitation that Mr. Otis was induced to use his persuasive eloquence in opposition to it. To them the result was as mortifying as it was unexpected, inasmuch, as they had confidently anticipated a different effect, from the popularity of Mr. Otis, and the consideration of the views involved in their report of the 30th of October, and were entirely unprepared for so marked and signal a defeat. They, however, gracefully submitted to the circumstances, and in conformity with the foregoing instructions, a meeting of the School Committee was held on the 16th of June, and the following gentlemen were chosen as the first Primary School Committee to carry into execution the vote of the town:

Ward 1. Rev. HENRY WARE, N. G. SNELLING, ROBERT FENNELLY.

Ward 2. REDFORD WEBSTER, LEWIS LELAND, SAMUEL HICHBORN.

Ward 3. JAMES W. BURDITT, JOSIAH MARSHALL, Captain SAMUEL HOUSE.

Ward 4. Rev. J. M. WINCHELL, BENJ. T. WELLS, NATHAN WEBB.

Ward 5. Rev. THOMAS BALDWIN, SAMUEL GORE, Dr. BENJ. SHURTLEFF.

Ward 6. Rev. PAUL DEAN, WILLIAM THURSTON, Rev. DANIEL SHARP.

Ward 7. Hon. Benj. Austin, Samuel Coverly, Dea. Moses Grant.

Ward 8. John Dorr, Shubael Bell, David W. Child.

Ward 9. Samuel May, James Savage, William Brown.

Ward 10. Thomas L. Winthrop, Henry Chapman, Gardner L. Chandler.

Ward 11. Elisha Ticknor, Benj. Rich, John Bellows.

Ward 12. William Dall, Benj. West, Thomas B. Wait.

1818.

The gentlemen thus appointed met on the 22d of June, 1818, and organized themselves by the choice of Thomas L. Winthrop, Esq., as Chairman, and James Savage, Esq., as Secretary.

At a meeting of the Committee, on Monday, July 20th, 1818, it was—

Voted, That the Secretary cause all the votes and doings of this Board, relative to the establishment of Primary Schools, so far as concern the duties of the several Ward Committees, to be printed and transmitted to each of them for their government.

In obedience to this vote, the Secretary transmitted the following to the several committees:—

Voted, That each School shall be opened and directed by the Committee of the Ward in which it is placed; consulting, if it stand near another Ward, the Committee of that Ward. To the same shall belong the duty of procuring a suitable room, of engaging competent Mistresses, and controlling all matters relating to the establishment. They shall visit, and inquire into the state of the school or schools under their charge at least once a month, and oftener if convenient. They shall make a statement, of all important matters relating thereto, at each quarterly meeting of this Board, to be holden on the third Tuesday of September, December, March and June.

It shall be the duty of the Mistress, besides the usual business of teaching, to keep account of the absence or negligence of the children, and make weekly reports to the Ward Committee, whose duty, thereupon, shall be to visit the parents and endeavor to secure regular attendance. She shall be also required to pay particular regard to the neatness and cleanliness of the children.

It has also been *Voted*, that for the purpose of general provision for instruction of children under our authority, between the ages of four and seven years, including the expenses of rent, fuel and all other charges for the year ending the thirtieth day of June next, the portion of this Committee nominated for Ward No. 1 be allowed to expend the sum of four hundred and eighty dollars, and no more; the portion nominated for Ward No. 2, the sum of seven hundred and twenty dollars, and no more; the portion nominated for Ward No. 3, the sum of seven hundred and twenty dollars, and no more; the portion nominated for Ward No. 4, the sum of two hundred and forty dollars, and no more; the portion nominated for Ward No. 5, the sum of two hundred and forty dollars, and no more; the portion nominated for Wards Nos. 6 and 7, the sum of seven hundred and twenty dollars, and no more; the portion nominated for Wards Nos. 8 and 9, the sum of four hundred and eighty dollars, and no more; the portion nominated for Wards Nos. 10 and 11, the sum of four hundred and eighty dollars, and no more; the portion nominated for Ward No. 12, the sum of seven hundred and twenty dollars, and no more — at the discretion of the several portions of this Committee thus divided respectively; provided, however, that the portions of the Committees for any two or more Wards or divisions may unite the whole or any part of the funds hereby to them assigned for expenditure, at their discretion, in establishing one or more schools on the Lancasterian plan, or in the usual mode, in any parts of the Wards or divisions they represent, for children of the age above specified, and that all the several sub-committees hereby constituted, make report of their provision in every respect to this Board at their next meeting.

Under these instructions, the several Ward Committees entered upon their duties, each of them electing a Chairman, Treasurer and Secretary; and the records of Wards Nos. 6 and 7 are presented as an example of the manner in which these duties were performed:—

"Boston, August 9, 1818. — Miss Maria Bates commenced teaching School No. 1, in Ward No. 6, situated in Leverett Street, at the rate of $170 per ann. for her services."

"August 10. — Hired of Mr. A. F. Lane, a room for the above school at $1 per week."

"Boston, August 10, 1818. — Miss Sarah Rice commenced School No. 2, in Ward No. 6, situated in Cambridge Street, at $240 per annum, she finding fuel and school room."

"Boston, August 10, 1818. — Miss Sally Jewett commenced teaching School No. 3, in Ward Nos. 6 & 7, at the rate of $170 per ann. Room hired of Mr. Taylor at $1 per week. Said school is situated in South Russell Street."

"Committee for the District composed of Wards Nos. 6 and 7, for 1818–19, commencing in June annually.

For Ward No. 6.	For Ward No. 7.
Rev. Paul Dean, *Chair'n & Treas.*	Mr. Samuel Coverly, *Sec'y.*
Rev. Daniel Sharp.	Hon. Benj. Austin.
Dea. Moses Grant.	William Thurston, Esq."

The Committee of Ward No. 6, for the establishmnent and superintendence of the Primary Public Schools, beg leave to Report—

That they have established two Schools in their Ward, and one in conjunction with the Committee of Ward No. 7.

The School No. 1, in Ward No. 6, is situated in Leverett Street, on the east side; is taught by Miss Bates; tickets of admission have been given to fifty-five scholars; and about forty-five attend daily.

School No. 2, in Ward No. 6, is situated in Cambridge Street, on the north side; is taught by Miss Rice; tickets for sixty children have been issued, and forty-five to fifty children attend daily.

School No. 3, for Wards 6 and 7, is situated in South Russell Street; is taught by Miss Jewett. This school is more immediately under the management of the Committee of Ward No. 7, who will make a report on the subject.

These Schools were put in operation on the first of August; and your Committee have pleasure in communicating the satisfaction they feel in perceiving the decent and cleanly appearance of the children generally, in their good conduct, in the good order and subordination introduced into the Schools, and the evident improvement already made by the children.

All of which is respectfully submitted.

PAUL DEAN, Chairman.

Boston, Sept. 15, 1818.

1819.

On the 31st of May, 1819, the Primary School Board presented their first report to the Town, of which the following is a copy :—

AT a legal meeting of the Inhabitants of the Town of Boston, held at Faneuil Hall, on Monday, the 31st day of May, A. D. 1819.

The following REPORT was read, accepted, ordered to be printed, and distributed for the information of the Inhabitants.   Attest,

THOMAS CLARK, Town Clerk.

REPORT.

PURSUANT to the vote of the Town on the 11th day of June last, the School Committee soon after nominated and appointed three gentlemen in each ward " to provide instruction for children between four and seven years of age, and apportion the expenses among the several schools."   Of these gentlemen all but two accepted, and have served.   The Board was organized on the 23d day of June, by choosing Thomas L. Winthrop, Esquire, Chairman, and James Savage, Esquire, Secretary.

On the 2d day of July, the Board resolved that the Committee of each Ward " ascertain, by personal inquiry, the number of children between the ages of four and seven; state who do, and who do not, attend any school, as also those, whose parents are desirous of availing themselves of this right; and report the names and place of residence." This was a very arduous duty; and the result of the inquiry was highly interesting to the Board.   The number between

four and seven years old, exclusive of about half of Ward
No. 7, from which the Committee made no return, amounted
to two thousand eight hundred and forty-three. Of these,
though five hundred and thirty-two only did not attend any
school, thirteen hundred and thirty were desirous of instruction at the new schools. The number who attended no
school was nearly double that of the return made the preceding year, but not larger than was expected to be found.
A comparison of the result, in each year, from all the Wards,
will assist us in judging of their correctness.

Wards.	1817.	1818.
No. 1	57	46
2	52	86
3	26	45
4	9	14
5	8	20
6	20	37
7	7	34
8	6	29
9	13	72
10	6	2
11	23	46
12	56	101
Total,	283	532

To provide instruction for that number, the grant of money
by the town was very liberal, and was indeed considered by
the favorers of the experiment adequate to furnish schooling
for seven or eight hundred children. But, when we ascertained that above thirteen hundred would demand the care
of the Board, it became a matter of great difficulty to divide
the sum granted in such a way as to approach nearest to a
fulfilment of the vote of the town, with which a perfect

6

compliance seemed utterly impracticable. We could not satisfactorily arrange this difficulty before the 20th of July.

As the pupils were of such tender age, they could not be required to go far from home; and schools must, therefore, be opened in sections of the Wards. To ensure health and improvement, their number in each school should be small; and to such an instructor, as alone ought to be employed, the compensation could hardly fall short of two hundred dollars. Rent, fuel, benches and other incidental charges might have reasonably been expected to exceed fifty dollars for each. But the Board were resolved to open twenty schools, and we were of necessity stinted to that amount. It was generally agreed by us, that the children in one school should not exceed forty-five, and be confined, if practicable, to forty. The money was divided by vote among the several Committees from the Wards, and schools were opened exclusively for such free scholars as the Committees received in every Ward but two. These two Wards were unitedly allowed from our fund enough to maintain two schools, or one-tenth of the whole; but it seemed expedient to the Committee of that united district to agree with mistresses, having already established schools to receive from the Committee an addition of pupils at a stated rate for each. Five teachers have been by them employed in this manner. The rate of ten cents per week, with allowance of two dollars for winter's fuel, for each child, making seven dollars and twenty cents a year, is now found to be much higher than that which the instruction in other Wards demanded, where the expense of each pupil has fallen short of five dollars.

Most of the schools were opened in August, and all by the first week of September, and all have continued without interruption.

The calculations, even of such citizens as were most solicitous for the establishment of these schools, have all estimated too low the number of children for whom we find it necessary to provide instruction. Though a large portion, probably half of our people would prefer to pay teachers of their own private selection for instructing their children of such an age; and though the never-tiring benevolence of many has provided schools for several hundred others, yet, in every instance, the schools opened by the Board have been filled beyond the limit we desired to prescribe. We should, however, observe, that several of the instructors, having daughters of age to afford assistance to their mothers, the Committees have been satisfied with permitting sixty, and in one instance seventy, in another eighty pupils in one school. In only two of those eighteen schools provided solely for the free instruction has the number been smaller than fifty; and on the second week of March, when our instructors returned all under their tuition, the amount was eleven hundred and eighteen. Large as this number will appear, the Board are satisfied, that a considerable addition should the current year be provided for; and from computation carefully made we conceive thirty-two schools for such children will be needed. At two hundred and fifty dollars each, a grant of eight thousand dollars would be requisite.

Two considerations, among several others more apparent, powerfully operate to produce, in the minds of the gentlemen at the Board the year past, a conviction of the importance and necessity of this system of free schools for young children, which they wish to submit to the consideration of their fellow-citizens. The first is, that our schools have been constantly pressed to admit a number of children in every part of the town above seven years old, who, having been unable to acquire a little acquaintance with English reading, or even the letters of our alphabet, are excluded from the Public Schools. This grievance we could not remedy; but if the new schools for children of younger age be continued, the evil will, in a great measure, soon be removed. The second is, that very many children, whose parents are able in summer to afford them schooling at nine-pence or a shilling a week, are deprived in winter, when fire money is asked by the instructors, which the parents cannot easily pay, of all teaching, and so lose, at that season, all their former acquisition in letters. Three private schools in one Ward, where the mistresses had twelve scholars each, have been, by this defect, reduced one to nine, and the other two to six pupils each. But the children for whom we have been required to provide instruction have attended with remarkable punctuality, not less in winter than in summer.

The result of our experiment has certainly been encouraging, and we confidently state that the improvement in all our schools has been far superior to our expectations. We found many parents, on our first inquiry, indifferent about sending their children to these schools, though they regularly attended no other. Perhaps mistaking the establishment for a charitable one, their pride revolted from acknowledging that they needed assistance; yet, since the operation has proceeded, they have almost invariably desired admission for them. Of the children received, one half in some parts of the town, and one-third in general, were ignorant of their letters, of whom many can now read in the New Testament, and several from each school are prepared for admission at the town grammar schools, who must have been, we are confident, otherwise rejected. In most of our schools, the girls have been taught knitting or sewing as well as reading. The several Committees are, by a regulation of the Board, required once a month, at least, to visit the schools under their particular care; and a return of the state of each is demanded at our quarterly meetings.

All which is submitted.

ELISHA TICKNOR.
BENJAMIN AUSTIN.
THOMAS B. WAIT.
NATHAN WEBB.
THOMAS BALDWIN.
HENRY WARE.
JAMES SAVAGE.

This is the *first* Annual Report of the *first* Committee of the Primary Schools, and it is exceedingly interesting, from the amount of general information it presents, and as developing the organization and arrangement of the duties of the Board, which were so wisely and carefully ordered, and have proved so well adapted to the purpose, that no *fundamental* changes were afterwards deemed advisable or necessary.

The proceedings of the Committee having been thus approved by the town, in conformity with the recommendation in their Report, an appropriation of $8,000 was voted for the expenses of the second year, 1819–20; and in June the School Committee appointed the Primary Committee for the year. Messrs. Webster, Wells, Burditt, Marshall, Gore, Dorr, Bell, Child and Rich having resigned, the following gentlemen were appointed in their place : Thomas Fracker, Dr. Horace Bean, James Davis, Thomas J. Bordman, Dr. Geo. C. Shattuck, Peter Mackintosh, Jr., Dr. Samuel Clarke, Edward Phillips, G. L. Chandler, and Pliny Cutler. At the first meeting, after their appointment, the Board reëlected Mr. WINTHROP as Chairman, and Mr. SAVAGE as Secretary ; and, encouraged by the confidence of their townsmen, proceeded with increased energy to perfect the arrangements for successfully carrying on their work.

At a quarterly meeting, December 21, 1819, a Sub-Committee was appointed " to consider of all subjects proper for the consideration of the Board ; " and in the reports of this Committee, which was presented and accepted March 21, 1820, a simple code of Rules and Regulations for the Committee and the Schools was adopted. The last section of this report particularly claims our attention as originating the Executive or Standing Committee, and defining its relation to the Board.

REPORT.

The Sub-Committee, appointed at the stated quarterly meeting of the Primary School Committee, on the 21st of December last, to consider of all subjects proper for the consideration of this Board, have attended to that service, and beg leave to report the following as the result of their inquiry, viz.:

1st. That each of the school-mistresses shall stand on equal terms in point of compensation.

2d. That all the schools shall be as nearly equal in point of numbers as may be, it being desirable that none have more than *fifty*, nor less than *forty*, as constant attendants.

3d. That the pupils in each of the schools shall be arranged into four classes, viz.: Those who read in the Testament shall be in the *First* Class; those in easy reading, in the *Second* Class; those who spell in two or more syllables, in the *Third* Class; those learning their letters and monosyllables, in the *Fourth* Class; and that the books be the *same* in every school, for each pupil *hereafter* entering.

4th. That no pupil shall be received into the Primary Schools without a ticket of admittance from one of the Ward or District Committees.

5th. That returns from each of the schools shall be made quarterly by the instructors to the District or Ward Committees, stating the ages and the number of male and female pupils, and the progress of each.

6th. That each Ward or District Committee shall meet, at least ten days previous to the quarterly meeting, to prepare from the returns of the several school-mistresses a report, to be made forthwith to the Standing Committee, with said returns, with such observations as they shall please to make.

7th. That a Standing Committee of *seven* be appointed by this Board, whose duty it shall be to meet on the second Tuesday of each month, to consider of every subject relating to the Primary Schools, and the same to visit semi-annually, and report at every quarterly meeting, recommending any improvements necessary to obtain the general objects of this Board.

Signed,   ELISHA TICKNOR, Per Order.

Although this is, doubtless, the origin of the Standing Committee, as such, yet the same duties had been previously performed by a Sub-Committee, corresponding in all respects with the Standing Committee now proposed, as is evident, from the *first* Annual Report made to the town in behalf of the Board.

The report having been adopted, the following gentlemen were elected as the Standing Committee by the Board: Elisha Ticknor, Rev. Paul Dean, Rev. Henry Ware, Deacon Moses Grant, James Savage, Thomas B. Wait, and Peter Mackintosh, Jr.

1820.

On the 25th of March, 1820, the first meeting of the Standing Committee, was held at the office of James Savage, Esq., at which all the members were present. After organizing themselves, by the choice of ELISHA TICKNOR, Esq., as Chairman, and P. MACKINTOSH, Jr., as Secretary, the committee proceeded to make arrangements for their "first semi-annual visitation;" and we deem the details of that meeting so interesting as the basis of all subsequent semi-annual examinations, that we cannot forbear introducing the entire record on this occasion, which is as follows:

It being the duty of this Committee to prepare a report relative to the Primary Schools, to be communicated at the adjourned meeting of the Primary School Committee; which report, when approbated, to be laid before the town for general information, it was judged proper that our first semi-annual visitation should be made as soon as may be, for the purpose of furnishing materials for said report, founded on an actual survey of each school by the Standing Committee. Therefore, on motion, made and seconded, it was

Voted, That the first semi-annual visitation of the schools in the several wards be made on Tuesday and Wednesday next, being the 28th and 29th instant, in conjunction with the respective committees in the wards. Also,

Voted, That this Committee be divided into *seven* Sub-Committees for that purpose, as follows:

Mr. Wait, for Ward No. 1, 3 Schools, and Ward No. 4, 2 Schools.

Mr. Ticknor, for Ward No. 2, 4 Schools, and Ward No. 7, 1 School.

Mr. Grant, for Ward No. 3, 4 Schools, and Ward No. 8, 1 School.

Mr. Savage, for Ward No. 6, 3 Schools, and Ward No. 5, 2 Schools.

Mr. Mackintosh, for Ward No. 12, 3 Schools, one of which is at South Boston.

Mr. Dean, for Ward No. 12, 2 Schools, and Ward No. 9, 3 Schools.

Mr. Ware, for Wards No. 10 and 11, 5 Schools.   Total, 33 Schools.

In order to produce something of uniformity in our inquiries, it was *Voted*, That each Sub-Committee should ascertain as follows:

1st. The whole number of scholars present at the visitation, designating the number of boys and girls.

2d. The number of children of seven years and upwards, designating the boys and girls.

3d. The number who are now qualified as candidates for the Grammar Schools.

4th. What number have been discharged and sent to the Grammar Schools, and there admitted during the past year.

5th. If any, and what number are admitted, as private scholars, from whom tuition money is received.

6th. The general state and condition of each school; stating in the report to this Committee whether it be good, bad, or indifferent; naming the ward, the number of the school, the name of the teacher, and her qualifications for her duty.

The Committee then adjourned to April 10th, at which meeting " reports from personal inspection of all the Primary Schools in town were made; and it was *Voted*, That the same be committed to Mr. Savage to prepare a condensed report thereon."

On the 25th of April, the *first* report of the Standing Committee was presented to the Board, and being approved by them, was read at the Town meeting in June. The brevity and comprehensiveness of the report, and the confidence with which still further claims were made upon the town, renders this report not less interesting than the first.

From it we learn that the whole number of schools in March, 1820, was 34, and " that from these nurseries 171 children had been advanced to the English Grammar Schools, and 177 more were found qualified for

7

admission therein," . . " making a total of 348 pupils, prepared for the English Grammar Schools" during the year. The whole number belonging to the Primary Schools was 1,666, of whom 1,409 were present at the examinations. The conclusion of the report is, " that, in the opinion of the Committee, the grant of $8,000 by the Town, made last year, for the purpose of enabling this Board to provide instruction for children between four and seven years of age, has been well appropriated, and that the good effects of its expenditure will long be experienced; but, inasmuch as that grant was made on a calculation of the necessity of having only *thirty-two* schools, for a number of pupils less than this Board has found itself obliged to provide for in *thirty-four* schools, the inhabitants of the Town will perceive the propriety, if the system is thought worthy to be persevered in, of making for the present year a grant larger than that of the last year, by $500, to support the increased establishment." This report is " signed, ELISHA TICKNOR, *Chairman.*"

In addition to this report, prepared for the town meeting, Mr. Savage also prepared a report of the returns made by the several members of the Standing Committee, which was presented to the Board at the quarterly meeting, April 25th.

At the town meeting, in June, the report was read, accepted, and the desired appropriation of $8,500 voted for the year 1820–21. In the annual appointment of the Primary School Committee, the following changes were made :

George Darracott,	vice	Robert Fennelly.
Isaac Harris,	"	N. G. Snelling.
Thomas Wells,	"	Rev. J. M. Winchell.
Reuben Richards, Jr.,	"	Thos. S. Bordman.
Samuel J. Armstrong,	"	Dr. Benj. Shurtleff.
Andrew Green,	"	Rev. Daniel Sharp.
Rev. Sereno E. Dwight,	"	Hon. Benj. Austin.
Isaac Mansfield,	"	Edward Phillips,
Samuel Norwood,	"	Henry Chapman.
Lewis Tappan,	"	Rev. Dr. T. Baldwin.
Thomas Jackson,	"	John Bellows.
Samuel Dorr,	"	G. L. Chandler.
William Jackson,	"	Benjamin West.

At the regular meeting of the Board, Mr. WINTHROP was reëlected Chairman; and as Mr. SAVAGE declined, Mr. PETER MACKINTOSH, Jr., was elected Secretary, and Mr. WILLIAM BROWN, Treasurer, of the Board. The Standing Committee was composed of the same gentlemen as the previous year, all the members having been reëlected. At a meeting of this Committee, July 20, 1820, ELISHA TICKNOR was chosen Chairman, and MOSES GRANT, Secretary. It was also " *Voted*, That one dollar per annum be appropriated to each school for the purchase of reward books, and tickets or medals.

" *Voted*, That Mr. Cutler's and Grant's bills for small reward books and tickets, and all similar bills now due, be paid by the Treasurer.

" *Voted*, That Mr. Mackintosh prepare the Rules and Regulations for the government of the Committee."

The Committee then adjourned to July 23d, at which meeting the first " Rules and Regulations of the Primary Board " were read and accepted. They were subsequently adopted by the Board July 27th, and printed in a pamphlet form. It appears from these "Rules" and the records, that at that time and previous to June, 1824, the officers of the Primary Board were a Chairman, Secretary, and Treasurer; the duties of the latter officer were defined in "Section IV. The Treasurer shall keep a fair and accurate account of the moneyed concerns of the Board. He is authorized to receive, from the Town Treasurer, all the moneys granted for the support of the Primary Schools; and pay the Instructors of the Schools quarterly, their bills being first approved by the Committee of the Ward or District to which they belong. His accounts shall be audited or inspected, whenever the Board may appoint a Committee for that purpose. At the close of the year he shall make a transcript, or an abstract of his accounts as audited, to be laid before the Board."

The books to be used in the Primary Schools were selected by the Standing Committee, and were adopted by the Board at the same time with the "Rules." They were, "the Testament, Child's Companion, Kelley's Child Instructor, Webster's Only Sure Guide, Pickard's Juvenile Spelling Book. and Child's First Book English Reader."

Notwithstanding the gratifying success which had attended the schools, and the large number of children which were brought within their salutary influence, the benevolent minds of the Committee were soon attracted to the importance of extending the benefits of education to that class of children who were too old to be admitted to the Primary, and were not qualified to enter the Grammar Schools. In pursuance of this object, at a meeting of the Board on the 16th of July, 1819, it was " *Voted*, That a Committee of one from each Ward be appointed to ascertain the number of children in this town over seven years of age, who are not qualified for admission into the Public Schools, and whose parents are not able to pay the expense of instruction; also of those children who are idlers, truants, and such as have no visible or known employment, and who do not habitually attend any school, and report at the next quarterly meeting; and also the form of a memorial to be presented from this body to the Board of Selectmen of this Town, requesting the adoption of such measures as they may deem proper to supply the want of Schools to those who are unqualified to enter the Public Schools."

The labor involved in this vote required considerable time, and the Committee were unable to complete their report and present it, until the quarterly meeting of the Board on Tuesday, April 25th, 1820. It was then read and accepted, as follows :

REPORT.

Your Committee, deeming it highly important, would state to their fellow-citizens, that in the discharge of their duty the past year, they have had many applications for the admission to the Primary Schools, of children over seven years of age, who were not qualified to enter the town schools, and consequently, could not be legally benefited either by the Primary or Public Schools.

This induced us to make a careful inquiry to ascertain the number of children in this town between seven and fourteen years of age, who are in this condition, and to our great surprise and grief, we have found the number to exceed *three hundred,* and we entertain no doubt that the real number is much greater. Some of these are truants; some of them employed in street-begging, and all of them ignorant; and if nothing is done for them, they seem destined forever to remain ignorant, and vicious, and wretched.

These children, be it remembered, were born in as free and as happy a land as the earth affords, and have, as we believe, undeniable claims on the public munificence for such an education as will enable them to know, defend, and enjoy the civil, religious, and social privileges of which they are born the distinguished heirs; and not only so, but if they are permitted to remain in their ignorance, insubordination, and vicious habits, they will not only go quickly to destruction themselves, but by their pernicious example and influence, they will draw many others after them to the same deplorable ruin.

A lively interest in the welfare of these unhappy youth, (which we believe is also felt by a humane and virtuous public,) has led us to consider whether something could not be done for their relief and the public good, both in a moral and social view; and the result of our reflections has been, that one or more schools might be opened at a trifling expense to the town, and instructed by persons competent to teach and govern them; and that nearly all these children, whose names, ages, and places of residence we are already in possession of, may be induced to attend, and thus escape the evils to which they are now exposed.

This evil, which has been accumulating for several years, from a want of Primary Schools, will be remedied in a few years, at farthest, in our opinion, after which the Primary and Public Schools will be fully adequate.

<table>
<tr><td>Elisha Ticknor,</td><td rowspan="5">} Sub-Committee.</td></tr>
<tr><td>Paul Dean,</td></tr>
<tr><td>Moses Grant,</td></tr>
<tr><td>Wm. Thurston,</td></tr>
<tr><td>Benj. Shurtleff,</td></tr>
</table>

This report was drawn up by Rev. Paul Dean, and appended to the Annual Report, made to the Town by Mr. Savage at the Town meeting in June. The report and petition were referred by the Town to the School Committee, and by them committed to a Sub-Committee. But, as no report was made by them, the Primary Board brought the subject again to the notice of the School Committee, who then recommended to the Town an appropriation of $1,000, to establish a School for Mutual Instruction, for the accommodation of such children. This was voted at a Town meeting, held July 2d, and the School Committee were authorized to establish the school; the matter was then referred by them to the Primary Board, and the school was organized in the basement room of the Boylston School House on Fort Hill.

This school was the *first* of that class of schools which subsequently became much extended under the name of "Intermediate Schools."

As exemplifying the careful supervision of the schools at this time, and the manner in which they were conducted, we present the report, of Mr. ELISHA TICKNOR to the Standing Committee, of his Semi-Annual visitation to four schools in Ward No. 2, and one school in Ward No. 7, in March, 1820:

GENTLEMEN: According to your directions, I have visited and examined, in company with Messrs. Fracker, Hichborn, and Leland, Committee of Ward No. 2, four Primary Schools, on the 28th instant.

	Whole No.	No. present.	Boys.	Girls.	Entered Gram'r School last y'r.	Prepaid for Gr Sc. this year.	Over 7 years.
School No. 1, kept by Miss Turner, ...	58	56	22	84	7	8	8
School No. 2, kept by Miss Ripley, ...	47	44	25	19	16	6	5
School No. 3, kept by Miss Marsh, ...	48	41	23	18	6	3	2
School No. 4, kept by Miss Fracker, ...	68	36	12	24	1	....	2
	221	177	82	95	30	17	17
I also visited and examined in company with Mr. Coverly, Committee of Ward No. 7, School No. 1, kept by Miss Jewett.	68	56	35	21	8	9	12

In visiting these schools, we proceeded to examine in the first place School No. 2, kept by Miss Ripley. Her pupils were neat and clean, respectful in their manners, and orderly in their behavior. They passed an excellent examination in reading and spelling, and repeating what they had learned by heart. The young lady, also, set an example worthy of her pupils' notice, and appeared to possess those qualifications both for governing and instructing, which are so desirable for one in her situation to possess. Her children, she observed, attended school punctually, and, with very few exceptions, were moral and civil in their manners, and generally clean and neat as we then saw them. Fifteen read in the Testament. The books she taught were Kelley's Spelling Book and the Testament. These she considered as sufficient to qualify her pupils for the Grammar School. She had no private scholars. She taught no knitting or sewing; and I was sorry for it, because I believe a little manual exercise will induce children to learn more, and better, and faster, and will give a spirit and animation to whatever they undertake to perform. This school is evidently well taught, and may be denominated a good one.

We then passed on to School No. 3, kept by Miss Marsh, successor to her mother, lately deceased. It was neat and clean, and there were evident marks of good government and proper subordination. It certainly appeared well; the pupils read and spelt excellently, and were desirous to show, by repeating long lessons from Scripture, that they had been no idlers in school, but had been orderly and diligent. The Instructress was mild and dignified in her manners, and her scholars exhibited marks of respect and attention which quite satisfied your Committee. Fourteen read in the Testament. She observed that she had no cause to complain of any immoral language, or expressions falling from the lips of her pupils, and they were punctual at school. The books taught were Kelley's Spelling Book and the Testament, which she thought, also, were sufficient to qualify her pupils for the Grammar School. In this school knitting and sewing were taught, although none was exhibited.

We then examined School No. 4, kept by Miss Fracker. This school is a new one, got up but a few months ago, and is not in that state of improvement we could wish; yet there appears to be no fault attached to the instructress. She is mild in her manners, and evidently possessed of a good mind; but whether she has energy enough in her government, and system enough in her mode of instruction, must hereafter be determined by the Ward Committee. This school is, however, far from being properly organized, and what course the Committee can take to compel or induce upwards of thirty children, irregular in their habits, to attend school punctually, as do the others, is beyond my experience to determine; but if any method can be devised, it will be a great acquisition, and a point gained in favor of the Primary School system. I think it may be done; but it will depend upon the exertion and perseverance of the Ward Committee. A complaint of vulgar language was brought against one, and him we called up, and trust that we shall hear nothing more on that subject. Knitting and sewing were taught here, and four read in the Testament. In books, the scholars were very deficient, evidently not half enough to serve the school.

We then visited, for the last school in this Ward, School

8

No. 1, kept by Miss Turner. She is, or I am greatly mistaken, one of the most accomplished and thorough schoolmistresses for a Primary School I have yet seen. On entering the school-room we were received with respect and attention, and all remained standing till we were seated; and during the time we were present, no disorder, and not the least deficiency of government appeared. I informed the young lady that I was commissioned to examine her school, and requested to propound to her a few questions previous to the examination. These questions she readily answered, and I then requested her to take her own way to exhibit to us the acquirements of her scholars, together with her own mode or system of instruction, that we might know exactly what the scholars had learned, and what might be the future prospect of improvement. She began by calling upon the Fourth or youngest class, which showed me instantly that she knew how to examine her pupils to advantage, and that she had already divided her school systematically into four classes, as the Primary Committee had agreed at their last meeting to have done. With this beginning I was pleased. The class then stood up in their places and read in words of one syllable, audibly and distinctly, which is not common for those of their standing. They were then ordered to close their books; each did it instantly, and put his book under his arm, and renewed his position, and order of standing. They then spelt in a distinct, and with a proper tone of voice, and sat down. The Third class then rose, and passing through similar ceremonies, read in words of three or four syllables, spelt, and were seated. During this period attention and perfect silence reigned through the school. The second class then rose in their place (for each class sat by themselves), and with like ceremonies they read in easy reading, and spelt quite to my satisfaction. The first class was then directed to rise. They read in the Testament excellently, and spelt, and sat down. At this moment I supposed the mistress had completed the exhibition of her pupils, and was preparing myself to address a few words to them; but observing a child, about six years of age, at my right hand, "Sir," said the mistress, "Will you please to hear the child repeat the rules she has learned?" The child handed me Kelley's Spelling Book, and repeated to me between 50 and 60 rules, being all it contained in relation to letters and pronunciation. At her remarkable memory and attention I was surprised, because she appeared, at the same time, to understand the nature of the rules. "Sir," said the mistress, "no child is allowed to pass from the second to the first class who is unable to repeat these rules." A second repeated to me all the reading part or lessons in Kelley's Spelling Book, principally made up of maxims and important sentences. A third, all the stops and marks used in reading; a fourth, the use of all the capitals; a fifth repeated a long catalogue of words of similar sound, but differently spelt; a sixth, a long catalogue of vulgarisms, such as *vinegar*, not *winegar*; *vessel*, not *wessel*; *wharf*, not *vaff*, &c.; a seventh, the use of the common abbreviations, such as A.M., D.D., LL.D., &c. No one in the second class can be advanced to the first who has not committed to memory, and actually repeated all the above rules. The First class appears to be the place for practice, in which the *use* of all these rules is taught. This class read so excellently, I imagine they might all enter a second standing in our English Grammar Schools. But the examination did not end here; the mistress sent us up a number of misses to show us wristbands they had stitched, and button-holes they had wrought in their leisure moments after they had learned their lessons. This work was neat and well done, and creditable to them and their instructress. But this was not all; a boy was sent up with a slate, on which he had written with his pencil the common figures, and printed the alphabet very handsomely; a second came with each of the stops and marks on his slate, and repeated to me their names and uses; a third came also and repeated to me the letters standing for numbers, such as V. for 5, VI. for 6, &c., all of which were very correctly explained.

Thus ended the examination; the pupils were neat and clean, and punctual at school. Knitting and sewing were taught; and profanity, I understand, was a stranger among these children.

School No. 1, in Ward No. 7, kept by Miss Jewett, is well taught. She is excellently well qualified, in my opinion, for an instructress, and exhibited the improvement of her pupils to great advantage. When I consider the part of the Ward from which her scholars are collected, I think she has done remarkably well, and but very few, if any, have surpassed her. Could she be induced to adopt the same system of instruction as that now in use in School No. 1, Ward No. 2, her school would in a short time be much improved; as it is now, the children read and spelt exceedingly well. Twenty-seven read in the Testament, which is unusual, considering the whole number in the school. The children were neat and clean in their appearance, and attended school pretty punctually; and the mistress spoke well of their morals, and generally as excellent children. Knitting and sewing are taught.

All which is submitted by

ELISHA TICKNOR, *Sub-Committee.*

In addition to this report, which was semi-annually made of each school, the teachers were also required to report quarterly to their district committees, the names, ages, and class to which each pupil belonged; the number of verses in the Bible learned by each pupil, and the needlework and knitting done by the girls during the quarter. In the first class, in one of the schools in Ward No. 3, the number of verses in the Bible learned by one of the pupils was 438, and the average for each pupil in the class, 267. And, as an instance of the industrious habits encouraged in the pupils, we learn from the report of another school in the same district, that, among the articles of work done by the twenty-six girls of the school during the quarter, there were made "30 shirts, 12 pairs of sheets, 6 pairs of pillow cases, 26 pocket handkerchiefs, 8 cravats, 10 infant's frocks, 5 coarse bags, 4 dozen towels, 4 pairs of socks, 3 pairs of mittens, and a number of small pieces of work."

1821.

On the 15th of March, 1821, a rule was adopted, requiring the teachers to report the visits of the Ward or District Committees; and, at the next monthly meeting of the Standing Committee, on the 10th of April, the Committees were appointed for the Semi-Annual Examination. A Committee was also appointed to obtain information, "relative to the means of instruction enjoyed by the colored children of this town, and report at the next monthly meeting."

At the quarterly meeting of the Board, April 28, the Annual Report, on the condition of the schools, was made by Mr. SAVAGE, and an abstract of the Teachers' returns by Mr. GRANT. From these documents, it appears that the schools had increased, during the year, to 36; that the whole number of children belonging to the schools was 1,909; the number present at the examination, 1,666. Mr. Savage was requested to make the usual report to the town, which was presented at the Town meeting, in Faneuil Hall, in June, 1821. This was the *last* Annual Report that was made by the Primary School Board to the Town; and the appropriation of $9,000, thereupon voted, was the last which was made by a direct vote of the inhabitants; as, on the 4th of March, 1822, the City Charter was adopted by a vote of the citizens, and the Town meetings became extinct.

At a meeting of the Standing Committee, May 8, it was "*Voted*, That the several Ward and District Committees shall, annually, on the day preceding the May vacation, make an election of Instructors, and report the same to the Standing Committee; and whenever they make any change of Instructor, at any other time, they shall report the same, and give a certificate of such election to each Instructor."

At the regular monthly meeting of the Standing Committee, July 10, 1821, the death of their Chairman, Mr. ELISHA TICKNOR, was announced in terms due to so worthy a citizen and active philanthropist. On motion of the Secretary, it was then "*Voted*, That a Chairman be now elected, by ballot, to fill the place vacated by the decease of our lamented friend, Deacon Ticknor."

The simple and affectionate manner in which the death of Mr. Ticknor was noticed by the Standing Committee, shows the estimation in which he was held by those with whom he was most intimately associated. He was the earliest, and one of the most ardent and devoted pioneers in the establishment of these schools; his hand penned the successful petition, which was granted by the Town; and, as the original Chairman of the Standing Committee, he devoted himself to the work with a vigor and energy worthy of the cause. The announcement of his loss to the Board, by his friend, coadjutor, and successor in the office, Mr. Savage, was a feeling tribute to his benevolence and public spirit, and was most sincerely responded to by his associates on the Board.

The long-continued and earnest efforts made by Mr. Ticknor, in behalf of the Primary Schools, justly entitle him to more than a passing notice; and we believe that a few facts in his history will be an interesting and agreeable episode.

Elisha Ticknor was born in Lebanon, Connecticut, in 1757, and lived there until 1774, when his father moved to New Hampshire, and, with some others, settled a town there, which, in regard and love for their old home in Connecticut, they named " Lebanon," a name the town still bears. Mr. Ticknor subsequently removed to Boston, and became the principal of the Town Grammar School at the South end, and continued such till about the year 1795, when ill health compelled him to seek more active occupation, in which he persevered until 1811. Having at that time acquired a moderate competency, he voluntarily retired from all active business. His leisure after this induced him to give much attention to the condition of the poorer classes in Boston. His early experience as a schoolmaster made him anxious that something should be done for the children between four and seven years of age, who were in a much less favored condition for education in Boston than in some of the country towns of the Commonwealth. His early impressions of the necessity of Primary Schools led him frequently to urge their importance upon the attention of his friends, many of whom had been long deeply interested in the subject, until, with their aid, the earnest desire of his heart was accomplished ; — the schools were established, and became a proud monument to his memory, and to the efforts and perseverance of himself and his associates.

Side by side with this noble pioneer, was our highly esteemed, but now venerable fellow-citizen, JAMES SAVAGE, whose public spirit in the cause of education and philanthropy requires no encomiums from us. His character and acts are a public record. It was his pen that pressed the subject on the public mind; it was he that defended the system through the public press, and replied to the arguments and the conclusions in the Report of the School Committee, against the establishment of Primary Schools; it was his pen that, year after year, drew up the reports of these schools, for the information of the inhabitants of the town, and in a manner to secure their confidence, and the necessary appropriations for their successful continuance. His unwearied labors through the trying period of its organization, and his devotion to the duties of the most laborious and responsible offices for many years, entitle him to the deep and lasting gratitude of his fellow-citizens, who have so long been the recipients of the benefits arising from this class of our schools.

It is with peculiar pleasure, therefore, that we are able to present several extracts from a letter of Mr. Savage, in answer to the inquiries of a friend, in February, 1841, in which he gives some invaluable reminiscences, of the motives and acts, of the prime movers in the establishment of these schools, and bears the most disinterested testimony to the early and active exertions of his friend, Mr. Ticknor. He says, "It was, I think, in May, 1818, that after conference, for many weeks, on the lamentable deficiency of instruction for a large class of our population, Mr. Ticknor, with myself and a sufficient number of others, caused the Selectmen of Boston to insert an article in the warrant for the Town meeting, in June, to see if the citizens would authorize the opening of schools, at the public expense, for children under the age of seven years.

" At the Town meeting, I remember, opposition to the object on the ground solely of expense, was made by Mr. Otis and Judge Thacher. Of support of the object, my memory is less confident. Mr. Thomas B. Wait, a printer, I am confident, spoke with some effect; probably Mr. Ticknor opened the discussion, and it may be he was sustained by Lewis Tappan, and perhaps by myself, but of this I have no positive recollection; I know, however, that the vote was carried by a respectable majority — at least, two to one. Five thousand dollars was voted by the Town to make true and sufficient experiments; and it was confided to a large committee, chiefly of the petitioners, perhaps to the number of twenty or thirty. The first action of the committee was to take a census of the town for such children who would *need* the instruction at the public expense, between the ages of four and seven years. Five thousand dollars would be adequate to the expense of twenty schools kept by females; and the number of pupils who could be easily obtained was not less than twelve hundred. The work of inquisition was most faithfully performed by two gentlemen, I believe, in each of the twelve Wards; and no house or hovel, except as by their occupants' known happy circumstances could not be expected to contain children whose education was a burden to their parents' purses, was unvisited. Perhaps the number of Dames' Schools was found to be equal to seventy or eighty, but a majority of them had children to teach for a weekly compensation of a shilling, or ninepence, or sixpence, or fourpence halfpenny each. Of course, there was great uncertainty in the payment of such fees; and many a benevolent teacher got not a penny a year, but furnished books gratis to the object of her favor.

" Almost infinite difficulty followed the selection of teachers, as all were most anxious to obtain the fixed and certain salary of the Primary Schools, although the yearly rate was put as low as two hundred dollars. But the natural result was to obtain the best teachers, and to improve their capacity annually. In the second year, I believe, an addition of fifty per cent. to the grant was made, and almost every year since the increasing population has called for greater grants, though not by so large gradation.

" A chief inducement to Mr. Ticknor's exertions was the success which had attended the early action of our Savings Bank, opened only in February, 1817, of which he was Trustee, and afterwards Treasurer.

" Since the success of the first year, nobody has believed that the money of the public treasury was better applied in any other direction; and I believe that no project could meet with more universal rejection than to abolish the provision for these Primary Schools. I have, for more than a dozen years, exonerated myself from the personal labor and responsibility that falls on the Primary School Committee, having been absorbed in other avocations. But, I believe, my services were given above ten years; and, in these humble labors, not a small part of my satisfaction arose from the knowledge that, to this beneficent course my first introduction was by means of Mr. Ticknor, who turned all his ardor and perseverance to the success of Primary Schools." ..

It is a gratifying circumstance to state in this connection, that the interest exhibited by the father was nobly emulated by the son (Prof. GEORGE TICKNOR), who, for a number of years, was an able and valuable member of the Board, and also a member of the Standing Committee, in which his active interest appears, from a Semi-Annual Report made by him, in the absence of Mr. Savage, to the Board, at the quarterly meeting Nov. 19, 1822.

In October, 1821, the Semi-Annual examination was made, and the Report for the Board was prepared by Mr. LEWIS TAPPAN. The number of schools was 36, and the whole number of pupils belonging 1,806, of whom 1,528 were present at the examinations. Of this number, 885 were girls and 921 boys; 261 had been sent to the Grammar Schools, and 139 pupils were reported in the schools who were over seven years of age. The Instructors were paid $240 per annum in quarterly payments, in full for compensation and school expenses, including rent.

1822.

On the 22d of May, 1822, two months after the organization of Boston, under a City Charter, the following petition was presented to the City Council, and

is evidently the first official introduction of the Primary
Board to the new government:—

To THE CITY COUNCIL OF BOSTON.

The undersigned, a Committee of the Board for providing
instruction for children between four and seven years of age,
appointed by the General School Committee, under a vote of
the Town, on the 11th of June, 1818, respectfully submit to
the Mayor, Aldermen and Common Council, that the appointment by said vote directed, may more usefully, in the opinion
of the Board, be made for Districts, other than Wards, or
without reference to Ward lines, but by Districts, to each of
which six gentlemen be appointed, if the Districts be six, with
an additional member for South Boston, or that the Board be
permitted to increase their own number by addition, as the
number of the schools increases.

THOMAS L. WINTHROP, }
JAMES SAVAGE, } *Committee.*
PETER MACKINTOSH, JR. }

Boston, May 22, 1822.

The Committee appointed to prepare and present
this petition was composed of the Chairman of the
Board, the Chairman of the Standing Committee, and
the Secretary of the Board. This petition was not
acted upon by the government, in consequence of the
pressure of business, arising from the many changes required to be made to bring the City Charter into effectual operation.

In June, the people of color at the northerly part of
the city presented a petition to the Board for a Primary
School in that section, which the Standing Committee
deemed it expedient to refer to the Grammar School
Committee; "and the Secretary was directed to signify

the willingness of the Primary Board to undertake the control of such African Primary Schools as the General School Committee may give them authority to institute in this City, with such expansion of powers as may thereby be deemed necessary. And they recommend a School in the North Section, and another in the West part of the City, to embrace the young Africans from four to seven years, and beyond that, if necessary, to qualify them to enter the regular African School in that quarter."

Upon the reception of this petition and recommendation, the Grammar Board appointed a sub-committee of their body, through whom a school was established for colored children at the North end. They also communicated a request and authority to the Standing Committee of the Primary Board to establish a Primary School for these children at the west part of the city. A sub-committee (Messrs. BENJ. GUILD and MOSES GRANT) was thereupon appointed to attend to the duty; and on the 7th of August, 1822, the first Primary School for colored children was opened in Belknap Street, in a room in the Rev. Mr. Paul's Church, at an annual rent of $72. At the commencement of this school, the number of scholars was 47 (19 girls and 28 boys), and it was placed under the charge of Miss Charlotte Foster (a young woman of color), whose success was satisfactory to the Committee, and the school soon became a useful auxiliary to the Grammar School. The increase of pupils rendered a second school necessary, and it was established in December, 1822, in Southac Street, with only 6 pupils, which number, however, in a few weeks was increased to 33. Two Silver Medals were purchased, with the inscription "Reward of Merit" on one side, and "African Primary School, 1822," on the other. The Committee visited these schools weekly for some time after their establishment, and much credit is due to them for their faithful services, for the children were, generally, very poor and ignorant, many of them ten and twelve years old, without knowing a letter of the alphabet. In a school of 50 pupils, 42 were in the Alphabet class.

The City allowed $240 to each school, which included the salary of the teacher, rent of room, furniture and fuel; but the condition of the children was such as to require charitable relief; and clothing, shoes and books were furnished by the liberality of the members of the Standing Committee, and particularly by the generous donation of $10 each quarter from the President of the Board (Hon. THOMAS L. WINTHROP), which continued until his resignation of the office. A private memorandum of the receipts and expenditures by the sub-committee is the only record of the active benevolence which reflects so much honor upon these members of the Board.

June 11, 1822, Rev. BENJAMIN B. WISNER was elected a member of the Standing Committee in place of Mr. THOMAS B. WAIT, who had removed from the city. The resignation of Mr. Wait was deeply regretted by the Standing Committee, of which he was one of the original members, and had performed the duties with great judgment and fidelity.

In the arrangements, made by the Standing Committee, for the semi-annual examinations, the rules adopted continued to evince the thorough supervision which they felt necessary to exercise for the interests of the schools. By these rules the Committee were required to "Examine the mode of teaching the pupils the Alphabet, to ascertain how long they are acquiring it, and if the method can be improved; to examine the School Register, and impress upon the teacher the necessity of accurate returns; to inquire if the School has been regularly examined each Month, and by *whom;* to allow the Teacher to conduct the examination a part of the time, that the Committee may judge of her capacity; to fill all the columns of the Blanks which are furnished, and to offer as many remarks upon the Schools as will render their Report interesting and useful." With these rules for their government, the schools in the several Wards " were assigned for examination, which was to take place *in fair weather only,* and previous to August 25th."

"At a meeting of the Committee, November 12, 1822, GEORGE TICKNOR, Esq., to whom was referred the Sub-Committee's Semi-annual Reports, to condense the same, read a very able and interesting report on the state of each of the forty Primary Schools, as they appeared at the late semi-annual visitation, which was accepted, and ordered to be presented to the Board, at the quarterly meeting on the 19th instant."

In October, 1822, a Sub-Committee of the Grammar School Committee made a report, from which the following is an extract: "Your Committee are bound in duty to express their great satisfaction at the zeal and diligence with which the gentlemen who have been chosen members of the Committee of Primary Schools, have hitherto discharged the duties assigned them."

1823.

In March, 1823, the City Council, by concurrent action, authorized the appointment of a sufficient number of Primary School Committee, to allow *one member for each school.* In a report of the Committee on Public Instruction, City Document No. 22, which was adopted, and ordered to be printed, April 17, 1852, the following paragraph occurs:

" The Grammar School Committee was instructed by the people in town meeting, in the year 1818, to appoint annually thirty-six gentlemen to take charge of the Primary Schools; but it does not appear by what authority this number has been increased from thirty-six to one hundred and ninety, or how it is that the Primary School Board came into the possession of powers which are not granted to the Grammar Board, and which that Board has never presumed to exercise; such for instance as that of filling its own vacancies — unless it be that not having its duties and privileges defined by law, it became a law unto itself."

This is a grave charge upon the reputation of the Primary Board, and emanating as it does from a Committee of high official position, we deem it our duty to present the official record of the petition, and the action thereupon of the City Government, as transmitted to the Grammar Board by the City Clerk, which, with the subsequent action of the Grammar and Primary School Committee, proves, that there was no ground for such a charge; but, that in this, as in all other acts, the Primary Board in no case transcended the proper legitimate authority with which it was invested.

PETITION OF THE COMMITTEE OF PRIMARY SCHOOLS.

*To the Mayor, Aldermen, and Common Council of the City of
　Boston:*

Humbly represent, the undersigned, that by a vote of the
Town of Boston, at a legal meeting, 11th June, 1818, the
School Committee were directed, in June annually, to appoint
three persons in each Ward to provide instruction for children
between four and seven years of age; that said appointment
has in subsequent years been annually made, and that great
attention to that trust has been bestowed by the several persons so appointed, and that the number of such little children
now amounts to about twenty-one hundred, instructed at
forty-two schools; that these schools being taught by females,
require very frequent visits and examinations, and that the
number of the Committee is not found sufficient, since it is
desirable that each School should have one member of the
Committee to direct the admission of pupils, and to watch
over the economy of the School; that in some Wards there
are but one or two Schools, in others, six or seven. Wherefore, they being thereunto directed by the general Committee
of the Board for Primary Schools, request that the School
Committee may be authorized to constitute such an additional
number of members for this purpose as may be adequate to
its object, not less than *fifty* being now needed, or that this
Board itself may be empowered to increase its number as to
them may seem good; and as in duty bound shall ever pray.

<table>
<tr><td>JAMES SAVAGE,</td><td rowspan="7">}

Standing
Committee.</td></tr>
<tr><td>MOSES GRANT,</td></tr>
<tr><td>P. MACKINTOSH, Jr.,</td></tr>
<tr><td>THOMAS WELLS,</td></tr>
<tr><td>LEWIS TAPPAN,</td></tr>
<tr><td>BENJ. B. WISNER,</td></tr>
<tr><td>BENJ. GUILD,</td></tr>
</table>

10

This petition is thus endorsed:

In Common Council, March 3, 1823.

Read, and committed to Messrs. John Welles and Amory, with such as the Board of Aldermen may join to consider and report.

Sent up for concurrence.

WM. PRESCOTT, President.

In Board of Aldermen, March 6, 1823.

Read and concurred, and Alderman Jenkins is joined.

JOHN PHILLIPS, Mayor.

The Committee, to whose consideration was referred the foregoing petition, are of opinion that the prayer of the petitioners ought to be granted, and that an order pass the City Council, authorizing the School Committee to appoint such additional number of Superintendents for the Primary Schools as they may deem proper.

By order of the Committee.

March 17, 1823. JOSEPH JENKINS, Chairman.

In Board of Aldermen, March 17, 1823.

Read and accepted, and ordered accordingly.
Sent down for concurrence.

JOHN PHILLIPS, Mayor.

In Common Council, March 17, 1823.

Read and concurred.

WM. PRESCOTT, President.

A true copy. Attest,

S. F. McCLEARY, City Clerk.

The foregoing petition was drawn up by the Chairman of the Standing Committee (Mr. SAVAGE), and adopted at their meeting on the 1st of March. The prompt action, in relation to the subject, by the City Government, is evidence that the popular influence of the Primary Schools had not deteriorated by the adoption of the City Charter. The Grammar School Committee having referred the communication of the City Clerk to the Standing Committee, at a meeting of that body on the 15th of April, it was "*Voted*, That the Secretary of the Board notify a meeting on the 29th, at 3 P. M.; and also request the members to select suitable candidates in the Districts, where they will be wanted to furnish one committee-man to each school."

The Board having, at this meeting, elected the proper number of members, on the 2d of July the Standing Committee held a special meeting, the object of which was to new district the city, so as to make *seven* districts, as nearly equal as possible, in conformity with the duty assigned them by the Board, and after due deliberation, arranged them as follows, viz.:—

Instructors' Names.	Location of Schools.	No.	Committee of District.
	District No. 1.		
Charlotte Emerson	Charter Street	1	Thaddeus Page.
Lucy Ditson	North Street	2	John Elliot.
Susan C. Adams.........	N. Bennet Street ..	3	Henry Fowle, Jr.
Sarah Domett	Ship Street	4	John Fenno, Jr.
Harriet B. Luce	Fleet Street	5	Thomas Fracker.
Mary A. Eaton..........	Battery Alley	6	Charles Lincoln, Jr.
	District No. 2.		
Eliza Barnes....	Back Street.......	1	Caleb H. Snow.
Mary A. Wilder	Middle Street	2	Ellis B. Green.
Ruth Bonner	Cross Street	3	Edward Page.
Hannah H. Hansell	Prince Street	4	John Farrie, Jr.
Eliza P. Snow..........	Ann Street	5	Joseph Lewis.
Aphia Turner	North Square	6	H. Bates.

Instructors' Names.	Location of Schools.	No.	Committee of District.
	District No. 3.		
Elizabeth Deshon........	Scott's Court......	1	Reuben Richards.
Sarah Deshon	Hanover Street ...	2	George Lane.
Mary M. Vallett........	Portland Street ...	3	Charles Hood.
Sarah Gragg...........	Pitts Court	4	Charles Ewer.
Maria H. Parmenter	Leverett Place	5	George Domett.
— Welsh	Leverett Street....	6	Dr. E. Maynard.
Mary A. Calvary	Brighton Street ...	7	Benjamin French.
Maria Bates	Spring Street	8	Peter Mackintosh, Jr.
	District No. 4.		
Elizabeth Ford.........	Blossom Street	1	William J. Spooner.
Sally Jewett............	S. Russell Street...	2	Lewis G. Pray.
Lydia Johnson	May Street	3	Daniel Henchman.
Harriet Gragg..........	Cambridge Street..	4	Charles G. Loring.
Charlotte Foster	Belknap Street ...	5	Wm. J. Spooner.
Naomi Jeffers	Southac Street	6	Robt. Ward.
	District No. 5.		
Mrs. Newmarch	Broad Street......	1	Dr. Z. B. Adams.
Miss Newmarch	Broad Street......	2	Isaac P. Osgood.
Margaret Fox..........	Purchase Street ...	3	Isaac Mansfield.
Sarah Blanchard	Pearl Street	4	Abiel Chandler.
Mrs. Bacon	Sister Street	5	J. A. Haven.
Lucy H. Greene........	Newbury Street ...	6	Wm. T. Andrews.
	District No. 6.		
Rebecca Beaman	Nassau Street	1	George Ticknor.
Sarah Mackintosh	Elliot Street	2	Samuel Greele.
Ann Hope.............	Pleasant Street....	3	Benj. A. Gould.
Mary A. Thaxter........	Rainsford Street...	4	Samuel Davis.
S. Siders & Mrs. Cazneau .	South Street Court.	5	Dr. Enoch Hale, Jr.
Mrs. Wakefield..........	Sea Street........	6	Wm. H. Prescott.
	District No. 7.		
Maria Hagar............	Warren Street	1	Gerry Fairbanks.
Mary A. Bell	Orange Street.....	2	Samuel Bradlee.
Elizabeth Groves	Washington Street.	3	Benj. Stevens.
Catharine Thayer........	South Boston	4	Rev. Lemuel Capen.
Charlotte Cole	South Boston	5	Rev. Theodore Edson.

This duty having been accomplished, it was then
"*Voted,* That the Committee, assigned to each district, be
requested to organize themselves by the choice of a
Chairman and Secretary, and to appoint one gentleman
to the particular care of each school, and make a re-

turn to the Secretary of the Standing Committee by the 12th inst." These returns were duly received, the schools being assigned, as in the preceding list, and the whole embraced in a report carefully prepared by the Chairman, and presented to the Board at the ensuing quarterly meeting.

The new organization of the Primary Board was attended with increased watchfulness and labor on the part of the Standing Committee; and it was fortunate that the principal care and responsibility rested upon those so eminently qualified for the duties. Relying upon the confidence reposed in them by the Board, — strict in their construction of the line of duty required to render the schools prosperous, — conscientious in the faithful discharge of their trust, — their reports are characterized by a fearless independence in relation to the delinquency of members, and the suggestions of reform. In their first Semi-Annual Report, after the reorganization, made at the quarterly meeting of the Board in August, the neglect in one of the districts is severely noticed. After giving the Statistics of the schools, the Report states, " that the Committee of District —— report to us ' that they have appointed a committee of three to examine each school once a quarter, in addition to the monthly visits.' This is gratifying information, and the more so because it is noted on the return of Miss —— that the Committee have not visited her school during the quarter! The same committee suggest that, 'When additional blank returns are printed for the instructors, they may contain other columns to include such facts as would be inquired for by the Board, and thereby save considerable labor for the District Committees.' We hope that improvement will soon be introduced in these forms; but the idea of *saving labor* to the Committee cannot be encouraged. Unfortunately, the Committee of this District have saved themselves too much of the proper labor of their office ; and, from the imperfection of their returns, we are obliged to confide in their assurance, 'that the instructors have continued to discharge their duty with industry and zeal,' and that 'the schools have continued to improve since the last quarterly returns.'

"It is with regret that we mark the deficiencies of their Report, or allude to some of its errors, except for improvement. Under the column of '*Times of Examination*' is written 'sundry times,' but we have no results of an examination in any one of the six schools at either of the 'sundry times.' We usually hope to find the errors of the instructor's returns corrected in the Committee's Reports, but in this instance we have seen the reverse, and we were led into such great mistakes by their Report, and so confused was our statement, drawn from it, that we were obliged to re-write two pages to make it intelligible."

In several of the other Districts, just praise was awarded, to the Committee and teachers, for the manner in which their several duties were performed. We find also in this, as in other of the early reports, a commendable conservatism in regard to the formation of *new schools*. The Committee at South Boston having petitioned for another school, the Standing Committee observe : "The two South Boston schools have only 51 and 53 pupils, while in the same District are three schools on this side of the bridge, with an average of 60; the Standing Committee, therefore, cannot omit to express their decided opinion, that, as the *largest* number *present* at either of these schools, on any of the nine visits, except one, was 48, another school cannot be more wanted in this district than in two or three others; and it seems to them, that at present, we had better continue with our forty-three schools, which is one more than our appropriation of funds is calculated for, and make no increase until the ensuing spring."

At this time the total number of pupils belonging to the schools was 2,294; being an average of over 53 to each school.

In the same report, the Standing Committee congratulate the Board that "the City Government have granted $10,500 for the support of this establishment for the current year, besides $500 to enable us to make some small additions to the Instructor's compensation;" and they suggest, that, "perhaps the best division of this additional sum will be to give ten dollars to each instructor, making the annual salary an even sum of $250."

This was adopted, and also a recommendation of the Committee, that "the vacation shall be on Wednesday afternoon, instead of Thursday, which will divide the week more equally." In consequence of the nonconcurrence of the Grammar Board, this recommendation was not carried into effect till 1829.

At the meeting of the Standing Committee, September 9, 1823, among the Rules to be observed at the Semi-annual Examination, "The number (and names, if thought best,) of all 'truants,' were to be reported;" "the appearance of the room and scholars as to cleanliness;" "the faithfulness of the Committee." The capacity of the teacher, &c., &c., were also to be noticed. The Examining Reports were made at the October meeting, when an unfavorable report of the African Primary School No. 2 having been made by Mr. Williams, the subject was referred to the Secretary, who subsequently reported that he "had visited the school, and found 25 children present, and from conversation with the local Committee, he had no doubt that every means would be used to restore the school to its former prosperity." A note was also received from the local Committee, "explaining the circumstances of its apparent decline, and that the number had now increased to about 35; and also, that he had endeavored to inform the instructress as to her duty, and to stimulate the scholars in their attendance and good behavior."

At the meeting of the Standing Committee, October 28th, the Chairman (Mr. SAVAGE,) was directed to "prepare a condensed report, according to his views, and offer such resolutions as the state of the schools require; and as the report of each District will be communicated to the Committee of the district, it will not be necessary to go into the character of each school, as heretofore."

In conformity with these instructions, Mr. Savage prepared a general report on the condition of the schools, from the Examiner's returns, and presented the following Resolutions, which were adopted by the Board :

Resolved, That the Chairman or Secretary of each District Committee be authorized and requested to call on

The subjects of inquiry were the following:

1. The children of each sex present, and belonging, of each class.

2. The number sent to the Grammar Schools during the last six months, and the number now qualified.

3. The number of Truants, and the effect, of former inquiries upon this class of scholars.

4. The Instructor's mode of keeping a record of tardiness and absence of her pupils, and of the visits and examinations by the District Committees.

5. The economy of the School-rooms, and the cleanliness of the children.

6. The School Hours.

7. Respecting Sewing and Knitting.

8. Deficiency of Books.

9. The discipline, mode of instructing, and proficiency of the scholars.

Each member of the Standing Committee made a written Report of all the subjects of inquiry, which will be delivered to the District Committees, and thus save the necessity of a voluminous report by the Standing Committee. They, however, recommend to the respective District Committees to circulate these reports among the members of their Boards respectively, and take such measures in relation to the schools under their charge, as may appear necessary.

The number of pupils present in all the schools was 2,171; 1,054 boys, and 1,017 girls. The number absent was 290; 122 boys, and 168 girls.

The grand total belonging to the schools was 2,463; 1,278 boys, and 1,185 girls. The increase since the last semi-annual examination, being the average number present in the schools, was $49\frac{15}{44}$; and the average number belonging was 56. One new school was established in District No. 1 the last six months, and one in District No. 7, since our examination, while making this report. No changes have been made in the Instructors during that period. A new school was found to be wanted in District No. 6.

The numbers present at the examination amounted to above 88 per cent. of the whole number belonging, which is unusually large, and highly gratifying. It is to be attributed to the greater attention of the District Committees, the vigilance of the Instructors, and it is hoped, to a better appreciation by the parents of the benefits derived from these seminaries.

The number sent to the Grammar Schools during the last six months was 76; all *boys*, of course, as the ancient and unnecessary custom of prohibiting *girls* from attending Grammar Schools in the winter season has not been abolished. It is a subject of congratulation, however, that the autumn term is prolonged, and the girls may now attend until December. When it is considered that the same expenses are incurred by the city, in winter as in summer, in the number of masters and ushers, that the custom of girls attending private schools throughout the year, is very general amongst us; and that the sentiment of the advantages of education to females is now very prevalent, it is to be hoped and confidently expected that a prohibition of our predecessors whose notions in regard to education and the claims of the other sex were less enlightened than those prevailing at the present day will be abolished. About 270 were found qualified.

The members of the Select Committee have in their reports expressed their opinions in regard to the numbers qualified agreeably to the Rules for admission into the Grammar Schools.

It is respectfully urged upon the District Committees to see that those who are recommended for admission into the Grammar Schools are thorough in the acquisitions required by the Rules, to the end that the reputation of the Primary Schools may be preserved, and a laudable impulse imparted to the Grammar Schools in keeping in advance of those who enter from lower seminaries.

It is probably known to many members of the District Committee, that children must now apply for admission into the Grammar School on the first Monday in the month. and that they cannot be received on any other day.

Truanting has diminished in these schools, and the admonitions given to truants have had a happy tendency. The *morals* of the pupils, so far as the Select Committee could ascertain, are as correct as could be expected, and illustrate the benign effects of good discipline, of intellectual and religious instruction, imparted by the lessons taught in these schools.

The *Journals* of the schools, though improved, are far from being uniform or perfect. Dr. Hale, of the Committee for District No. 6, has devised a plan, so excellent, that the Standing Committee recommend it as a form for all the schools. It is a folio book, calculated for recording the names of all the scholars on one page, so as to give at one view the name, date of entrance, age, parent's name, rewards, tardiness and absence. A *Diary* is also kept, in the same book, giving the day of the month, day of the week, section of day, state of the weather, number present, number absent, and remarks. It occasions but little trouble to the Instructor to keep such a book; it, in fact, *saves* her time, and prevents perplexity in giving a *verbal* account of her school to the Visiting Committees, and written accounts on the quarterly returns; it is of great use to the Committees, inasmuch as they can, on inspecting it, ascertain the attendance of each half day, between their examinations; and it furthermore serves to record the visits and examinations of the District Committee.

The only part of the plan about which a difference of opinion might exist, is the columns for best and poorest scholars each half day. So many circumstances are to be taken into consideration, in deciding these facts, such as natural abilities, industry, proficiency, behavior, &c., that an Instructor would be perplexed to decide every day out of 50 pupils.

It affords great pleasure to the Standing Committee to state, that the effects of new districting the city, new organizing the Committees, introducing more system into the superintendence, supplying the Instructors with Walker's Dictionary and the Pronouncing Testament, have been very important and encouraging. The schools were never so regularly and faithfully examined as they have been the last six months. A conscientious spirit seems to have pervaded every Board, and the members have given evidence that they will not hold offices without discharging the duties of them, nor be unfaithful to the responsible and important interests committed to their charge. The Instructors, with some exceptions, have better qualified themselves to be good teachers, their pronunciation is improved and more uniform, and the discipline and instruction of their pupils more judicious and thorough.

There appears to be a deficiency of books, especially in the Third and Fourth classes, in many of the schools. The Standing Committee attribute it, to a considerable extent, to the expectation of a new Spelling Book, to supersede the Child's Companion and Instructor. They have the gratifi cation to notice the publication of Mr. Fowle's Rational Guide, a copy of which has been sent to each member of this Board. If it has appeared, on examination, to you as it has to the Standing Committee, it will be adopted in the Primary Schools, and be greeted as the most systematic, correct, and useful Spelling Book that has been published in this country.

An accurate and uniform edition of the New Testament is much wanted in these schools. The editions now used are so numerous, and many of them of such bad paper, so badly printed, so various in punctuation, that much perplexity is occasioned to the instructors, and to the pupils.

It may be questioned, whether it is useful to require the Fourth class to obtain books. To such small children books are mere playthings. No child ought to be entrusted with a book, who does not know its *value,* and feel ambitious of preserving it in good order. The *habit* of treating books lightly ought not to be formed. *Cards* are cheaper and equally useful for such children as books.

Heretofore the school *hours* in the Primary Schools have not been uniform, nor the half *holidays* universally on the same days. Some schools have had but one session in a day, viz.: from nine to three o'clock. This practice has prevailed also in some *private seminaries* in the city; but it has been introduced to accommodate the hours of dining of parents, and against the opinions and inclinations of intelligent and humane instructors.

As this Board are the guardians of the physical as well as intellectual wants of the children under our superintendence, it behoves us to guard scrupulously against injuring their constitutions by allowing instructors to seclude them from recreation and wholesome air for too long a period at a time. Experience teaches that such a practice will be detrimental alike to body and mind; and it is believed a great and irreparable injury will be done to these pupils if long continued sessions are for any reasons permitted. It would be well also if the half holidays were alike, and if the school hours could be the same. When companions are roaming abroad in play, it naturally produces discontent in those who are at schools. These subjects are necessarily committed to the wise discretion of the District Committees. It is obvious that there is much waste of time in nearly all these schools. There is little study, and not a third of the time is allotted to recitation of each pupil. For the largest part of the day the school-room is more a place of confinement than of study. This applies particularly to the youngest classes, and is true, with various degrees of exception, to all the schools. It becomes then a natural inquiry, whether the children cannot be more constantly *occupied* without injuring them. The well attested experience in the schools of mutual instruction bears evidence that young persons of the tender age of seven years may be actively employed six hours a day, properly divided, without rendering instruction tiresome or hurtful; on the contrary, no scholars receive instruction, or apply themselves with greater pleasure or success. Children of all ages are incessantly employed out of school, without fatigue or disgust; and the reason is, there is perpetual *variety* in their amusements and occupations. If their instructors and Committees will take a hint from *Nature*, they will perceive that if instruction be made a system of diversified amusement, and the discipline is maternal, an untiring interest can be preserved in the minds of the pupils.

The usual mode of teaching the *Alphabet* appears to the Standing Committee to be inefficient and improper. The first step in the path of knowledge should be associated with pleasurable ideas, and made as interesting as possible; the young pupils should be allured, not driven. There will ever be truanting, tardiness, and inattention when in school, where instruction is accompanied by frowns, scolding and frequent chastisement.

It is scarcely necessary to observe that the ancient mode of teaching A B C, which is the prevailing mode at present in most of the Primary Schools, is anything but alluring or pleasant to the pupils. Some improvements have been introduced; in the alphabet wheel, alphabet sheet, and sand forms, wherever sufficiently tried, these experiments have succeeded admirably well. They interest and improve the learners better than any other mode known to the Standing Committee. Besides, they do not engross the time of the instructor so much as the ancient system. The excellent mode of teaching the Alphabet by Mrs. Hope and Mrs. Thaxter, of District No. 6, may be recommended to the Board as worthy of adoption in all the schools. The children form a semi-circle near the wheel; at the foot of it is placed the large printed Alphabet, and affixed to the shaft of the wheel is the small printed Alphabet, taken from a spelling book. One of the children holds the board on which the letters are *painted*, and another turns the wheel. The instructor points to a letter on the printed sheet, and the pupil is required to name it, and afterwards to find the same letter at each of the other places, naming the large and small letters. By this operation, the same letter is seen in *four* places, and the same letter, in two forms, at each place.

A monitor is taken from the first class to superintend the pupils at the sand form, when the children learn to *make* a letter at the same time they learn its name. It is ascertained that months' labor is saved by these modes of teaching the alphabet, and that it is a pleasant exercise to both teacher and learner. There is no doubt but the introduction of *other* parts of the popular and excellent system of Mutual Instruction into the Primary Schools, and into each class, would be attended with important benefits.

Monitorial instruction relieves the instructor, and permits her to be more thorough in teaching the elder scholars.

It is a subject of considerable complaint, with many inhabitants, who take great interest in the good of society, that knitting and sewing are not more attended to in the Primary Schools. It is declared by respectable ladies, that the poor are sadly deficient in the arts of sewing and knitting, a knowledge of which is so necessary to the comfort of their families. Frequently this subject has been

12

alluded to in the Primary Board. In many schools sewing is attended to in a sufficient degree to be recorded in the quarterly returns, and to comply with the Rules. There are difficulties arising from the want of *materials* among the poorest people, particularly for knitting, and an indisposition on their part to aid their children in these industrious habits. Still, a skilful use of the needle, and a facility in knitting, are as useful to the poor as instruction in reading or spelling, and probably more so; and it seems as much the duty of society to afford the means of instruction. Another obstacle arises from the large numbers in the average of schools, and the impossibility in some, for one instructor to teach sewing and knitting, in addition to a faithful attention to the other branches required. But it is thought that if no school is allowed to exceed fifty in number, the instructor would be able to form a *sewing and knitting class*, to include all the girls belonging to the school, who are of sufficient age; and that two afternoons in each week, at least, if not every afternoon, should be exclusively devoted to these useful branches of female education. After subtracting so considerable a portion from the time allowed to girls, a recompense might be made to them for the advantage the boys would have over the girls in devoting all the school hours to study, in procuring the abolition of the custom of girls not being allowed to attend the Grammar Schools during the winter months; a custom very unnecessary in this city, if necessary anywhere, and contrary to the usage prevailing in the higher classes of society, whose children attend private schools throughout the year, without distinction of sex.

The Ward Vaccinating Committees recommended to the City Council to prohibit the admission into the Grammar Schools of all children who have not had the kine pock. That body, for wise reasons, deemed it injudicious thus to visit the neglect of parents upon their offspring; but the object is important, and may probably be attained by another and less objectionable way.

If the District Committees, before giving tickets of admission to the Grammar Schools, will ascertain whether the scholar has been vaccinated; and in case it has not been done, will devote a little friendly aid to the accomplishment of this desirable object, the wish of the Ward Vaccinating Committees will, in a great measure, be attained, the child be greatly benefited, and the community protected.

The Standing Committee deem it to be their imperious duty to notice, in this Report, the case of those children, of both sexes, over seven years of age, who are not qualified for admission into the Grammar Schools; many of them, by indulgence, are suffered to remain in the Primary Schools. A few are permitted to enter after arriving at the age of seven, and a considerable number are debarred from all instruction, except at Sunday Schools. It will be recollected that a year or two since a Lancasterian school was opened on Fort Hill, under the patronage of the general School Committee, for the accommodation of this description of youth. It succeeded remarkably well, was doing great good to the pupils and to society, when suddenly it was discontinued by order of the School Committee, on account of the master, Mr. Fowle, resigning his office for the purpose of commencing a private school on the same principles. Another gentleman, well qualified, stood ready to succeed the first master; but for some reason, not known to the Committee, was not appointed, and the scholars were dispersed. That in this city a considerable number of youth should be suffered to grow up destitute of the advantages secured to the children generally, and be abandoned to idleness, vagrancy, ignorance, and crime, reflects no honor on the citizens or our institutions, and demands prompt attention.

The schools are in better condition this spring than at any

previous examination. The system has been gradually advancing to excellence throughout every department of it, and may now be contemplated with satisfaction and pride. The healthy appearance of the children, their general neat attire, their happy faces, their good conduct and proficiency in study, afford additional proof of the wisdom that established these schools, and commend them to the continued vigilant and persevering superintendence of the committees, and the liberal support of the city authorities.

The Standing Committee beg leave to submit several Resolutions, embracing several topics noticed in this Report, which are offered for the consideration and disposal of this Board:—

1. *Resolved,* That the Chairman of every District be requested to prepare a diary for each instructor in his District, similar to that in Messrs. Siders and Cazneau's School, Essex Street, in District No. 6, and that each instructor in the Primary Schools be required, from and after the expiration of the present quarter, to keep the records of her school agreeably to said plan, with the omission of the columns for *best* and *poorest* scholars.

2. *Resolved,* That Dr. Hale, Dr. Ware and Col. Fairbanks be a committee to inquire and report at the quarterly meeting in May next, on the expediency of having new Testaments in a uniform edition, gradually introduced for all the pupils in the first classes in the Primary Schools; and also which edition may most conveniently and satisfactorily be adopted.

3. *Resolved,* That the Chairmen of the seven Districts be a committee, to examine into the most approved methods of teaching *the alphabet;* that they be authorized to adopt a uniform system, together with such improvements from the *monitorial* system as they shall deem proper; and that they make a report of their doings at the next quarterly meeting.

4. *Resolved,* That the Chairmen of the District Committees

be a committee to prepare suitable reading and spelling lessons *on cards* for the use of the fourth classes in the Primary Schools, to supersede the use of *books*, and to cause the same to be introduced into all the schools.

5. *Resolved*, That it be recommended to the several District Committees to ascertain that each pupil, before receiving a ticket of admission into a grammar school, has been vaccinated; and if said pupil has not had the kine pock, to befriend said pupil, so that it may be vaccinated.

6. *Resolved*, That Mr. J. Savage, Dr. Hale and Mr. J. R. Adan be a committee to draw a respectful memorial to the School Committee of this city, praying them to take into consideration the case of the youth over seven years of age, and not qualified for the Grammar Schools, and to provide for them instruction on the Monitorial System, or such other as they may consider best adapted for these children.

7. *Resolved*, That henceforward all the girls in the Primary Schools, who have arrived at the age of six years, shall devote the afternoons of every Tuesday and Friday to sewing or knitting.

This Report and the Resolutions were adopted by the Board, and the first change was made in the originally selected school books by the adoption of "Fowle's Rational Guide" as a reading book, to be introduced into the Primary Schools on and after the 1st of May.

At the quarterly meeting of the Board, May 18th, Mr. Savage, in behalf of the Standing Committee, read a memorial to the City Government for an appropriation of $11,200, for 47 schools at $240 each, which was adopted, and the Standing Committee directed to present the same to the City Council, who, in June, appropriated the required amount.

Mr. Savage having resigned as Chairman of the

Standing Committee at the close of the school year in June, the Committee was organized August 10, 1824, by the choice of THOMAS WELLS, Esq., as Chairman, and MOSES GRANT as Secretary. The members elected by the Board were Rev. B. B. Wisner, Thomas Wells, Moses Grant, Benjamin Guild, J. P. Osgood and William T. Andrews.

The schools for colored children continued to be a source of great trouble and anxiety to the Committee; and in consequence of the ill success of the teacher of the African School No. 2, she was superseded on the 1st of July "by the appointment of Mrs. Catherine Paul, the wife of the Rev. Mr. Paul, the esteemed colored clergyman, who immediately entered upon the trust, and was permitted to change the location of the school from Southac to George Street, her place of residence. The room is not so large as the former, but is more airy and central; and the advantage to be derived from its being under the roof of the Rev. Mr. Paul determined the Committee in its favor. The change, in all respects, is for the better. The numbers have increased from 40 to 60, and the average attendance from 30 to 50. The school has a more orderly and cleanly appearance; and in the studies and manners of the children there is much improvement. The influence of Mr. Paul, which is kindly and judiciously exercised both in and out of school, is of great service; and, judging from the month during which Mrs. Paul has had charge of the school, the Committee believe that the result will satisfy their highest expectations." The success of Mrs. Paul was very good, and the Committee induced her to continue the charge of the school for several years, and then she was succeeded by her daughter, Miss Susan Paul, under whose care the school remained until 1838.

It will be recollected, that in July, 1820, at the solicitation of the Primary Board, a school for Mutual Instruction, for children between seven and fourteen years of age, was established in the Boylston School House. This school had been quite successful, but was insufficient to accommodate the increase of children whose education had been neglected, and those who were continually arriving from other countries; and in November, 1824, a Special Committee of the Primary Board was appointed to apply to the School Committee, respecting *further* provision, for the instruction of such children who were too old for the Primary, and were unqualified for the Grammar Schools. This petition was referred by the Grammar School Board to a subcommittee, in whose hands the subject remained unattended to until February, 1826, when they made a report, recommending an application to the City Council for means to establish one or more schools for pupils of the above description, and the application was made accordingly; but the City Government declined doing anything in regard to the matter.

1825.

From the Report of the Semi-Annual visitation of the Standing Committee, made by the Chairman, Mr. THOMAS WELLS, in March, 1825, we find that the number of schools had been increased to 48, and the whole number of pupils was 2,686; and it is a singular circumstance that, at this time, there was an equal number of each sex in the schools, viz., 1,343 girls and 1,343 boys.

Mr. Wells was a member of the Standing Committee from 1820 to 1830, and was a worthy successor to Mr. Savage as Chairman of that body. His reports to the Board are characterized by a careful, but somewhat elaborate, exposition of the state of the schools, — mature suggestions in regard to improvements, — and a faithful adherence to the rules and regulations of the Board. As an example of his earnestness in regard to the duties of the Committee, we present an eloquent appeal to them, in the concluding portion of the report from which the preceding statistics are obtained ; the interest in which will undoubtedly be increased, from the appreciating record of the valuable services of one of his associate members, who was well known and beloved as a Christian pastor, and whose memory is still endeared to many now among us:—

By the appointment of Providence, we have been placed in a situation in which we are enabled to act an influential part. We have it in our power to produce some effect upon the character and hopes of society. By the wisdom and prudence of our ancestors, we are in the possession of the institutions of civil and religious liberty. To these institutions we are indebted for all that we have. They rest on the broad basis of universal intelligence. To preserve this basis firm and unbroken is a duty that, in some degree, has devolved upon us. Let it not be the reproach of this generation, that they were so much occupied in the *enjoyment* of blessings obtained by the labors and the sacrifices of their ancestors, that they could not *find time* to preserve them for the benefit of their children. Let it not be the reproach of any individual at this Board that he lingered at the very threshold of duty, and gave an unwilling aid to the maintenance of these institutions, which are at once the glory and happiness of our land.

We do not make these remarks under an impression that they are particularly called for at this time. On the contrary, we have been much gratified with the attention which has generally been paid to the schools by the district committees; and were it not for an invidious distinction which it does not belong to us to make, we could point to individuals whose zeal and fidelity have excited within us feelings of admiration and gratitude.

In making this remark, we are forcibly reminded of the loss that our own number is about to sustain in one who has probably contributed as much as any individual towards advancing the schools to their present prosperous condition. The Rev. Mr. WISNER, having been elected to the Board of the General School Committee, will necessarily relinquish the connection that he has long held with us. We should feel deep regret for this loss, were it not attended with the knowledge that his labors will still be continued in another part of the great vineyard, in which we are employed, and where his experience, — his well-tried fidelity and discretion, — will be particularly useful.

It appears from this report, that, at this period, it was not customary for members of the Primary School Committee to hold any other office in the City Government. The resignation of Mr. Savage was caused by his election to the Grammar Board ; and from Mr. Wells's allusion to Mr. Wisner, it is evident that the members of the Primary Board were considered City officers, and as such, the holding of any other office was regarded as incompatible with the City Charter.

We notice another peculiarity in the early history of the Board, and which continued as late as 1838, that on the election of any one as a member of the Standing Committee, it was usual for him to be relieved from the supervision of any particular school; and, in most cases, another was elected to his school by the Board. There does not appear to have been any rule of the Board requiring this, but it would seem to have been at the option of the individual, *after* he was chosen to the Standing Committee, whether he would continue to act as a local committee or not. The same privilege appears to have been extended to the President and Secretary of the Board. From 1830, this custom began to be discontinued, and in 1839, *all* the officers, including the Standing Committee, had special charge of particular schools.

At the Semi-Annual examination in October, 1825, the number of schools had been increased to 50, and the number of scholars to 2,716. In making this examination, the committees were required to report " the number of truants and profane scholars, and also the mode of punishment practised by the instructors." In regard to the latter, the Standing Committee, in their report, judiciously observe, " In our investigation as to the nature and degree of punishment practised in the schools, we were under the impression that too much variety existed in these respects, and that much of the inequality in the character of the schools was attributable to this. It is obvious that but little advance in education can be expected unless order is preserved, and that order can only be the effect of judicious discipline. We have not found so great diversity in the

tee to reconsider the subject, of "providing means of instruction for those children who are excluded from the existing schools." The report was accepted, and the same Committee were instructed to represent the subject to the General School Committee, agreeably to the report and resolution.

The subject of Sewing having been again urged upon the attention of the Board, in the report of the Standing Committee, a vote was passed that the Committees of the several Districts be requested, forthwith, to take measures for the establishment in their District of one or more schools for instruction in Sewing, on Thursday and Saturday afternoons, and that the Secretary be directed to send a copy of this vote to the Chairman or Secretary of each District. In compliance with this vote, a number of schools for Sewing were formed in the several Districts, with good effect; particularly was this the case in the Broad street District No. 5, in which the attendance of the children was very regular, and their improvement was such as to gratify the desires of the Committee.

In October, 1826, the Standing Committee suggested to the Board, the expediency of introducing something of the plan of Monitorial Instruction into the Primary Schools, and their suggestions were referred to a Sub-Committee, consisting of Messrs. Blanchard, Pray and Spooner, to consider and report; this Committee, on the 17th April, 1827, presented a detailed report and plan, which was printed and referred to a subsequent meeting, May 10th, when the plan recommended by them was again referred to a Committee of twelve, who were directed to make such experiments of the plan as they should deem expedient. Accordingly, this Committee proceeded to introduce the plan of Mutual Instruction into one school in each District, and the result was so favorable, that in their report presented to the Board on the 22d of January, 1828, they recommended a continuance of the experiment in the schools which had already been placed under that system, and the authorizing of the several District Committees to introduce it as they should deem best, into their schools. The Board accepted the report, and authorized the District Committees, in conformity with the recommendation.

Towards the close of the year 1827, the public mind was considerably excited in regard to the Small Pox; and at the quarterly meeting of the School Committee, held at the office of the Mayor, on Tuesday, November 13, 1827, the following Preamble and Order was passed:

WHEREAS, great apprehensions were entertained, in the early part of this year, of the spreading of contagion by Small Pox, and the cities of New York and Philadelphia, and others with which the commercial intercourse of our citizens is very frequent, are often subject to that evil, and whereas the best security against contagion of that loathsome and deadly disease is furnished by a diffusion of the mild remedy of cow pock through the community, and the City Government have adopted measures for the universal extension of this benefit, without expense, to all such persons as would feel an inconvenience in paying the usual fees, and the remedy may most satisfactorily be obtained by children;

It is therefore *Ordered* by the School Committee, that after March next the instructors of all the Public Schools in this city be directed to ascertain by probable evidence that every child, who is offered for admission at any of said schools, shall have been secured from contagion of the Small Pox; and no child, not so secured, shall be received at any such school, unless on return from the master the School Committee shall order such child to be received.

This action of the Grammar Board was communicated by the following courteous letter from the Secretary:

Moses Grant, Esq., *Chairman of Committee for Primary Schools:*

Dear Sir,—In communicating the within order of the School Committee to you, as Chairman of the Committee for providing instruction for children between four and seven years of age, I feel great pleasure, because the efficacy of the measures adopted will be so materially dependent on the faithful services of your Board. These services never fail. It will be most easy, before granting any certificate for admission to a Primary School, for the member of the Committee to ascertain that the child, in whose favor the desire is made, has been secured by the Cow Pock; or if not, to obtain a certificate from any member of the City Council, or Overseer of the Poor, to secure the services, gratuitously, of any physician, if the parent or guardian *need* such favor.

The devastation which this last year has been extended by the Small Pox at Halifax, and the loss of above one hundred a year, for the last two years, in each of the cities of New York and Philadelphia, and the occasional advances in various directions in smaller towns, not to mention our own loss of two or three, must put us on our guard.

With highest regard, yours,

Boston, 3d Dec., 1827.　　　　　　　　　JAMES SAVAGE.

The foregoing communications, having been presented at the quarterly meeting of the Primary School Committee, Jan. 5, 1827, it was *voted*, that,

14

Whereas, a communication has been received by this Board of an order of the General School Committee relating to the important subject of requiring the protection of the cow pock inoculation for the children in the schools under our care, and we are deeply conscious of the importance of such a measure, and anxious to give our coöperation towards carrying it into effect, —

Therefore, Voted, That it be considered the duty of each member having the charge of a school to see that the order of the School Committee, respecting the admission of children into our schools not protected by the kine pock inoculation or otherwise from the contagion of the small pox, be carried strictly into effect; and that they be earnestly requested to interest themselves to see this protection extended to all those who are now members of the schools, who may not be thus protected.

Voted, That the district committees be requested to obtain the assistance of some physician for this purpose, it being understood that all the physicians have offered their gratuitous services in such cases, where necessary.

Voted, That to every certificate or order for admission furnished to children applying for admission to the schools after the above order shall take effect, shall be added the words " said (A. B.) being secured from being subject to the small pox."

Voted, That the above votes, with the order of the School Committee, be printed, and a copy of the same distributed to the members of the district committees and the instructors of the several schools.

By the subsequent action of the City Council, Feb. 4, " any member of the School Committee, and of the Primary School Committee, is authorized to issue certificates to any member of the Boston Medical Association, to enable any inhabitant of Boston to enjoy the advantage of gratuitous vaccination, for him or herself, or his or her child, in the form, and of the import, specified in the resolve of the City Council, passed March 12, 1827."

1828.

JAN. 15.   The following officers were elected : —

Chairman — MOSES GRANT.

Secretary — WILLIAM T. ANDREWS.

Standing Committee — Thomas Wells, *Chairman;* Moses Grant, *Secretary;* Joseph Tuckerman, B. B. Wisner, J. P. Blanchard, John P. Spooner, Lemuel Capen, Sebastian Streeter.

Monitorial instruction having been introduced with considerable success into several of the Primary Schools, in conformity with the recommendation of the Board, the subject was regarded with such favor by the Grammar School Committee that a sub-committee of that body reported, "that, in their opinion, the number of schools could be reduced, and much advantage derived, from reorganizing *all* the Primary Schools upon that plan.   This report was accepted, and the recommendation of the Committee was referred to a sub-committee, as expressed in the following vote : —

In School Committee, Feb. 21, 1828.

Voted, That the Mayor, Messrs. Savage, Armstrong, Fowle, Barrett, Adams and Farnsworth be a Sub-Committee, with authority to communicate to the Primary School Committee the views contained in the preceding Report, and in conjunction with that Committee, to devise such modifications of the present system of those schools as shall be deemed expedient and practicable, and lay the same before the Board for its consideration and sanction.

This vote was communicated to the Secretary of the Primary Board, in a note from the Mayor, as follows:—

Boston, Feb. 26, 1828.

Sir:—I have the honor to enclose a vote passed by the School Committee of the City of Boston, appointing a Committee on the subject therein expressed.

I am directed to request that a meeting of the Primary School Committee may be called, for the purpose of appointing a Sub-Committee, to meet, discuss and arrange with the said Sub-Committee of the School Committee the subjects specified in the above vote.

The Report alluded to in the vote will be ready to be delivered to the members of the Primary School Committee *to-morrow*, and a sufficient number of copies will be delivered to you for the purpose of distribution.

Respectfully, I am your humble servant,
JOSIAH QUINCY,
Mayor and Chairman of School Committee.

W. T. Andrews, Esq.,
Secretary Primary School Committee.

P. S. — The Sub-Committee of the School Committee will meet the Committee of Primary Schools at any time they may appoint.

A meeting of the Primary Board was accordingly held on the evening of March 3, at which Messrs. Moses Grant, Thomas Wells, Gerry Fairbanks, Geo. B. Emerson and Dr. Chandler Robbins were appointed a Committee of Conference on the subject proposed.

At a meeting of the Sub-Committees on the 11th of March, the representatives of the Primary Board urged as preliminary to any action, the necessity of suitable school-rooms being provided by the city; inasmuch as the rooms now furnished by the teachers were, many of them, not adapted to their object, — often too small, badly ventilated, crowded, and, in consequence, unhealthy and unpropitious for discipline; that the difficulty of obtaining even these rooms was already very great, and this difficulty would be much increased by the adoption of the system of Mutual Instruction; by which it was proposed to have rooms of sufficient size for 80 to 100 children, to be under the charge of one teacher. That the school-rooms should be provided directly by the city was also evident, from the fact that the present arrangement operates very unequally, and with great injustice, upon some of the teachers, because, while the compensation of all of them is the same ($250 per annum), the rent they are obliged to pay for rooms in suitable locations varies, in different parts of the city, from $40 to $80. If this difficulty could be obviated, and the school-rooms located so as to be convenient for the children to attend, and the number of scholars in each school continue to be regulated according to the judgment of the Primary Board, and the change in the system *gradually* introduced, the Sub-Committee expressed their opinion that the modification proposed by the Grammar School Committee might be advantageously made; and, as the teachers would be relieved from the rent of their rooms, their annual salaries could properly be reduced to $200.

The Sub-Committee of the Grammar Board acknowledged the propriety of these considerations, and expressed their entire concurrence in these views; and, on the 14th of March, the report of the Sub-Committee was made to the Primary Board, accompanied by a series of resolutions in favor of the plan. The report and resolutions elicited a long discussion, which continued, by adjournment, through several evenings, during which strong doubts were expressed as to the propriety of any action, until the result of the application of the Board respecting school rooms was ascertained. This and other reasons, adverse to the project, derived from the experience of the Committee, caused the Board to finally vote an indefinite postponement of the whole subject.

The subject having been thus disposed of, renewed efforts were made to induce the City Government to make provision for school-rooms; and on the 15th of March, a Committee, consisting of MOSES GRANT, THOMAS WELLS, and Rev. Dr. JOSEPH TUCKERMAN, presented a memorial to the City Council, " respectfully representing the serious evils, and bad consequences, resulting from the want of suitable rooms in various parts of the city for the accommodation of the Primary Schools, and praying that some measures may be adopted to remedy the evils."

This memorial was referred, March 31, to a Committee of the City Council, which, on the 14th of July, reported, " That, having examined into the subject, they are satisfied that it is for the interest of the city to provide school-rooms for the Primary Schools; and that, as they have heretofore been provided by the school-mistresses, a proportionate deduction should be made from their salaries on that account. They find by a report made to them by the Primary School Committee, that the present whole number of these schools is 57; the annual rent paid for which is $2,673, and that the

During this period, 622 qualified pupils have been removed by the Committee, with recommendations to the Grammar Schools, besides those who have left without such recommendations, or who have removed elsewhere; whose number it is not in our power to ascertain exactly, but we think ourselves safe in assuming 10 to each school that was in operation at the commencement of the year, making the total of 530; which, added to the numbers now in the schools, and the numbers sent to the Grammar Schools, will give an aggregate of 4,506 pupils, who we hope have derived benefit from the Primary Schools during the year.

Respecting the aggregate number of pupils admitted, and distinction of those who came from other Public or Primary Schools, it is not easy to determine; for, although in each school a Record is kept of the admissions and removals, yet it does not, nor cannot always explain whence they come or whither they go. We estimate, however, that about 1,500 pupils who did not before belong to the Public School establishment, have been admitted into the Primary Schools during the year, from April 1, 1827, to April 1, 1828.

The average annual expense for books to each pupil we estimate at about 50 cents, which, on the present numbers, will give an aggregate of $1,677, which, added to an equitable estimate, for those who have left during the year, may raise the aggregate on this head to about $2,000. All other expenses are paid by the city.

Yours, very respectfully,

THOMAS WELLS.

At the quarterly meeting, July 15, Mr. WILLIAM T. ANDREWS resigned the office of Secretary of the Board, which he had discharged with great ability and satisfaction, and Mr. FREDERIC T. GRAY was elected.

15

Mr. J. P. Blanchard, from the Committee appointed at a previous meeting, reported an amendment to "Rule V. That two dollars shall be annually appropriated to each school for the encouragement of the children, and a sum proportioned to the number of schools in each District, shall be placed at the disposal of the respective District Committees, which they shall expend and apply as they may judge most effectual for that purpose."

A communication was received from Hon. H. G. Otis, and fifteen others, inhabitants of Ward No. 6, representing that there were more than 40 children in their vicinity of suitable age, not provided for in the existing Primary Schools, and praying that a new school may be established. The subject was referred to the Committee of District No. 4, with authority to establish a new school as soon as 40 children are found of suitable age.

October 21. Rev. Messrs. Wisner and Tuckerman having resigned as members of the Standing Committee, Messrs. Gerry Fairbanks and Francis Jackson were elected to the vacancies; and it was "*Voted*, That the thanks of this Board be presented to Messrs. Wisner and Tuckerman for their valuable services."

It was also "*Voted*, That Messrs. Parkman, Hatch and Robbins be a Committee to take into consideration the subject of supplying vacancies that may occur in the Standing Committee."

1829.

JANUARY 20. The officers elected were as follows:

Chairman — MOSES GRANT.

Secretary — FREDERIC T. GRAY.

Standing Committee — Thomas Wells, *Chairman.* Moses Grant, *Secretary.* Lemuel Capen, J. P. Blanchard, John P. Spooner, John P. Bigelow, Francis Parkman, Gerry Fairbanks.

The Committee appointed last October, on the subject of vacancies in the Standing Committee, reported " That it was expedient to amend the Rules, so as to authorize the Standing Committee to select candidates to fill any vacancies which may occur in their number;" which report was unanimously accepted. At the meeting, Dr. DAVIS and Messrs. GRAY and WELLS were appointed a Special Committee "to prepare and have printed a correct table of the organization of the Primary Schools; to procure a suitable number of copies of the Rules and Regulations, as they now exist; to furnish each member with *two* copies of the same; to have printed such blanks as may be necessary, and to cause the table above referred to to be published in several of the newspapers of this city."

APRIL 21. Rev. MELLISH I. MOTTE was elected on the Standing Committee, in place of GERRY FAIRBANKS, Esq., resigned. The Semi-Annual Report of the Standing Committee, giving a statement of the several schools, drawn up with great care, and presenting a detailed account of the several Districts, was read by the Chairman, Mr. Wells, and accepted.

In addition to the circumstances usually attended to in the Semi-Annual Examinations, the Standing Committee were particular in their inquiries relating to some objects especially occupying the attention of the Board.

In regard to the character of the rooms, on which a petition from the Board is now before the city, it is ascertained that of 57 schools examined, about 28 are held in rather commodious rooms, and 29 in those which are poor and inadequate. Of the 28 good ones, however, there are but about one-third which are of large size.

Of 12 schools now taught on the Monitorial System, none are reported as having decidedly deteriorated since its adoption; some are represented as improved under it, and others are represented as doubtful, or equal to their former state.

Tuition in Needlework is yet strictly maintained in some Districts, but in general this branch of education has fallen into decline.

By Section 3, Rule 8, the several District Committees will soon be called upon to discharge a very important duty, viz.: on the week preceding the May vacation, to elect the instructors for their respective schools, and report the same to the Standing Committee within ten days. The utility of this rule is apparent, and affords an opportunity for the District Committee to suspend a choice, or elect on a limited term such instructors as do not advance their schools to that rank which is so generally attained.

The Committee on School-rooms, which was appointed to carry into effect the vote of the City Council, July 14, 1828, reported, " that they had attended to the duties assigned them, and had done all that lay in their power to procure suitable rooms, but as some other course appeared to them necessary, they begged to be discharged from further duty." The report was accepted, and the request granted.

After some discussion upon the want and necessity of school-rooms, it was "*Voted*, That a Committee of five be appointed to memorialize the City Council and School Committee, that school-rooms should be purchased or built on account of the city, in places where they cannot be now obtained on leases of suitable character or location." Messrs. J. P. Blanchard, John P. Bigelow, Dr. McKean, Dr. C. Robbins, and John Gulliver were chosen on this Committee.

Considerable discussion having ensued upon a motion to change the hour of commencing the schools in the afternoon, it was finally "*Voted*, That the District Committees have permission, during the months of May, June, July and August, to commence their schools at 2 or 3 o'clock, and keep three hours." The necessity of uniformity in the conducting of *all* the schools being apparent to the Committee, this permission does not seem to have been acted upon by the District Committees.

JULY 21. Mr. GEORGE B. EMERSON, Chairman of a Committee on the subject of appropriations for Rewards, made a verbal report, recommending that the money be appropriated in all the districts to the establishment of small libraries for the use of meritorious scholars.

The Committee on Rooms reported, "That they had addressed a letter to the City Council, but no answer had yet been received."

OCTOBER 20. At the regular quarterly meeting, Mr. GEO. A. SAMPSON, of the Committee appointed at the last meeting, to consider the expediency of amending Rule 8, Section IV., made a report, recommending that the schools shall hereafter be kept on Thursday afternoon, and a recess be allowed on Wednesday afternoon, in order to conform to a similar change recently introduced into the Grammar Schools." The report was accepted, and the change ordered to be made after the first of November next.

This change had been recommended by the Standing Committee, and adopted by a vote of the Primary Board, in August, 1823; but in consequence of the propriety of having a uniform rule in this respect for *all* the public schools, and the Grammar Board objecting to make the change at that time, the Primary Board deferred any action on their vote, until the change had been made in the Grammar Schools.

Messrs. Lincoln and Edmands having informed the Board that they had lately published an improved edition of "Emerson's First Lessons in Arithmetic," and requested that it be introduced into the schools, in place of the one now in use, it was "*Voted*, That this subject be referred to the Standing Committee, with power to act thereon, as they may judge expedient."

The Semi-Annual Report of the Standing Committee, giving the results of their last examinations, was presented by Mr. JOHN P. BIGELOW. After a faithful exposition of the state of the schools, Mr. Bigelow concludes his report with the following judicious remarks.

The Standing Committee have thus endeavored to present an accurate, though succinct, view of the situation of the Primary Schools. In doing so, they regret exceedingly the necessity of speaking, as they have done, with some severity, in relation to the management and condition of a few of the individual schools. They are satisfied, however, that most of the evils which they have noticed are not of so deep a character but that they may be thoroughly corrected by a little wholesome advice and caution to the teachers, and by a little more attention in some of the districts on the part of the gentlemen who compose the local committees. The cause in which we are engaged is a *good*, and it may almost be said to be a *holy* one. By earnest, untiring, and disinterested efforts in this cause by our predecessors, immense benefits have redounded to the community in which we live. Let us be careful, then, that the institution shall not essentially deteriorate nor languish while under *our own* auspices; and may we redouble our diligence and watchfulness under the unerring conviction that, in advancing the cause of education, we are promoting, by the surest methods, the greatest and best interests of our country and our religion.

Mr. J. P. BLANCHARD, Chairman of the Committee appointed April 21, 1829, to petition the City Council to erect suitable School-rooms at the expense of the city, read a copy of a petition, which had been presented to that body, which he submitted as a report of progress, and for information. At a special meeting of the Board, Nov. 18, "the Report of the Committee on Rules and Regulations was taken up, acted upon by sections, and, after some amendments, was accepted, and ordered to be printed for the use of the Board."

Dec. 29, 1829, the Standing Committee held a special meeting to act upon the subject of introducing the

"North American Arithmetic," referred to them, and after due consideration, directed Mr. J. P. Blanchard to report the following resolution to the Board : —

Resolved, That the "North American Arithmetic" be substituted for the "Primary Lessons" in all cases where new books are wanted; and with all, as soon as they can be obtained without inconvenient expense to the parent.

It was also

Voted, That Mr. Grant and Dr. McKean be a Committee to see that a regular and correct list of all the members who intend to serve another year be presented to the Grammar School Committee for their consideration and appointment.

1830.

JAN. 19. The Secretary of the School Committee having informed the Board of their reappointment, they proceeded to organize themselves by the choice of the following officers : —

Chairman — MOSES GRANT.

Secretary — FREDERIC T. GRAY.

Standing Committee — Francis Parkman, *Chairman;* Lewis G. Pray, *Secretary;* Joshua P. Blanchard, John P. Spooner, Lemuel Capen, John P. Bigelow, Chandler Robbins, and Joseph W. McKean.

Dr. SPOONER, of the Standing Committee, read the Semi-Annual Report, drawn from the returns of the District Committees, which was unanimously accepted. From this we learn that there were 57 schools, to which there were 3,583 pupils belonging, viz., 1,757 girls, 1,816 boys; and in addition, 1,031 had been qualified, and left for the Grammar Schools, during the past six months. The number of visits, or examinations, by the Committees was 277, which is nearly an average of five to each school. The report closes with the following deserved tribute to the memory of two of the early and faithful friends of the Primary Schools: —

It is with much regret that it becomes our duty to notice the loss which the Board has sustained in the death of Mr. THOMAS WELLS and Mr. GERRY FAIRBANKS. Mr. FAIRBANKS was for many years previous to his death connected with this Board. We lament his loss, for his sober judgment, his influence in society, and his interest in everything which served to improve the character of the community, and establish on a firm basis our republican institutions, rendered him a very important member of this Committee.

Mr. WELLS has been connected with this Board almost ever since the establishment of the schools in 1818; and for several years has acted as the Chairman of the Standing Committee, which office he held at the time of his decease. He was a man of whom it can be truly said, — He was scrupulously faithful to every trust committed to him. All who were acquainted with him in connection with our schools, knew the deep interest which he felt in their welfare; and there is no one among us who gave to those schools more thought, and time, and labor than he did. He has left behind him too many evidences of his usefulness to stand in need of our praises. We feel that more than we can give is due to his memory, and we offer thus much from a sincere regard to the worth of his character."

On motion of Dr. Davis, it was

Resolved, That it is expedient to cause the several schools belonging to this establishment to be provided with signs of sufficient size, affixed to some part of the buildings in which such schools are respectively located, or to some conspicuous place in the vicinity, and that a committee be appointed to apply to the city to meet this expense. Messrs. Davis, Hatch, and Blanchard were appointed the Committee, and they reported at the next meeting, April 20, that they had attended to the duty, and had caused the signs to be affixed to all the schools except those in District 8 (South Boston). Upon which the thanks of the Board were voted to this Committee for the very prompt and satisfactory manner in which they have discharged their duties.

At a meeting of the Standing Committee, Feb. 9, Rev. FRANCIS PARKMAN was chosen Chairman, and Mr. J. P. BLANCHARD, Secretary of the Committee. Mr. Blanchard declining this office, Mr. LEWIS G. PRAY was chosen in his place.

Mr. MOSES GRANT having performed the arduous duties of Secretary of the Standing Committee from 1820, and the duties of Chairman of the Board from 1825, resigned the former office at this time; but the Committee, being desirous of retaining his valuable experience in their body, "*Voted*, That the Chairman and Secretary of the whole Board be requested to attend the meetings of the Standing Committee, and aid the members in the discharge of their various duties by their experience and advice; and the Secretary is hereby directed to notify said officers of the meetings of the Committee."

At the quarterly meeting of the Board, Rev. Mr. CAPEN read the Semi-Annual Report of the Standing Committee on the state of the schools, which were represented as being generally in a flourishing condition. But the Committee regretted to find, "that in many schools, there appeared to be a disposition in the instructors to bring forward the upper classes in branches not prescribed in the Rules and Regulations. Exercises in geometry, geography, and natural philosophy have been introduced, to the manifest neglect of what, in a *primary* school, should be considered of *primary* importance, viz., correct reading and thorough spelling. Another evil of great magnitude has also resulted from this procedure; that many instructors, emulous to advance the children under their care to a higher rank than those in other schools, have greatly exceeded the regular school hours, to the manifest injury of the health and constitutions of the children." For these reasons the following resolution was offered by the Standing Committee to the Board:

Resolved, That the instructors in the several schools be forthwith directed to conform strictly to the hours for beginning and closing the schools, specified in the Rules and Regulations of the Primary Schools; and also to the course of instruction there laid down for the several classes of children under their care.

The Report of the Committee was accepted; the resolution was unanimously adopted, ordered to be printed, and a copy to be distributed to each of the Committee, and teachers connected with the Board.

This is a marked instance of the ever-watchful care exercised by the Standing Committee, whose prompt and timely warnings tended so often to guard the schools from impulsive innovations, and confine elementary education to its legitimate and proper sphere.

Among other benevolent enterprises which were connected with public education, "Infant Schools" had occupied considerable attention, and at this time were quite popular and successful, under the auspices of societies and individuals. These schools were started with the laudable object of taking charge of those children, from two to four years of age, whose parents were dependent upon their daily labor; and during school hours to interest them in some way adapted to their age and capacity. To render the school attractive, pictures and natural objects, singing, marching, and other exercises were introduced, which were made the means of imparting instruction to the pupils; and it was also thought, by its friends, that the instruction and discipline to which the children were thus early subjected, would be advantageous to the Primary Schools. This idea of partially relieving the poor parents from the care of their little ones was highly commendable, and worthy of the kind hearts that projected and encouraged it; but the attempt to learn children of this tender age spelling lessons, and even lessons in arithmetic and geography, by singing them in concert, while marching to time, gave them a restless habit and a sing-song style which it was subsequently found almost impossible to eradicate, and caused more trouble to the teachers of the Primary Schools than all the advantage the pupils had derived from the instruction they had received. The bad effects of these habits gradually became so marked, that at the quarterly meeting, in April, 1830, on motion of Mr. G. B. Emerson, it was "*Voted*, That each instructor be directed to ascertain, when children enter her school, whether they have attended any 'Infant School,' and for what length of time; and if they have, to note these facts by placing a particular mark against their names in the record book of the school."

For the purpose of acquiring correct information upon this subject, ·the Standing Committee passed an order Sept. 3, 1830, that at the Semi-Annual examination, the several committees shall ascertain "how many children are from Infant Schools, and whether they are more forward than others of the same age." In conformity with these instructions, the Committees reported the result of their inquiries; and although the numbers varied in the different schools, yet there was a remarkable similarity in all the reports respecting the character and influence of those children who had been admitted from Infant Schools. The report of Mr. JOHN P. BIGELOW, on the schools in District No. 4, expresses the views and experience of the teachers, and of the examiners, in such a manner as to answer for the reports of all of them. He observes: — "With regard to children from 'Infant Schools,' it is the decided opinion of every instructress in the district, who has had any experience on the subject, that it is better to receive children into the Primary Schools who have had no instruction whatever, than those who have graduated with the highest honors of the Infant Seminaries. It is stated that these children are peculiarly restless in their habits, and are thereby the cause of restlessness and disorder among the other children; and it does not appear that their previous instruction renders them, in any respect, peculiarly proficient or forward in the studies of the Primary Schools."

In other reports, these pupils are spoken of as intractable and troublesome, restless from want of constant excitement, and their attention with difficulty fixed upon their studies. From the evidence which was thus obtained, the Standing Committee were satisfied that "no good effect had resulted from the new and popular system of 'Infant Schools,' regarded as a means of discipline and instruction, preparatory to admission into the Primary Schools." This Report was made to the Board by Dr. CHANDLER ROBBINS, and unanimously accepted at the quarterly meeting, Oct. 19, 1830.

1831.

JAN. 18. The Board was organized by the unanimous election of

Chairman — MOSES GRANT.

Secretary — FREDERIC T. GRAY.

Standing Committee — Rev. Francis Parkman, *Chairman;* Mr. Lewis G. Pray, *Secretary;* Dr. John P. Spooner, Dr. Joseph W. McKean, Dr. Chandler Robbins, Mr. John P. Bigelow, Mr. Daniel Henchman, and Rev. Samuel Capen.

The thanks of the Board were voted to Mr. JOHN P. BLANCHARD, for the very faithful manner in which he had so long discharged his duty as a member of the Standing Committee, and Dr. DANIEL HENCHMAN was chosen in his place.

A vote was passed directing the Secretary, when notifying gentlemen of their election as members of the Board, to furnish them with a correct copy of the Rules and Regulations, and of the organization of the Board.

At a meeting of the Standing Committee, Jan. 10, the Secretary was "instructed to inform the Committee of District No. 5 that a complaint had been made to them of a violation of the Rules of the Board, by the instructor of School No. 3, in the use of a Catechism not authorized by their Regulations, and by which one parent had been deterred from exercising his privilege in the school." On motion of Rev. Mr. Capen, this subject was ordered to be noticed in the Semi-Annual Report to the Board, which was made by Dr. J. P. SPOONER, Jan. 18. This portion of the report occasioned considerable discussion, but the action of the Standing Committee was sustained, and the Secretary of the Board was directed to address a note to the several districts, requiring strict conformity to the Rules in regard to the books and studies authorized in the schools. By a subsequent vote, the Standing Committee were requested to take into consideration an alteration of the " Rules " to render them more restrictive in this respect. In conformity with this vote, the Standing Committee reported a recommendation that "Rule 7, Sect. 4, be made absolute by striking out the words 'without the permission of the District Committee,' and that to Rule 5, Sect. 5, be added the following: 'provided that no publications of a sectarian or controversial character be admitted,' which were unanimously adopted by the Board April 19, 1831.

At this meeting the resignation of Rev. LEMUEL CAPEN, as a member of the Standing Committee, was communicated to the Board, and Mr. GEORGE B. EMERSON was chosen to fill the vacancy. The thanks of the Board were " presented to Mr. Capen for his able and faithful services, for many years, as a member of the Standing Committee." A Committee of one from each district was appointed to consider the expediency of introducing instruction in vocal music into the Primary Schools.

At a meeting of the Standing Committee, Oct. 11, Mr. G. B. Emerson was requested to prepare the Semi-Annual Report for the Board, and "was instructed to embody in the report, the opinion of the Standing Committee, that it is expedient to divide the schools, so as to enlarge the number of districts to *ten*, exclusive of South Boston;" and that the Rules and Regulations should be amended, so that it shall be the duty of the Standing Committee to make the Semi-Annual examinations in the months of April and October instead of March and September. Messrs. Emerson, McKean and Grant were appointed a Committee to prepare a plan of the proposed new districts to submit to the Board.

The Report and plan were submitted to the Board at the quarterly meeting, Oct. 18, who adopted the recommendation in relation to the change of time for the semi-annual examinations; but, after some discussion, deferred action upon the increase of districts until a subsequent meeting (Dec. 6), when it was voted to be "inexpedient to alter the present arrangement of the Primary School Districts." But, to relieve the Standing Committee of their onerous duties, they were "authorized to nominate to the Board such, and so many, members of the Standing Committee as they shall deem necessary."

The Committee to whom was referred the subject of the delinquency of members, reported, through Mr. J. W. Ingraham, their Chairman, "That it is expedient to amend the Rules, so that any member neglecting the required duties for *three* consecutive months shall be considered as having resigned his office, unless the Secretary of the district shall receive satisfactory evidence that he was prevented from attending by sickness, or absence from the city; and the District Committee shall proceed forthwith to nominate some person to fill the vacancy." This Report was adopted, and ordered to be incorporated into the Rules.

An adjourned meeting of the Board was held Dec. 6, 1831, at which Mr. LEWIS G. PRAY reported "That their memorial to the City Government, in relation to establishing 'Intermediate Schools,' had been for some time in the hands of the School Committee, and that the City Solicitor had been requested to give his opinion in relation to the power of the School Committee to establish such schools; and that a copy of the memorial had been placed in the hands of a member of the Common Council, which was awaiting the decision of the Committee."

A Report was read by Mr. G. B. EMERSON from the Committee of Conference with the Grammar Board, appointed at the last meeting, on the subject of a want of conformity between the Regulations of the Grammar and Primary School Boards, accompanied by a communication from the Secretary of the Grammar Board, enclosing the following votes passed by that body Nov. 23, 1831, viz. : —

Voted, That the rules be amended so as to read " children may be admitted into the English Grammar Schools at the age of seven years, bringing a certificate from a Primary School, or having received the necessary preparatory instruction at other schools. Their qualifications shall be ascertained by the master, &c., as in the printed rules."

Voted, That it is expedient that a Joint Standing Committee of three from each of the two Boards of the School

17

Committee, and of the Committee on Primary Schools, be annually appointed to secure the introduction and continuance of a uniform system of instruction in the Public Schools, and to confer, as occasion may arise, on subjects of common interest; and that the first appointment of said Committee be made in each Board on the acceptance of this report, and notice thereof be reciprocally communicated by the Secretaries of the two Boards. These votes having been adopted, the Rev. Ezra S. Gannett, Alderman Henry Farnum and Rev. Sebastian Streeter were appointed a Standing Committee of Conference on the part of the Grammar Board.

S. F. McCleary. Secretary.

The first proposition of the School Committee, in relation to the admission of children in the Grammar School, was *not* accepted, although it was earnestly recommended in Mr. Emerson's report. The ground of objection was, that it abrogated the certificate of the Primary School Committee, and made the Grammar School Master the sole judge of the qualifications of the child.

The second proposition was accepted, and Messrs. L. G. Pray, G. B. Emerson, and Samuel Howe were appointed the Standing Committee of Conference, on the part of the Primary Board.

<h1 align="center">1832.</h1>

At the regular quarterly meeting of the Standing Committee, January 10, on motion of Mr. J. P. Bigelow, the semi-annual returns of the Districts were referred to the Chairman, Rev. Dr. Parkman, to make an abstract, and report for the use of the Board. From this report it appears that on the 31st of December, 1831, there were 64 schools, containing 1,759 girls and 2,010 boys—total, 3,769, being an average of 59 to each school. That in the course of six months there were 358 examinations, and 350 visits, by the Committees, being an average of between five and six examinations to each school. In regard to the introduction of new experimental studies into some of the schools, or the change of school books, as suggested in several of the District reports, the Standing Committee observe, " that all such improvements, whatever their value, can only be properly introduced as a part of a general system, and with the consent and approbation of the whole Board. Uniformity in the system of studies and instruction is supposed by the very establishment of our Board, and is essential, not less to the order of the schools themselves, than to the public confidence in them. The faithful examination of the schools, which is the most important duty of the District and Standing Committee, absolutely requires the strictest *uniformity*; without it it is impossible to form any just or satisfactory comparison of their condition or progress. Parents and the whole community, moreover, have a right to know what is to be taught; nor can the general confidence, so essential to its usefulness, be expected for any system that is not distinctly understood, or which is left in any of its essential parts, to the various opinions, taste or experience of the individuals to whom may be entrusted the instruction or superintendence of them. The Committee also suggest, that in the changes and improvements which may be adopted, reference should ever be had to the primary object for which these schools were established — the *preparation of the pupils for the Grammar Schools.* Nor should it be overlooked, that as no inconsiderable proportion of the children are of families in the poorer classes, unless public provision be made for their supply, frequent changes or the introduction of new studies, requiring many books, will be found inconvenient and burdensome."

The Secretary of the Board and Messrs. Pray and Grant were appointed a Committee to revise the list of the organization of the Primary Board. Rev. ASA RAND and GEORGE A. SAMPSON were nominated to fill the vacancies in the Standing Committee, occasioned by the resignation of Dr. Spooner, who had removed from the city, and the election of Dr. J. W. McKean to the General School Committee.

JANUARY 17. The Board having been notified of their appointment, proceeded to organize for the ensuing year, by the unanimous choice of the following officers and Committee:

Chairman — MOSES GRANT.
Secretary — FREDERIC T. GRAY.
Standing Committee — Francis Parkman, *Chairman ;* Lewis G. Pray, *Secretary ;* George B. Emerson, Chandler Robbins, John P. Bigelow, Daniel Henchman, Charles Walker, D. H. Storer.

In the Semi-Annual Report of the Standing Committee, allusion was made to the severity of the winter, and the unprecedented price of wood, which subjected the instructors to a heavy tax in supplying their schools with fuel, and recommended that application be made to the City Government for relief. After some discussion, it was unanimously "*Voted*, That the Chairman and Secretary be a Committee to present a memorial to the city authorities, petitioning that the sum of *ten dollars* be appropriated to each of the instructors of the several schools for the purchase of wood." This petition was presented to the City Council, February 23, and an order was passed by the Common Council, March 8, making the appropriation. In the following November, another application was made to the City Government, to make an *annual* appropriation of $14 for fuel for each of the schools, to be expended under the direction of the several District Committees. This was committed to a Joint Committee, of which Alderman HENRY J. OLIVER was Chairman, who reported, December 6th, "That the prayer of the memorialists appears to be reasonable, and that the public interests would be promoted, by yielding to the request therein contained; and they recommend the passage of the following order:"

Ordered, That there be allowed to each of the Primary School teachers, in addition to their salary, a sum not exceeding $14, to be expended by them under the direction of the several District Committees for fuel for the current year.

The Mayor and Aldermen passed the order after substituting $10, instead of $14, in which the Council refused to concur, but subsequently receded, and passed the order as amended. This annual appropriation was eventually superseded by the city supplying the fuel, through the "Joint Standing Committee on Fuel."

The Standing Committee voted that the following, among other inquiries and duties, should be embraced in the Semi-Annual examination in April:

The moral character of the school; the record book examined, and the number of examinations made by the District Committee the last six months, and by whom; whether the children are properly supplied with books; if explanations are given of the lessons, and questions asked; obtain the written answer to the circular, as to the methods of teaching the alphabet, for the information of the Sub-Committee on that subject; whether the room is ventilated, and how; if the teachers are in the habit of obtaining leave to close their schools on Training days, or other casual holidays, and how many instances have occurred the past year. The Secretary (Mr. Pray) and Mr. G. B. Emerson were appointed a Committee to prepare and forward a circular to each of the teachers, to ascertain their respective modes of teaching the alphabet; the answers to be ready, in writing, for the Examining Committee.

At a meeting of the Standing Committee, April 24, Mr. Grant, the Chairman of the Board, informed the Committee that he had received from Noah Webster, Esq., a gift to the Primary Schools, of more than one hundred copies of a book entitled, " Biography, for the Use of Schools," the author of which is the donor; whereupon it was " *Voted*, That the Secretary be a Committee to examine the book, and to report upon the disposition which should be made of the same." The letters from the teachers on the subject of teaching the alphabet, were referred to the Secretary and Mr. Emerson to consider and report.

At an adjourned meeting, April 30, the Secretary made a report on the 'book referred to him, stating objections to it, on account of the sectarian views expressed by the author, which, by the rules of the Board, would render it inadmissible for distribution among the schools. The report was accepted, and Dr. CHARLES WALKER was requested to notice the gift, and the cause of its rejection, and also to notice in his report to the Board, the deficiency of the binding of the books used in the Primary Schools, and suggest that means be taken to obtain a remedy. At a subsequent meeting, Messrs. Robbins and Sampson were appointed a Committee to advise with the publisher of the books, and obtain, if possible, more attention to the binding of the same. From the abstract and report of the Semi-Annual Examination, by Dr. Walker, it appears that there were 63 Primary Schools in the city, containing 3,927 pupils; averaging 62 to a school. Three new schools were established during the past year, with 109 pupils.

At the quarterly meeting of the Board, May 1, the Rule was changed, by which the Chairman or Secretary of each District was required to receive the salaries of the instructors; and the teachers were "required to present their bills, quarterly, to the City Auditor, made on the printed forms, provided for that purpose, and approved by the Chairman or Secretary of the District Committee."

Mr. Pray submitted several votes, by which the District Committees were relieved of the labor of preparing *monthly* reports; and in lieu thereof, were required to prepare a tabular abstract from the teacher's reports, and forward them to the Standing Committee during the first weeks of January and July. Also, requiring " each instructor, on the last days of June and December, to make returns to their District Committees, agreeably to the blanks furnished by the Board, in which they shall state, with precision and accuracy, the number of examinations and visits made to their schools, discriminating between the two, and by whom made; the number of pupils admitted, left, and belonging to the school; the average attendance and absence during the previous six months; the number sent to the Grammar Schools; with such remarks on the condition and wants of their schools as they may consider interesting and important." These votes were unanimously adopted, and the Standing Committee were directed to have the proper blanks prepared. This arrangement was very judicious; and as it was continued during the existence of the Board, a large amount of valuable statistical information in relation to these schools is thus placed in a permanent form.

1833.

As the schools increased, the necessity of a strict uniformity in the books, studies and other matters pertaining to the schools, became more and more apparent. This subject had been especially alluded to in the report of the Standing Committee at the beginning of the year, and the sentiments therein expressed had been concurred in with great unanimity by the Board. From the number of new members, which were continually being added to the Board, it is not surprising that there should have been occasional infractions of the rules in respect to books or studies, which, at the request of a publisher, author or teacher, were inconsiderately introduced, by permission of a Local Committee, into his school. The confusion which would ensue from the exercise of any such power, by the different Local or District Committees, rendered the Standing Committee peculiarly sensitive upon this point; and whenever an instance came to their knowledge, their admonitions were promptly given, and were generally received with courtesy and cheerfully corrected.

At this time, however, an instance occurred, in which a district assumed the responsibility of introducing certain books and apparatus into the schools in their district, and refused to recognize the propriety of any interference by the Standing Committee, with what they regarded as *their* prerogative. Under these circumstances, the Standing Committee held a special meeting on the evening of January 10, 1833, and appointed Dr. Charles Walker and Lewis G. Pray a Committee to confer with the Committee of the District upon this subject, and if necessary to call a special meeting of the whole Board, and lay the case before them for their decision. The result of the conference not being satisfactory, a meeting of the Board was accordingly held, by order of the Standing Committee, on the evening of January 18, when they made the following statement:

At a special meeting of the Standing Committee of Primary Schools, held on the evening of Jan. 10, at the house of the

18

Chairman, to consider some complaints which had been made to different members of the Committee, of an alleged violation of the Rules relating to the course of instruction prescribed for the Primary Schools, after the subject had been considered, it was *Voted,* unanimously, that, in the opinion of the Committee, there had been a violation of the Rules, which violation was of sufficient importance to make it the duty of the Standing Committee to call a special meeting of the whole Board to consider the subject, unless measures were taken by the Committee of District No. 6 to have the causes of complaint removed. A Sub-Committee was appointed to bring the matter before the Board, provided a special meeting was held; in the discharge of which duty that Sub-Committee would offer this statement: —

Representations having been made to members of the Standing Committee, that the regularly prescribed course of instruction had been departed from in some of the schools in District No. 6 at the instigation of a member lately elected to that district, and it appearing that there was danger, if permitted to continue without any notice having been taken of it, that it would lead to very serious difficulties, it was thought to be a part of their duty to make inquiries, and find out precisely how far these complaints were founded in truth. They consequently called at the several schools in the district, and made inquiries of the teachers on these points; from which visits they ascertained that the regularly prescribed course of instruction had been departed from in three or four of the schools — in some to a greater, and in some to a less extent.

In School No. 8, Peter Parley's Geography, with Maps and a Globe, had been introduced; also Geometrical cards and models of various figures. The Geography was used as an occasional reading book by the children; and the other things were also used by the teacher. In three other schools, more or less of the same things had been introduced. It appeared further, that, all of them had been given to the schools, though, in some cases, the parents had been requested to purchase the Geography for their children.

It also appeared that the gentleman elected at the last quarterly meeting to take charge of School No. 8, District No. 6, had been the cause of the introduction of those studies. The Committee consider these acts as violations of Rule 1, Sect. iv., which says that, " The instructors are to teach their pupils agreeably to the course of instruction hereinafter prescribed; " and also of Rule 6, Sect. iv., which says, " The instructors are forbidden to permit any tracts or other publications to be distributed in their schools; " also, of the circular dated April 20, 1830, which directs the instructors to conform *strictly* to the hours for beginning and closing the schools, specified in the Rules and Regulations, and also to the course of instruction therein laid down for the several classes of children under their care.

From a careful examination of the Rules and Regulations of the Board, the Committee are at a loss to discover where the authority has been obtained to introduce new subjects of study. They had supposed that the regular way of accomplishing this object was to introduce the subject at a regular meeting of the whole Board, and if it was there approved of, then the proposer would be at liberty to introduce it, but not till then. They do not think that it is proper to consider whether these things, if properly introduced, would be likely to be beneficial to the schools or not; that they conceive will be a proper subject for consideration when it is regularly brought before them; neither do they think it is material whether *much* or *little* use has been made of these things, so far. They think the question is simply this — Has an individual member of this Board, or any District Committee, authority to make such alterations in the course of studies, as either may think best? Or, have either the

authority to make *any change* in the course of studies prescribed by the whole Board?   These are the questions which
the Committee think should be answered at this time.   They
believe it has always been understood by the Primary School
Committee, that the whole Board, and *that* only, should decide
on the course of instruction; and it appears to them that a
little reflection must satisfy any one that this is the only safe
and proper course.   For it is obvious, that if *one* has the
right to vary, or alter the course of instruction, every other
one has the same right; and this being once conceded in a
Board constituted as this is, changing from month to month,
we should be liable to have the different schools managed in
as many different ways as there are gentlemen having charge
of them; for probably every one would think that he could
improve his school in some particular.

There is one more subject which the Committee think calls
for the action of this Board.   They have learned that one
or more of the teachers consider *themselves* as having a discretionary power to make use of such books, pamphlets,
papers, or other means as *they* may think most likely to
benefit their pupils.

As the duty of the Sub-Committee is simply to bring these
subjects fairly before this Board for their consideration and
action, they abstain from going into any argument on the
general merits and bearings of these questions, believing that
this may be done with more propriety in another form.

To this statement, Mr. Rand, in behalf of the Committee of District No. 6, and other gentlemen of that
district, replied that the Books, Maps, Globes, &c., alluded to, were not introductions of books and studies
contrary to the laws of the Primary Schools; they were
not *new* books or studies *substituted* for the old, but were
introduced to illustrate and explain, more clearly, those

lessons which were taught in the books prescribed by the Rules of the Board; that the children had taken greater interest in their schools since this mode of illustration was adopted. Mr. Rand also read the report of a Sub-committee of District No. 6, which substantially admitted the charges made by the Standing Committee, in which they maintain that the books, &c., were introduced as mere *aids* to the instructor, and that they had found them very beneficial; that the District had a right to introduce them for this purpose; and that the Standing Committee, by their interference, had transcended their legitimate powers and duties.

After much discussion, the meeting was adjourned to Tuesday evening, Jan. 22d, when the question was again warmly debated, after which the following resolutions, proposed by the Standing Committee, were adopted:—

1. That neither the District Committees, nor teachers of the Primary Schools, have any authority to introduce new books, studies or means of instruction, into their respective schools without first obtaining for the same the approval of this Board.

2. That this Board acknowledge no discretionary power in the teachers of the Primary Schools to use, or permit to be used, as a part of the course of instruction, any books, pamphlets, newspapers, or other publications, or means of instruction, but those which have been sanctioned by this Board.

3. That these Resolutions be printed, and sent to each member of the Committee and Instructor connected with these schools, to the end, that the violations of these Rules, to which complaint has been made, may be forthwith redressed, and to prevent their violation in future.

By this action of the Board, the conservatism of the Standing Committee was fully sustained, which is a stronger evidence of their power and influence than would at first appear; since their interference in the present case was in opposition to a wide-spread popular sentiment in favor of Oral instruction. At this period, the " Lyceum System " was in the full tide of successful experiment. This was peculiarly a New England institution; and, appealing to that love and desire for popular education, inherent to our people, the idea of an association for mutual improvement by the dissemination of general information in science and the arts, was responded to with such zeal and enthusiasm that the most attractive places of amusement were neglected, to throng the various lyceums which had sprung up as if by the waving of a magic wand, in the cities, towns and villages of many of the States. The excitement of the ball-room, and attraction of the drama, paled before the more powerful influence of the lyceum lecture. In five years from the formation of the first lyceum, by Mr. JOSIAH HOLBROOK and a few citizens of Worcester County, Massachusetts, in 1826, the system had spread through all the various forms of society; and in 1832–33, the number of institutions on this general plan in the several States appears almost incredible. Besides the lyceums formed in the towns, which were designated usually by the name of the town in which they were located, there were the National Lyceum, State Lyceum, County Lyceum, Teachers' Lyceum, Farmers' Lyceum, Mechanics' Lyceum, Seaman's Lyceum, Ladies' Lyceum, Mother's Lyceum, Social Lyceum, Juvenile Lyceum, School

Lyceum, and Family Lyceum, all of which had been formed under the auspices of Mr. Holbrook, who was the indefatigable promoter, if not the originator, of the system.

It was under these circumstances and at this time, that Mr. Holbrook was admitted a member of District No. 6, in the Boston Primary Schools; and it is not surprising that he should soon have attempted to introduce his peculiar ideas and system of lyceum education into the Primary Schools, with which he was particularly connected. Sanctioned by the other members of his own District, and encouraged by the teachers, who were undoubtedly more or less influenced by the popular pressure in favor of the system, he presented to several of the schools a variety of illustrative apparatus, and introduced and encouraged the children to obtain some of the interesting works of " Peter Parley," and others. Trifling and unobjectionable as this proceeding appeared to be, it was, nevertheless, a serious innovation. The Primary Schools were established for *elementary* instruction, and particularly for the benefit of the poorer classes; the great object of its friends was to make the expense as reasonable as possible, to the community for instruction, and to the parents of the children for books. It was in pursuance of these ends that the Standing Committee opposed the proceedings in the schools of District No. 6; and it was upon this ground that they were sustained by the whole Board. Like other enthusiasts, Mr. Holbrook and his friends attempted to introduce innovations, without a due regard to the consequences and effect upon the schools, as a whole, the experience of the past, or the rights and privileges of their associates.

The lyceum system was, and has proved, a boon of great value in elevating the intellectual character and tastes of our people; but time and experience have sanctioned and sustained but *one* of the many classes of its projector; and a few town lyceums now remain as the only representatives of a system which, but a few years since, was deemed so potent and universal as a means of education.

On the 5th of February, the School Committee having appointed the members of the Primary Board, the quarterly meeting was held, and the Board was organized for the ensuing year:

Chairman — MOSES GRANT.

Secretary — EDWARD G. DAVIS.

Standing Committee — Rev. F. Parkman, *Chairman;* Lewis G. Pray, *Secretary;* John P. Bigelow, Charles Walker, George W. Otis, Rev. Asa Rand, Charles Choate, George A. Sampson.

The Semi-Annual Report of the State of the Schools, founded on the returns of the District Committees, was read by Rev. Dr. PARKMAN, and accepted.

Mr. George H. Snelling, after some explanation, submitted the following vote: "That each District Committee be allowed to select one school in their District, in which new methods of instruction may be experimentally introduced; provided, however, that the prescribed studies of the school be in no degree neglected for such object, nor the prescribed hours exceeded." After some remarks of Mr. Pray on the difficulty of carrying out any such arrangement of the schools, the motion was laid upon the table.

Mr. Clement Durgin, of District No. 6, asked leave of the Board to introduce, at his own expense, in school No. 2 in that District, certain articles for the purpose of instruction, viz.: "a Blackboard, a number of Slates and Pencils, and some forms suitable for children to write at, on the Slate." Unexceptionable as this application appeared, the Board refused to grant it, without considering its effect upon other schools, and it was accordingly laid upon the table.

Messrs. Davis, Rand, Pray, Marvin, and Snelling, "were appointed a Committee to consider the expediency of compiling or recommending a new book for the use of the First Class, to be used in connection with the New Testament."

At a meeting of the Standing Committee, April 30, the reports of the Semi-Annual examination were committed to Dr. CHARLES CHOATE, to make an abstract for the use of the whole Board. He was also directed to call the attention of the Board to the subject of physical instruction, and to state the results of the inquiries as to the time requisite to teach the alphabet in the Primary Schools.

On the 13th of March, a petition was presented to the Board of Aldermen by the citizens residing on the Mill Dam, for a school to be located on that avenue, which was transmitted to the Standing Committee of the Primary Schools, and by them referred to Messrs. Pray and Otis to consider and report. At the next meeting, May 6, the Committee reported, recommending "that $125 per annum should be allowed for a school upon the Mill Dam, which school should be placed under the management of a Local Committee, resident upon the Mill Dam; this Committee to be appointed by the Standing Committee, and the instructor to be approved by them. The school, in other respects, to be managed in the same manner as other Primary Schools, excepting that the Local Committee shall have the power to retain children over *seven* years of age, and advance them in their studies, according to the Rules and Regulations of the Grammar Schools." This report was read to the whole Board at the quarterly meeting, May 7, and accepted; and the Standing Committee was directed to organize the school, in conformity with the plan proposed. The school was accordingly established, and Messrs. Samuel Fowle, Benjamin Simmons, and Joshua Seaver, Jr., were appointed a Committee to take charge of the same.

On motion of Mr. Pray, the Board appointed a Committee of eleven, viz.: Messrs. Pray, Choate, Sumner, Hobart, Marvin, Snelling, Loring, Stebbins, Walker, Ingraham, and Durgin, "to consider whether any and what improvements, in regard to physical education, means of instruction, or books for study, can be made in the Primary Schools."

At a meeting of the Standing Committee, July 30, a note was received from Rev. Dr. PARKMAN, resigning his place as a member of the Committee; and "the Secretary was directed to offer him the thanks of the Standing Committee, for the faithful and courteous manner in which he had discharged the duties of member and Chairman of this Committee." The Committee then proceeded to ballot for a Chairman, and made choice of Mr. Lewis G. Pray.   Messrs. Pray and Walker were then appointed a Committee to select a candidate to supply the place of Mr. Parkman, and they reported in favor of Mr. Theophilus R. Marvin being nominated to the whole Board.

August 6.   Quarterly meeting of the Board.   Mr. Marvin was elected to fill the vacancy in the Standing Committee, caused by the resignation of the Rev. Mr. Parkman; and the following vote was unanimously passed by the Board; "*Voted*, That the thanks of this Board be presented to the Rev. Francis Parkman, for his faithful, efficient, and very acceptable services, both as a member of this Board, and of the Standing Committee, continued as they have been through many years; and that a copy of this vote be presented to him by the Secretary, as an expression of our regret at his retirement from the Board."

The Committee appointed, February 5, on the subject of a Reading Book for the First Class, reported in favor of "The First Reader," compiled by Rev. John L. Blake.   The subject was recommitted to the same Committee, with instructions to make inquiries respecting the price at which the work could be furnished, the manner of binding, &c.   The Committee were also directed to furnish each member of the Board with a copy of "Blake's First Reader" for examination, and also a copy of "Pierpont's Young Reader."

Messrs. J. W. Ingraham, A. A. Gould, and L. S. Cragin were appointed a Committee "to have the Primary School papers duly filed and arranged in such order as to be conveniently consulted."

The following recommendation, by the Standing Committee, was adopted by the Board: "In future, all children requesting permits of admission to the Primary Schools, shall be required to produce a certificate from a physician, of their having been vaccinated."

An order was also made known to the Board, as adopted by the General School Committee, whereby "all children over eight years of age, who are *not* qualified by their attainments, shall be admitted into the Grammar Schools; provided that their parents or guardians shall first obtain permission of the Sub-Committee of the school where it is proposed they shall be admitted."

November 5. Quarterly meeting of the Board. The Semi-Annual Report of the Standing Committee was read by Mr. T. R. Marvin, and accepted.

A communication was received from Mr. Mulkey, teacher of a new system of Orthoepy, requesting permission to make trial of his system in one of the Primary Schools, and referred to Messrs. Ingraham, Gore, Brown, Otis, Marvin, Gulliver, Loring, Stimpson, Pray, and Walker, with instructions to report at an adjourned meeting.

The salary of the teacher of the Mill Dam school was raised to the same sum as that of the other Primary School teachers.

The report of the Committee, recommending Blake's "First Reader" as a First Class Book, was accepted; and the Secretary was "directed to inform the publishers of the work of its adoption, and propose to them to reduce the price to $1.75 per dozen for such a number as may be wanted for immediate supply;" and also "to inform the publishers that the same will be retained in the schools only so long as the Board shall deem it expedient."

The Committee on the subject of improvement, appointed May 7, made a report, and recommended the adoption of the following Resolutions:

1. That the district committees and instructors of all the Primary Schools, jointly and severally, be directed to have the seats of their respective schools so arranged as to secure the greatest amount of support and comfort of position to the greatest number of their scholars.

2. That the following be adopted as Rule 10, Sect. v., of the Rules and Regulations. It shall be the duty of the instructors to attend to the physical comfort and education of the pupils under their care; and to this end, the ordinary duties and exercises of the schools shall be suspended for a portion of time not exceeding fifteen minutes each part of the day. This time shall be taken together, or divided, at the discretion of the teacher; and occupied according to the state of the weather, the season of the year, and the situation and convenience of the school-room; and in such manner as each instructor shall judge best adapted to relieve weariness, strengthen the physical constitution, excite a love of order, and associate with the school ideas of cheerfulness as well as improvement.

3. That a Committee be appointed to prepare a card, or cards, on the principles of this report, for the use of the 4th class.

4. That the schools be furnished with a sufficient number of slates and pencils for the use of the 4th class.

5. That the study of Arithmetic be introduced in *all* the classes as a part of the course of instruction.

All the foregoing resolutions were adopted by the Board, and ordered to be incorporated into the Rules and Regulations.

At an adjourned meeting of the Board, November 12, Mr. T. R. MARVIN, from the Committee on the request of Mr. Mulkey, read a report, recommending "that the same be granted, under the direction and supervision of a Committee of three persons, to be appointed by the Board." This report was accepted, and Messrs. Marvin, Pray and Walker were chosen as the Committee.

On motion of Mr. Pray, the Secretary was directed to purchase a sufficient number of slates and pencils, and have the following Orders printed and sent to each of the Committee and instructors:

Ordered, That the fourth classes in the Primary Schools be hereafter furnished with slates and pencils (which may be procured on account of the City at the bookstore of Mr. Samuel G. Simpkins, No. 79 Court Street), and when not engaged in the study or recitation of their lessons, be employed in using them to imitate some mark, letter, or other object placed thereon, or in copying from a card suspended before them for the purpose.

Ordered, That Numeration, or counting 1 to 100, be taught to the fourth class; the combination of these numbers, so as readily to find the page in any book, to the second division, third class; that the arithmetical tables be commenced in the first division, third class; that the same be completed, and the study of the rules and examples begun, in the second class; and that the study of the "North American Arithmetic" be completed by the pupils in the first class, before receiving a ticket of admission to the Grammar Schools.

Under the Resolutions adopted on the 5th of November, and the foregoing Orders, measures were effectually introduced for promoting the health and comfort of the children, and for systematizing the study of arithmetic, which had been heretofore almost entirely at the discretion of the teacher.

The Secretary submitted an offer from Messrs. Russell, Odiorne & Co., to furnish " Blake's Reader " in any quantity to the Primary Schools at $2 per dozen, which was accepted by the Board.

The necessity of having something done in relation to school-rooms, became more and more apparent; and, notwithstanding the ill success of previous efforts, the subject was again brought before the Board at their quarterly meeting, August 6,* when, on motion of Dr. Walker, Messrs. Walker, Choate, Ingraham, Palfrey, Sumner, Marvin, Hartshorn, Snelling, Hatch, and Stebbins, were appointed a Committee to make application to the City Government "for an appropriation of money for the purpose of building and furnishing suitable rooms for the accommodation of the Primary Schools, whenever suitable opportunities may offer in any of the Districts."

This Committee, by a Sub-Committee, presented their

---

* This movement, which resulted in a successful application to the City Government, is due to Mr T. R. Marvin, who was a member of the Committee, appointed May 6, in " regard to the improvements in education in the Primary Schools." This Committee met May 7th, and after they had finished their business, a conversation took place on the subject of school houses, when Mr. Marvin proposed that a new effort should be made to prevail upon the City Government to do something in the matter. His views were advocated by Dr. Walker and Mr. Ingraham, and resulted in a determination to again bring the subject to the attention of the Board.

application in behalf of the Board, to the City Council, and the subject was referred to the Joint Committee on Public Instruction, August 22, 1833. On the 14th of November, a report was made by the Mayor, Hon. CHARLES WELLS, as Chairman of the "Joint Standing Committee on Public Instruction," in which he states, " That the Primary Schools of the City have been conducted so judiciously by the several Committees, under whose superintendence they have been placed, and the teachers have discharged their duty with so much ability, that these schools have been a prominent part of our School System, and will, undoubtedly, always be supported at the expense of the public. The experiment has exceeded the most sanguine expectations of its warmest advocates, and its permanency, as a part of our Public School education, is firmly established. Under these circumstances, it appears to your Committee that such rooms as are not occupied in the lower story of the Grammar School-houses, as will be convenient for Primary Schools, ought to be appropriated to their use."

" And at the next annual appropriation, the sum of $10,000 should be applied to the purchase of land and the erecting of buildings for the same object; this sum will be sufficient to provide six buildings, (including the land,) which may be so constructed as to accommodate two schools in each building; and should this course be adopted the ensuing year, and repeated for the next four years, at that period the city will own a sufficient number of buildings to accommodate all the Primary Schools."

This report was read and accepted by both branches

of the City Government, November 14, 1833; and in the next annual appropriation in May, 1834, $12,500 was appropriated for the purchase of land and the erection of Primary School-houses. At this time there were sixty-four schools, all of which were held in hired rooms. The *first* Primary School-house was erected in South Margin Street in 1834;* it was built of wood and brick, two stories in height, and adapted for two schools. The cost of it was $2,528 69, exclusive of the land. In pursuance of the policy thus decided upon by the City Government, four more schools were built during the ensuing year, 1835–36. They were located on North Margin Street, Tileston Street, Castle Street, and Purchase Place. Each of these were adapted for two schools, and the cost of the whole was about $12,500, of which sum about $4,000 was paid for the land. From this time the City Government have continued to make annual appropriations for this object; and in 1854 there were fifty-two Primary School-houses owned by the city, in which one hundred and fifty-three schools were located.

1834.

The first meeting of the Primary School Board, after their appointment, was held February 4, at which they proceeded to organize the Board as follows. The

---

* It is proper to mention, that in 1830–31, a small school-house, with one room, was built by the city, on the "Western Avenue," at a cost of $468; but this was not strictly a Primary School, as Grammar School studies were taught, as well as the Primary. In 1832, a small building was purchased on the "Neck," and fitted up for a Primary School.

Chairman (MOSES GRANT, Esq.,) having declined a reëlection.

Chairman — LEWIS G. PRAY.

Secretary — EDWARD G. DAVIS.

Standing Committee — Chas. Walker, *Chairman*; Geo. W. Otis, Jr., *Secretary;* George A. Sampson, Charles Choate, Theophilus R. Marvin, Samuel Tenney, Lewis G. Pray, John P. Bigelow.

Committee of Conference — Messrs. Walker, Marvin and Davis.

On motion of Mr. Hatch, it was unanimously "*Voted*, That the thanks of this Board be presented to Moses Grant, Esq., for his able and faithful services as Chairman, and for the continued interest he has manifested in the welfare of the schools connected with this Board."

Formal, and in accordance with custom, as this vote may appear, yet probably no tribute of the kind was ever passed in this Board, if in any other, which was more deserved. Living as he now is in our midst, and with head and heart engaged, as ever, in the active duties of philanthropy and benevolence, we feel obliged to refrain from speaking of his public labors as they merit; but we deem it our province and duty to place, on this humble record, the evidence of his unremitting devotion to the interests of the Primary Schools.

Deacon GRANT, was one of the active friends, and original petitioners for this class of schools, — he was a member of the *first* Primary School Committee appointed in 1818, — and a member of the Standing Committee from its first organization in 1820, until 1834. From March, 1820, to January, 1830, he was

Secretary of the Standing Committee, and was present at all but *five* of the regular monthly, and adjourned meetings, during the whole of that time. From February, 1830, until 1834, he was Chairman of the whole Board, and *ex officio* member of the Standing Committee. In addition to all this, his official position as Secretary of the Standing Committee, caused him to be placed on almost every sub-committee which was appointed, during his term of office. His labors were arduous, but by his prompt attendance, and systematic discharge of his various duties, none were neglected; and while he commanded the respect and esteem of his associates, his long experience and calm judgment rendered his services invaluable to the schools. Such a record is honorable to him as a good citizen, and worthy of the self-sacrificing spirit of the Patriot and the Christian.

At this meeting of the Board, a Standing Committee on school-rooms was elected, consisting of one member from each District, and two from the Standing Committee.

Mr. T. R. MARVIN, Chairman of the Committee on Mr. Mulkey's request, presented a report which was accepted.

From this report, it appears, that after a conference with the Committee, Mr. Mulkey was allowed to try his system in School No. 4, District No. 5, kept by Miss Cragin, " and that he had given twelve lectures to the children of about half an hour each. The children were also instructed by their teacher, in Mr. Mulkey's system, one hour and a half each day; and made as much proficiency as could have

been expected for the time." The Committee, however, state, that "from the limited time, which has
been spent on this subject, they are not prepared to
give a very definite opinion of Mr. Mulkey's system
of teaching. They believe that some part of it may
prove useful, particularly to the teachers. They
cannot, however, at present, recommend its introduction into the Primary Schools. It is so great an
innovation upon the common system, that they think
if it should be introduced at all into the schools, it
ought to be done in a gradual manner, as it will
require considerable attention, on the part of the
teachers, to become familiar with it. It appears,
also, that the whole of Mr. Mulkey's system has not
been developed; that part on which he has been
lecturing being more particularly adpated to teachers.

The Committee conclude their report by recommending, "that the system be continued in Miss
Cragin's school, under their control, and that they be
directed to report further at the next quarterly meeting of the Board."

Another report was accordingly made at the quarterly
meeting May 6, upon which, on motion of Mr. J. P. Bigelow, it was "*Voted*, that the experiment be continued in
Miss Cragin's school," and "that other teachers duly
qualified, have liberty to employ the system in the instruction of their 4th classes, with the consent, and
under the direction of their Local Committees."

It does not appear from the Records, that under
these Votes, the system of Mr. Mulkey was introduced to any considerable extent into the Primary
Schools, as no further report appears to have been

made upon the subject. That it was fairly tested, there is no doubt, as the influence exerted in its favor was very great. The Grammar School Board had already taken action, by appointing a Committee, in October, 1833, to consider the expediency of employing the Rev. Wm. Mulkey to lecture to the teachers of the several Public Schools, on the accent and pronunciation of the English language. This Committee reported by their Chairman, Rev. George W. Blagden, " that after due examination, they considered the system of Mr. Mulkey, as a simple and interesting process for understanding the important principles of English Orthoëpy, and that in their opinion, it was expedient and proper, to employ him to lecture to the teachers upon this subject. And they recommend that the Board do, by their Chairman, respectfully ask the City Council for an appropriation sufficient to carry this design into execution."

This Report was accepted, and on the application of the Mayor, (*Chairman ex officio*) the City Council passed an order Nov. 14, 1833, authorizing the School Committee to employ Mr. Mulkey, and appropriating Five Hundred dollars for these lectures.

Thus recommended by the Grammar Board, which at this time comprehended the entire Board of Aldermen, — endorsed by the Professor of Elocution at Harvard University, and many other eminent literary gentlemen, — and sanctioned by a liberal appropriation of the City Government, — Mr. Mulkey presented his request to the Primary School Committee. The request was granted, and the experiment placed under the direction of an experienced and judicious committee, a portion of whose reports have been already presented, and affords another illustration of the careful conservatism of this Board, upon the introduction of any new project, however influentially urged upon their attention.

Mr. Mulkey's system of Orthoëpy was similar to those which have been often attempted, in various forms, but more recently under the name of "Phonetics;" in which the real elementary sounds, which constitute the syllables, are at once taught, instead of first teaching the conventional sounds or names of the letters. In theory such a system commends itself to our judgment, but, to reduce it to practice, renders the changes and innovations in our language so radical and extensive, as to preclude the possibility of its successful introduction. We should, however, do great injustice to those friends of education, through whose instrumentality these various experiments have been tried in our schools, were we not to admit that great advantages have accrued to the process of education, from the valuable ideas which, by this means, have been suggested or obtained.

At a meeting of the Board, Aug. 5, the Standing Committee announced the death of Mr. GEORGE A. SAMPSON, who had been, for some years, associated with the Board as a member of the District, and of the Standing Committee; the duties of which, he had performed in a most faithful and exemplary manner; and on their recommendation, Mr. FRANCIS BROWN was chosen as a member of the Standing Committee to fill the vacancy occasioned by the decease of Mr. Sampson.

A model of a "Punkah," or fan for the ventilation

of school-rooms, having been exhibited, Drs. Otis and Stebbins, and Mr. Austin, were chosen a Committee to examine the same, and if they judged it expedient, to have one erected for trial.

At the quarterly meeting Nov. 4, the Chairman communicated to the Board, the resignation of Dr. Edward G. Davis as Secretary, whereupon, Mr. Gustavus Horton was elected.

Dr. Thomas Gray, Jr., having resigned his place as Committee of School No. 5, District No. 3, and Mr. John P. Lathrop, a teacher in one of the Public Grammar Schools, having been proposed as a substitute, an incidental discussion ensued, on the propriety of teachers in these schools becoming members of the Primary School Committee. It was accordingly moved, that the subject be referred to a Committee to report upon at the next meeting. This motion was decided in the negative, and Mr. Lathrop was admitted, and remained upon the Board until Nov., 1836. At the next meeting, Mr. Charles Fox, another Grammar School teacher, was nominated to fill a vacancy in District No. 7; but after rather an elaborate debate, a ballot was taken, and Mr. Fox was rejected. No objections were made to the character or qualifications of Mr. Fox, but the rejection of his nomination was simply an expression of the opinion of the Board as to the principle involved in the election of Grammar School-masters as members of the Primary Board. Subsequently a Committee was appointed upon the subject, and upon their report the Board "*Voted*, That it was inexpedient for the teachers of the Grammar

Schools to be elected as members of the Primary School Committee."

1835.

FEBRUARY 3. This being the regular meeting for the choice of officers for the ensuing year, the Board proceeded to organize as follows:

Chairman — LEWIS G. PRAY.

Secretary — GUSTAVUS HORTON.

Standing Committee — George W. Otis, Jr., *Chairman*; Frederic A. Sumner, *Secretary*; Lewis G. Pray, John P. Bigelow, Francis Brown, Theophilus R. Marvin, Samuel Tenney, George Rogers.

Committee of Conference — T. R. Marvin, G. W. Otis, Jr., F. A. Sumner.

At the quarterly meeting, May 5, an order was passed, appointing Messrs. Thomas Hunting, Henry Hatch, and Samuel Tenney, a Committee to attend to a division of District No. 7. This Committee subsequently reported, August 4, in favor of dividing the district, so that District No. 7 should contain schools Nos. 1, 3, 7, 8, 9 and 10, and the new District No. 9 should consist of schools Nos. 2, 4, 5, 6, 11 and 12, the last being a new school. On the recommendation of the Standing Committee, Dr. JOHN FLINT was chosen in place of Mr. Marvin, who had resigned as a member of that body; and Dr. AUGUSTUS A. GOULD was elected for the new District, No. 9, as members of the Standing Committee.

At this meeting a report was made by Mr. Pray, approving of the study of Ethics, in some simple form, as a part of the course of instruction in the Primary Schools. This report was accepted, and the mode of its introduction referred to the same Committee; but it does not appear to have been introduced into any of the schools.

A petition was presented to the Board, November 3, from the inhabitants of East Boston, requesting the establishment of a Primary School in that section of the city. This petition was referred to the Standing Committee to make inquiry, and if found expedient, to establish a school on the same plan as that on the Mill Dam.

A petition was also presented from the teachers of the schools, under the care of the Primary Board, setting forth the duties and responsibilities devolving upon them, and requesting that their compensation might be increased. Whereupon, it was unanimously "*Voted*, That the Standing Committee be instructed to petition the next City Council to increase the pay of the teachers from $200 to $250 per annum."

It was also "*Voted*, That a Standing Committee on School Books be appointed, the Committee to consist of five." Messrs. L. G. Pray, C. F. Barnard, A. A. Gould, J. P. Lathrop, and G. Horton, were elected as the *first* Committee under this vote.

At a meeting of the Standing Committee, November 11, the following Resolutions were adopted, viz.:

1. That the Semi-Annual examinations shall be made during the first three weeks in the months of April and October.

2. That each member of the Standing Committee shall report in writing on the condition of the district assigned him.

3. That the Report shall give a brief statement of the condition of each school examined, and at the close a summary of the condition of the whole district.

4. That each member of the Standing Committee, in turn, beginning with the Chairman, and proceeding according to seniority of office, shall make up the quarterly abstracts for the use of the whole Board, and no member shall be at liberty to decline the duty, but may procure a substitute by exchange or otherwise.

The school at East Boston was then organized by the choice of Mr. Guy C. Haynes and Mr. Benjamin Brown as a Committee for the school, and Miss E. L. Pierce as teacher.

1836.

FEBRUARY 2. A communication was received from Samuel F. McCleary, Esq., Secretary of the School Committee, containing a vote of that body, confirming the present members of the Primary Board in office another year, and authorizing them to fill any vacancies which may occur in their numbers during the year.

Mr. LEWIS G. PRAY having declined standing as a candidate for the office of Chairman another year, on motion of Mr. J. W. Bourne, it was "*Voted*, That a Committee of one from each District be appointed by the Chairman to nominate a candidate for that office." The Committee subsequently reported the name of Dr. GEORGE W. OTIS, Jr., as a suitable person to fill the office of Chairman of the Board; which nomination was confirmed by Dr. Otis receiving nearly all the ballots of the Board. Mr. GUSTAVUS

Horton was unanimously reëlected Secretary, but declined the office at the next meeting. All the members of the Standing Committee were reëlected, and the same Committee of Conference were reäppointed.

The subject of paying a salary to the Secretary of the Board and Standing Committee for the ensuing year, was referred to a Committee.

The Standing Committee reported that they had established the school at East Boston, and also that another school, of the same character, had been petitioned for, to be located in the same section. Upon the suggestion of the Standing Committee, the Board " *Voted*, That the subject of another school be referred to the Standing Committee, with authority to confer with the Grammar School Committee, as to the propriety of establishing such schools in which other than primary studies are taught; and whether the Primary Board is justified in organizing them."

The Chairman of the Standing Committee subsequently addressed a note to the Committee of Conference, on the part of the Grammar Schools, requesting that a time and place may be appointed by them to meet a Sub-Committee of the Standing Committee, in reference to the school at East Boston. At a meeting, March 29, Mr. Pray, from the Committee of Conference, reported " that a Conference had been held with the Committee of the Grammar School Board, and that leave had been obtained to receive into the schools at East Boston, such children as did not strictly come within the Primary School Regulations." Upon which, Mr. Pray and Dr. Otis were appointed a Committee to ascertain " if there was a sufficient number of pupils to warrant the establishment of another school at East Boston; and if so, to make the necessary arrangements for its organization, such as obtaining a room, selecting a teacher and Committee to take charge of it. The Secretary was also "directed to notify the City Auditor, at the proper time, of the formation of the new school, and the names of the Committee and teacher, that the salary of the latter could be properly provided for."

We have entered into a detail of the proceedings in regard to the formation of this school, to illustrate the cautious manner in which new schools were established by the Primary School Committee, and their respect for the prerogatives of the Grammar Board; and also as an indication of the reciprocal courtesy which characterized their intercourse upon questions of mutual interest.

At the quarterly meeting, May 6, the thanks of the Board were tendered to Mr. LEWIS G. PRAY for the acceptable manner in which he had performed the duties of Chairman, and to Mr. GUSTAVUS HORTON for his faithful and laborious services as Secretary of the Board.

Messrs. R. W. Bayley and L. G. Pray were appointed a "Committee to call upon the publishers of the several books used in the Primary Schools, and remonstrate against the *binding* of them; and if necessary, to state that unless a remedy is applied, other books must be substituted for them in the schools." This Committee reported at the next meeting that they had attended to the duty, and the publishers had promised immediate improvement. On motion of Mr. S. H. Walley, the teachers were allowed to use Gallaudet's " Mother's Primer " for teaching the alphabet, by way of experiment, and requested to report to their District Committees their opinion of its value.

The Secretary was directed to apply to the City Government for a suitable and safe depository in one of the public rooms of the city, for the books and other property belonging to the Primary Committee.

The number of schools at this time was seventy-three, and the duties of the Secretaries of the Board and of the Standing Committee had become so arduous, as to require great personal sacrifices on the part of the members who accepted those offices. Under these circumstances, the Board, at their first meeting in February, appointed a Committee, who, in May, presented a petition to the City Government for an appropriation of $200 per annum to compensate, in some degree, for the labor performed by these officers. While this petition was under consideration, the Board deferred electing a Secretary; and as it was not acted upon by the City Council, the records of the Board were made by Secretaries *pro tem.* during the entire year.

1837.

FEBRUARY 7. Notice of their appointment having been received, the Board was organized by the election of the following officers and Committees:

Chairman — GEORGE W. OTIS, Jr.

Secretary — JOSEPH CURTIS.

Standing Committee — Sam'l Tenney, *Chairman;* Frederic A. Sumner, *Secretary;* George W. Otis, Jr., E. Weston, Jr., Gustavus Horton, George Rogers, A. A. Gould, J. B. Stebbins, R. W. Bayley.

Committee of Conference — George W. Otis, Jr., F. A. Sumner, Josiah F. Bumstead.

At a meeting of the Standing Committee, January 31, " the Chairman communicated the resignation of Mr. JOHN P. BIGELOW, and also his best wishes for the success and prosperity of the Board." Dr. JOHN FLINT having also tendered his resignation, the Committee nominated Mr. E. WESTON, Jr., and Dr. J. B. STEBBINS to the Board, to fill the vacancies occasioned by the resignation of Messrs. Bigelow and Flint.

Mr. Bigelow was elected as a member of District No. 6, in March, 1828, in which capacity he continued to act until his election to the Standing Committee in January, 1829. From this time until his resignation, a period of *nine* years, he was a prompt, efficient, and valuable member of the Committee, having made during that time *all* of the Semi-Annual examinations and Reports of the Districts assigned to him, besides a number of interesting quarterly and other Reports of the Standing Committee to the Board.

MAY 2. The City Council having appropriated $100 for the services of the Secretaries, Mr. Pray offered the following : " *Voted,* That the Secretary of this Board be authorized, in conformity with a vote of the City Council, to present, quarterly, to the proper authorities, a bill for $25, as payment for his services." The adoption of this vote being opposed, it was amended by the mover, so as to allow $60 per annum to the Secretary of the whole Board, and $40 per annum to the Secretary of the Standing Committee, and the vote was then adopted.

Some dissatisfaction was expressed with the small amount appropriated by the City Council; and on motion of Mr. Walley, " the Chairman of the Board was authorized to apply to the City Authorities for additional compensation for the Secretaries, whenever he may deem it expedient."

The Standing Committee on School Books reported that they were unanimously in favor of a better book for the highest classes, and commended to the favorable notice of the Board, " The Mother's Primer," by Gallaudet. The report was accepted, and the Secretary was directed to procure a sufficient number of copies for the use of the schools.

The Secretaries of tne Districts were requested to furnish the Secretary of the Board at least one month before each quarterly meeting, with a correct list of the names and residences of each member of their respective Committees and teachers.

In 1834, a Standing Committee on school-rooms was added to the organization of the Board; but, although this Committee had, since that time, been annually elected, their specific duties had not been defined. In the early part of the present year, (1837,) a Committee was appointed to define the powers and duties of the Committee on school-rooms. Their report came up for consideration at the quarterly meeting, November 7, and after the adoption of sundry amendments, was accepted, and ordered to be incorporated into the Rules as Section I., Rule 7, of the Rules and Regulations of the Board. The duties thus defined remained unaltered until the dissolution of the Board.

The subject of school books having excited considerable interest, from the difficulty experienced in obtaining those which were satisfactory in all respects, a special meeting of the Board was held, November 21, at which it was

Resolved, That a Committee of five be appointed by the Board to prepare or procure a Reading Book for the First Class in the Primary Schools; and that they be instructed to give the preference, in their selections, to the Scriptures, and American authors; the book decided upon, or the selection made, to be subject to the approval of the Board before printing.

Pending the consideration of this resolution, Mr. J. W. Ingraham offered the following as a substitute:

Resolved, That a premium of five hundred dollars be offered to the author or compiler of the best series of School Books for use in the Primary Schools of this city; the copy-right to belong to this Committee; or if the author prefer to retain the copy-right, that to be considered in lieu of the premium.

After discussion the substitute was negatived, and the first resolution was adopted, and the Committee was appointed. This Committee reported at a subsequent meeting in favor of placing the subject in charge of the Standing Committee on school books; and at their request, were excused from a further consideration of the subject.

1838.

FEBRUARY 6. This being the annual meeting of the Board, it was organized as follows:

Chairman — GEORGE W. OTIS, Jr.

Secretary — JOSEPH CURTIS.

Standing Committee — Richard W. Bayley, *Chairman;* F. A. Sumner, *Secretary;* George W. Otis, Jr., A. A. Gould, J. B. Stebbins, Francis Brown, George Rogers, J. F. Bumstead, J. W. Bourne.

Committee of Conference — George W. Otis, Jr., F. A. Sumner, J. F. Blanchard.

After the report of the Standing Committee had been read by Dr. J. B. STEBBINS, the following vote was passed: "*Voted*, That Messrs. Pray, R. W. Bayley, Bumstead, Cobb, Wales and Otis, be a Committee to consider and report upon the expediency of making it the duty of the Standing Committee to call together the teachers and members of the Board of the Primary Schools, Semi-Annually, in the week succeeding the meetings of the whole Board, in April and October of each year, for the purpose of communicating to them the Semi-Annual report and such other information as this Board may direct, or the Standing Committee may think useful and necessary."

The same Committee was instructed to inquire and report if any other method can be adopted in the Semi-Annual examinations of the schools, by which their condition may be improved, and a better knowledge obtained by the Board of their relative standing.

An adjourned meeting was held, March 6, at which a report from the Committee on Books was made, re-

22

commending Abbott's " Mount Vernon Junior Reader," for the Third and Second Classes, and " Pierpont's Young Reader," in place of " Blake's Reader," in the First Classes. The Secretary was also instructed to request the teachers and Committees of the several Districts to have these books introduced on the first Monday in May.

On the 13th of March, the Committee, to whom was referred the expediency of Semi-Annual meetings of the teachers, to hear the reports of the Standing Committee, made a report in favor, and recommended several additional sections to the Rules and Regulations, all of which were adopted by the Board. As these meetings were a peculiar feature of the Primary School Board, we present a few extracts from the Committee's Report, which will express their views and those of the Standing Committee, upon the subject:

The object proposed is to open between the members of the Board and the teachers of the schools a more direct and constant communication, by which they will become better acquainted with each other; there will be created between them a stronger sympathy in advancing the object they have mutually in view, viz., the improvement of the schools; and by communicating to the teachers, through the Standing Committee, the doings of the Board, its Semi-Annual reports, the votes which are passed in relation to the duties of the teachers, and all other information appertaining to the wishes of the Committee or the wants of the schools, there will be a uniformity of feeling and action produced, which cannot fail to have the most salutary influence.

To make these meetings effectual, two things are necessary, first, that *all* the teachers be present; and secondly, that the meetings be conducted in such a way that they shall be instructive and useful. To accomplish the first purpose, it should be made the *duty* of *all* the teachers of the Primary Schools to attend these meetings. To secure this, it would be obviously inexpedient and improper to take *their* time on Wednesday and Saturday afternoons, or on any evening in the week, as it might be inconvenient or impracticable for them to attend. Your Committee, therefore, recommend that these meetings be held on Tuesday afternoons, and that the schools be dismissed for the purpose. As it will require but two afternoons in the year, they are of opinion that the time lost by the children will be more than compensated by the good that will accrue to the teachers.

To accomplish the second purpose, that is, to render these meetings useful and instructive, it is proposed that it shall be the *duty* of the Standing Committee to call two meetings of the teachers on the second Tuesday afternoons of April and October, at some central and convenient place; the teachers and members of the Board to be notified by the Secretary; and when assembled, the Standing Committee shall communicate to them the reports of the examinations of their schools. They shall also make known to the teachers and fully explain to them any votes passed by the Board, appertaining to their duties or expressive of its wishes in regard to any improvement which they may desire to effect. The occasion may also be embraced, if time permits, for communications or addresses by themselves, or others invited by them, on the subject of education in general, or the improvements in study, discipline or modes of instruction.

The same Committee reported in favor of the Standing Committee being empowered and instructed to examine the schools by bringing together in succession the two highest classes of the schools in each District, for the purpose of comparing the proficiency of the classes in the several schools of a district with each other, and to ascertain their discipline and the condition of the lower classes, by subsequent visits to each of the schools.

Heretofore, the First and Second Classes had been examined in their own school-rooms, which usually occupied a whole session for each of the schools, besides more or less of another session, which was required for the lower classes. The effect of this was to bring the examination of the schools at different times and in different states of the weather, by which, in the opinion of the District Committees and teachers, their classes were so affected as to receive, sometimes, a less favorable report than their actual condition entitled them to.

To obviate any feelings of this nature, and being authorized by a vote of the Board, the Standing Committee decided to make their arrangements for the April examination, on the plan proposed. Accordingly, all the First Classes of the schools in each district were brought together in one of their school-rooms on a certain day selected by the examiner, and examined in the presence of each other, and in the presence of their teachers and Local Committees. On a subsequent day, all the Second Classes were brought together, and examined in the same manner. The result of this course was, that a more accurate idea was obtained by the Examining Committee, of the relative proficiency of the several schools; the teachers were enabled to compare the success of their own efforts with those of their associates; the Committees had an opportunity to judge of the efficiency of their respective teachers, and it had a tendency to excite a laudable emulation among the teachers and the pupils, to the advantage of all the schools. This mode of examination having proved eminently successful, continued to be practised until the close of the labors of the Board.

Year after year, from the first establishment of these schools, the Primary Board had endeavored to obtain the necessary authority to admit to their schools those children who were more than seven years of age, and were not qualified to enter the Grammar Schools. Frequent appeals had been made to the Grammar School Committee, and to the City Council, all of which had proved unsuccessful, until, finally, after nearly twenty years unremitted effort, the following Order was passed by the City Council on the 22d of March, 1838:

Ordered, That the Primary School Committee be, and they are hereby, authorized to admit into one school, to be by them selected, in each of the school districts, any child who is more than seven years of age, and is not qualified for admission to the Grammar Schools.

This order of the City Government was communicated to the Board by the City Clerk, at the quarterly meeting, May 1st, and was referred to a Committee, consisting of Messrs. Pray, Flint, Sumner, Gulliver and McBurney, to make the necessary arrangements to carry the same into effect. This Committee subsequently reported, " that the object of these schools being only for the accommodation of those who, coming from abroad, or who, from misfortune or neglect, are excluded from the Grammar Schools on the ground of qualification, and from the Primary Schools on account of age, — they deem it unnecessary to establish a school for special instruction in *each* of the districts; and are of opinion that the formation of a school of this kind in each of the Districts Nos. 2, 5, 7, and 8, will be sufficient for the present time."

When this order was first passed, it was supposed that there were about 700 children who were proper subjects for such schools; but in November of the same year, there were 963 in the schools, or 13 per cent. of the whole number of scholars.

This was the origin of our "Intermediate Schools," or "Schools for Special Instruction," which were subsequently established in the several districts, with great advantage to the other schools.

The Committee on Books were instructed to consider the expediency of furnishing each of the Primary Schools with a "Blackboard," and to report upon the proper mode of procuring and using it. The Chairman of the Standing Committee was also requested to call upon the publisher of the "Mount Vernon Reader," and ascertain the cause of the bad binding of many copies supplied to the schools.

After the adjournment of the Board, the Standing Committee held a meeting, and appointed Messrs. Bayley and Brown as a Committee of Arrangements, in regard to the meeting of the Committee and teachers of the Primary Schools on the afternoon of Tuesday, May 8. This *first* semi-annual meeting of the teachers to hear the reports of the examinations of their schools, was accordingly held at the County Court House, (now occupied as the City Hall,) at which seventy-eight of the eighty-three teachers, and forty-two members of the Committee, were present. After the reports were read, several addresses were made by members of the Standing Committee, and other eminent friends of education. A highly favorable report of this meeting was made to the Board at their meeting on the 18th of May; and from this time these meetings of the teachers were regularly held semi-annually, and have been always regarded as an interesting and important auxiliary in the improvement of the schools. By invitation of the Standing Committee, they were frequently attended by the Governors of the Commonwealth, and other State officers, — by the Mayors of our city, and those connected with the Municipal Government, — by the Secretaries and members of the Board of Education, and by the clergy and others, who, by their eloquent addresses and judicious advice, have often encouraged the hands and hearts of the Committee and teachers in their arduous work.

We have now arrived at a point in the history of the Board, from which we may trace the commencement of the opposition, that finally resulted in the destruction of the Primary School organization.

The Primary Board, as we have seen in the preceding pages, were frequently called upon to exercise great judgment and discretion in regard to the many professed reforms which, under the specious name of " educational improvements," were being constantly pressed upon their attention. In the decision of these questions they were calm and deliberate, but firm in opposing all innovations which appeared unnecessary, or were incompatible with the general system which long experience had shown to be well adapted to its end.

The official intercourse between the Grammar and Primary Boards had ever been characterized by a courtesy and regard for the duties and privileges of each other, which was highly honorable to both parties. We do not intend to imply that there had not been differences of opinion upon various matters, during the many years the Public Schools had been in the joint charge of the two Boards; for this could not be reasonably expected of two coördinate branches of government, whose duties were so intimately interwoven; but, as in other similar cases, whenever the two Boards found that they entertained different views upon subjects affecting their schools or organization, it was referred to Committees of Conference, and by this means all differences were courteously considered, and were generally satisfactorily arranged. At this time, however, the Committee of Conference of the Grammar Board proposed to the Standing Committee of Conference of the Primary Board, the expediency of certain changes in regard to the latter organization, which were considered by them as too important for their action, and requiring the appointment of a *Special* Committee. For a proper understanding of this subject, it will be necessary for us to show its origin.

In April, 1837, the Board of Education of the State

of Massachusetts was established by the Legislature, and it was organized in June of the same year. This Board consists of ten persons. The Governor and Lieutenant-Governor, for the time being, are *ex officiis*, members of the Board. In the act establishing the Board, they were required to appoint a Secretary, to "collect and diffuse information of the most approved and successful methods of arranging the studies, and conducting the education of the young, to the end that all children in the Commonwealth, who depend upon Common Schools for instruction, may have the best education which those schools can be made to impart."

In pursuance of these duties, the Secretary of the Board turned his attention to the Boston Public Schools, and appears to have succeeded in impressing upon the Grammar School Committee a portion of his spirit and independence as a radical and uncompromising reformer, which they, in turn, attempted to impress upon the Primary Board. Accordingly, the Grammar Board, through their Committee of Conference, presented certain propositions, made by the Secretary of the Board of Education, to be considered by the Committee of Conference of the Primary Board, but the latter, justly regarding the subject beyond their province, brought the matter before the Primary Board at a special meeting, May 23, which resulted in the appointment of a Special Committee, consisting of Messrs. Pray, Wales, Bumstead, R. W. Bayley, Flint and Otis, into whose hands the whole subject was placed. As this Committee declined to confer, except with a *Special* Committee of the Grammar Board, the

23

Standing Committee of Conference of that body took umbrage, and insisted upon the Special Committee of the Primary Board conferring with them alone, as no other Committee would be appointed by the Grammar Board. The Committee declined a conference thus dictated to them, and proceeded to make a report, on their own responsibility, which was submitted to the Board, July 3, 1838.

We regard this report as a very important document in our history, as it not only expresses the views of the Primary Board at that time, on several matters which have since been consummated by the Grammar School Committee and the City Council, but because we believe that the same sentiments were entertained, and the same principles substantially endorsed by their successors on the Primary School Board. Under these circumstances, it is with no little pride that we transcribe the clear and masterly manner in which the subjects were analyzed, and their fallacies exposed, by the Committee, and their noble vindication of the faithful and valuable services of the members of the Board.

The Committee, after stating for the reasons we have given, that this report is from necessity *ex parte*, proceed as follows:

The subject, as originally presented by the Secretary of the Board of Education, was simply that of adopting some plan in this city for " qualifying teachers to take charge of our Public Schools." In consultation, however, with that gentleman, it appears that he suggested to the Grammar School Committee " that a suitable person be engaged to visit regularly all the *Primary* Schools; to give the present teachers such assistance as they may desire in the discharge

of their duties, and to hold himself ready to instruct and
qualify a class of those persons who may desire to prepare
themselves for the office of teachers." It further appears
that the suggestion in this form met with the approbation
of *that* Committee, — a suggestion which excluded *their*
schools from any participation in the benefits to be derived
from the plan! In this stage of the case it would have
seemed perfectly natural if that Committee had felt themselves relieved from any further care of the matter, except,
perhaps, to suggest through *their* Committee of Conference,
to *ours*, the propriety of giving the subject a proper consideration. But they determined otherwise, and forthwith proceeded to " unfold the details " of a plan for this Board, the
germ of which had thus been brought under their cognizance.

The plan, as unfolded by the Committee of the other
Board, and upon which they ask a conference with us, is
divided into two parts ; first, as to the agency, which the
individual proposed to be appointed, was to have in assist-
ing the teachers and relieving the Primary School Board
of the duties devolving upon them; and secondly, his duties
in taking charge of a class of persons who may desire to
become qualified for the situation of teachers.

As for the first duty proposed for this agent, there is great
indistinctness in the manner in which it is unfolded by the
Committee. By a careful analysis of it, however, they are
brought to the conclusion, that, as the Committee express
the opinion, that " most of our teachers enter upon the office
with very little experience or *preparation ;* " and as they are
represented to be " very grateful for every exertion that is
made to render their labors *more easy* and more effective," it
is the intention of the Committee that this agent, if appointed,
shall go into all *our* Primary Schools, and impart instruction
there to all *our* teachers. We infer this, because if our teachers, as there asserted, have little preparation before they
enter upon their duties, they require additional instruction

somewhere; and their proposition is, not that they should visit him, or receive instruction at his school, but that he should visit all the Primary Schools, and give the present teachers such assistance as they may desire in the discharge of their duties, so as to render their labors more easy and more effective. Your Committee regret the indistinctness with which this proposition is shadowed forth in the report. But if they have divined its true import, they are prepared to say to this feature of the plan, there are numerous and fatal objections. They need not be given in detail. It will be sufficient only to name them; and the *first* objection is, the interruption which such an agency would constantly be to the regular instruction of the schools. The *second* is, that it would lead to repeated experiments of new methods of instruction, which could not be sufficiently understood, when acquired under such circumstances; and the consequence would be, that their schools would suffer more by the new methods, though better, than by the use of the old methods, though not so good; but with which the teachers were perfectly familiar. The *third* is, that it would lessen the respect of the pupils for their teachers, when they should find that, like themselves, they were the subjects of instruction; and lastly, that there would be constant danger that this agent would come in conflict with the opinions and requirements of the Committees of the several schools, which would not only perplex the teachers, but increase their labors and anxieties, and do more harm than any good that could be effected for the schools by this measure.

But there is another aspect in which this part of the proposition is to be regarded that calls for still more particular consideration. It would seem as if by this arrangement, it was the intention of the Committee who made the report, now under consideration, to substitute, if they could, the labors of this person or agent, for the labors of the Primary School Committee. This is the direct inference from the language of the report, which is, "It may be urged that the necessity of such an appointment is superseded by the establishment of the Primary School Committee, whose duty it is to visit the schools, and direct and superintend their progress. We reply, that the schools are so numerous as to demand, in our opinion, nearly the whole time of a single individual." That is, if there is any force in language, it *is* made the duty of the Primary School Committee "to visit their schools, direct and superintend their progress;" but, as these schools are so numerous that the ninety gentlemen who are the Committee, either cannot, or *do not*, take care of them, therefore, in their opinion, they require nearly the whole time of one individual for the express purpose. We are fortified in this opinion by another circumstance, to which we would now advert. In the March number of the "Annals of Education," there appeared a gross and false attack upon the character and management of the Primary Schools, and upon the character and fidelity of the Primary School Committee. In this article, after many misrepresentations of the condition of our school-rooms, and of the neglect of the Committee in this respect, — of our books, studies and the moral culture of our pupils, — we have the following language: "We have heard of late that it is in contemplation, of *some*, to secure the appointment of a sort of City Missionary of Instruction, whose office it shall be to inspect minutely all schools, in all their circumstances, and report respecting the same to the proper authority;" and this, especially, on account of the Primary Schools. Now, in the proposed appointment, we have the identical City Missionary of Instruction, whose creation and agency is supposed to be necessary, because of the neglect of the Primary School Board.

By this means an opportunity is afforded us for the first time to meet these accusations in an official manner, and give them the answer they require. It is only necessary to allude to what this Committee has done in past years, to show, not only their general fidelity, but that no agent, however talented or efficient, could possibly perform the duty which is required of the gentlemen who compose this Board; and what is of still more consequence to the city, that there can be no necessity for the appointment of such a *salaried* agency, when the work can be as well or better done by the responsible, intelligent, and gratuitous labors of a voluntary Committee. We say this with the less reserve, as the praise will mainly be upon those who are now serving the public in other spheres of action, or on those who have gone to their final award — the Ticknors, the Savages, the Wells, the Grants, the Tappans, the Parkmans, the Blanchards, the Hales, the Emersons, and others, who, in previous years, have been the active and efficient members of the Board.

In the first place, then, what have this Committee done in respect to the procurement of suitable school-rooms? A single glance at their records will give ample proof of their fidelity and vigilance. From 1818, when the schools were first organized, to 1827, the whole work of selecting, hiring and furnishing these rooms, was the business of the District Committees. At this period, when the whole number thus obtained was fifty, an increasing difficulty was felt in obtaining rooms of a proper size, and of convenient location. A Committee was therefore raised by the whole Board to represent to the City Government the serious evils resulting from the want of suitable rooms, and praying that measures might be adopted to remedy the difficulty. This application was not successful. In 1828, another memorial was presented to the City Government, for an annual appropriation of $3,000, for the erection of Primary School-houses; but that body was not yet prepared to recognize the principle of erecting houses for the use of these schools. This application, however, resulted in a vote authorizing the Committee to *hire* a suitable number of rooms on leases of *ten* years; the city, and not the teacher as before, being responsible for the rent. This power was used with great alacrity by the Committee, and to great advantage, so that a large number of better rooms were obtained. But finding this insufficient for their purpose, they memorialized again in 1829, that "school-rooms should be purchased or built on account of the city;" but the city authorities still had doubts of the policy of erecting buildings for this purpose, and the application again failed. From this time till 1833, we have the record of frequent applications to the City Government for the use of rooms, not otherwise improved, such as the unoccupied rooms in Grammar School-houses, gun-houses, engine-houses, and ward-rooms. By this means, and the use of vestries in churches, their most pressing wants were supplied, and the schools for the most part were well accommodated. But as the schools were constantly increasing, and the difficulty of obtaining rooms became greater every day, on account of the increased value of property, the Board, in August, 1833, made another application to the city by a Committee of ten, "for an appropriation of money for the purpose of building and furnishing rooms for the accommodation of Primary Schools, whenever suitable opportunities may offer in any of the Districts." This application was supported by all the influence of the Board, both without and within the Council; and in 1834, they recognized the principle, and erected one house at the expense of the city. In 1835, an appropriation of $12,500 was made, which it was understood was to be set apart for this purpose, until all the schools should be suitably provided for. This sum has been so appropriated and expended for this purpose every year, with the exception of one, until of the eighty-two schools, there are only a few remaining which need better rooms. And the Committee are prepared to say that the rooms occupied by *our* Primary Schools have at all times been equal to, and will now compare advantageously, with those used by any city in the United States. In view of these facts, they would ask if this is such a kind of *neglect* that a special and salaried agent is required to supply their deficiencies; or if one were appointed, he could do more, or better?

So with regard to books. When these schools were first established, few or no books had been published suitable for children from four to seven years of age. A card, a small spelling book, and the New Testament were the books originally used. Soon after, at the solicitation of the Board, a new spelling book was prepared by Mr. W. B. Fowle, and the " Rational Guide " was introduced. In 1826, an " Easy Reader " was compiled expressly for this Board by Mrs. Nathan Hale, (Governor Everett's sister,) called the " Boston Primary Lessons," which was introduced with a new spelling book, adapted to their use, by Mr. Lee, in the place of Fowle's, which had been found too difficult. In the same year, the study of arithmetic was introduced for the First Class, and "Emerson's North American Arithmetic " adopted. In 1827, a new elementary card was introduced; and in 1830, another on the Edinburgh Sessional School plan was prepared by a Committee of the Board, and adopted. In 1833, a new reading book, " Blake's Reader," for the First Class, in connexion with the New Testament, was introduced. Since which, Arithmetic in all the classes, a Numerical Calculator, Slates for the Fourth Class, Gallaudet's Mother's Primer, Abbott's New Reading Books, and Pierpont's Young Reader, have been added to the number of books and the means of instruction in these schools.

Now these are *facts* hastily gleaned from our records, in relation to this branch of the subject; and your Committee would confidently ask if *these* are such evidences of neglect, as to require a *special* agent to increase their number or improve their character?

It is the same with regard to studies. The Committee have always regarded these schools as strictly preparatory to our Grammar Schools, and have uniformly acted upon the principle, that the studies provided for in the books above named, were amply sufficient for a class of pupils from four to seven years of age. They find them, upon comparison, quite equal in all respects to those in the schools of New York, or those in the celebrated schools of Prussia, for children from six to eight years of age; and quite sufficient to qualify them for admission to our next higher grade of schools. It is notorious, indeed, and has been so for years, that the pupils of the Primary Schools lose ground after entering the Grammar Schools, as the studies of the latter are not in advance of the former. As a proof of this, we have the testimony of one of the grammar masters, who, in answer to a recent circular from the Grammar School Committee, uses the following language: Many of the pupils offered from the Primary Schools are well qualified to take a higher rank in the Grammar Schools than the lowest divisions of those schools; and are to be considered as better capable to study the higher branches than those divisions." This is confirmed in a different way, by another of those teachers, who says: " Generally speaking, however, I must do the teachers of the Primary Schools the justice to acknowledge that the children that come from those schools, are, for the most part, *better taught* in the rudiments than those of the same age, who come from private schools, or from the country." Another of these masters proffers the following testimony, which will speak for itself: " In conclusion, I must do the schools the justice to say, that, judging by the children, who come from them to the Hancock School, and by my recent visits to them, they appear to be admirably conducted, and to stand in no need of any change important enough to be called a *reform*. The discipline appears to be excellent, and the children seem to be perfectly happy." Your Committee do not mean to be understood by these remarks, that they consider these schools as by any means perfect; or that these grammar masters, in

24

other parts of their communications, do not speak of deficiencies and faults that need correction; but they do mean to ask, with such opinions before them, as it regards the general results of our labors, coming from those who may be considered as impartial witnesses, whether it is probable that the appointing of an agent to supersede the Primary School Board, will produce better results than has been, and is now obtained.

There is one other portion of their duties to which it is necessary to advert for a single moment. It is made the duty of the Primary School Committee to " visit the schools and superintend their progress." In the discharge of this duty the Rules require a monthly examination of one school from *each* member of the Board. In recurring to one of our latest reports, we find those examinations for six months, or one half a year, to have been three hundred and forty-nine, or about seven hundred for one year. Besides these examinations, which usually occupy from one to two hours each, there were made to the schools by the several District Committees, four hundred and forty-seven visits, or about nine hundred in a year, giving an average of seven examinations and eleven visits to each school per annum. Besides these, there are the Semi-Annual examinations of the Standing Committee, who give two or three hours to each school twice a year, occupying the best portion of eighty days annually. Suppose this agent to be appointed, what would be the result in this one particular? A slight calculation will make it apparent. After deducting Sabbath days, Wednesday and Saturday afternoons, and vacation days, it will appear that the schools are kept about two hundred and thirty-six days in a year. Let this agent then visit and examine these schools every day in the year, and both parts of the day, when they are kept, so as to occupy his whole time; and the total number of his examinations could only be four hundred and seventy-two, in

contrast with seven hundred, now made by the Committee, —
which number is independent of their ordinary visits, and the
thorough examinations of the Standing Committee. We say
nothing now of the advantage of a Local Committee, who it
may be, is a parent to some of the children, or a neighbor
to all; we say nothing now of the necessity of having a Committee, whose residences are near the schools, with whom the
teachers can advise in any case of a difficulty; we say
nothing of the influence of such a Committee with the whole
community in giving confidence to the public in the system
they support; we only state these simple, undeniable facts
drawn from public documents, and ask whether there can
be a necessity for the creation of such an office, or the
appointment of such an agent, the effect of which, if not
intended to supersede their labors, would be to paralyze
their efforts, to produce an apathy, and to render their
office apparently a nominal, if not a useless one.

Your Committee entertaining an undoubting assurance
of the willingness and fidelity of the members of the Board
to perform the duty assigned them in time to come, as in
time past, answer, without any hesitation, in the *negative.*

It now remains for them very briefly to consider the
second part of the proposition, in relation to a Normal
School. The idea of a Normal School, or a school for
qualifying teachers, is rather a new one to this community. They have been established, however, in other countries, especially in Prussia and France, with success and
advantage; and there is no reason to doubt that their establishment in this country would be attended with corresponding good results. They are intended to make the business
of school-keeping as much of a profession as that of law,
medicine, or theology, and a peculiar course of study as necessary to its successful practice, as either of those. We, therefore, express the hope that the Secretary of the Board of
Education may be enabled to establish one or more of these

schools in the State, so as to test satisfactorily their practical utility. But whether it is necessary or expedient for this city, in her municipal character, to establish or maintain such an institution at her own expense, as your Committee do not understand that any portion of the legislative provision or fund for this purpose will be appropriated for the use of this city, is a question upon which this Committee are not called upon to express an opinion. For themselves, as a Board, they are not prepared to entertain or carry forward such a proposition; but if the other School Committee, or any of the city authorities, shall deem it expedient to establish such an institution, they are ready to proffer them any aid which it is in their power to give." * * * *

This report and the accompanying resolutions, which embodied the views and sentiments expressed in the report, were adopted by the Board at a special meeting, held July 3, 1838, and we do not find that any further action was taken by the Grammar Board upon these subjects at that time.

In pursuance of an idea which had been suggested by the Standing Committee, the Primary Boards, at this time, established a "Model School," for the purpose of trying experiments in Primary School instruction. This school was placed in charge of a Special Committee, who, after due deliberation, and with reference "to the size of the room, its central situation, and the character of its teacher," selected the school in District No. 4, kept in the Derne street school-house, by Miss Mary Torrin. This school was continued with varied success until 1842, when it was abandoned, as not having proved so advantageous to the schools as had been anticipated.

A vote was also passed, authorizing the division of any district by the District Committee, when the same shall contain more than nine schools.

1839.

MARCH 5. The list of members of the Committee, appointed by the Grammar School Board, was read by the Secretary, and he was instructed to place the same on file. The Board then proceeded to ballot for a Chairman, which resulted in the choice of Mr. JOSIAH F. BUMSTEAD. Mr. Bumstead having declined serving, GEORGE W. OTIS, Jr., was elected *Chairman*, and JOSEPH CURTIS was reëlected *Secretary*.

Standing Committee — R. W. Bayley, *Chairman;* F. A. Sumner, *Secretary;* George Rogers, J. F. Bumstead, George W. Otis, Jr., Augustus A. Gould, J. B. Stebbins, Francis Brown, J. W. Bourne, Samuel McBurney.

Committee of Conference — George W. Otis, Jr., F. A. Sumner, J. F. Bumstead.

Among other business acted upon at this meeting, a Resolution was adopted, " That when any school shall have remained for a considerable time, with a smaller number of pupils than it can accommodate, the cause shall be made a particular subject of inquiry by the District Committee, and a remedy applied, either by changing its location or its teacher."

At the quarterly meeting of the Board, June 4, the Committee on Books reported in favor of introducing " My First School Book," prepared expressly as a spelling book, for the Third and Fourth Classes, by Josiah F. Bumstead, which was adopted, and ordered to be used, instead of the " Mother's Primer," in those classes.

A petition of Samuel P. Scott and others, to have sewing and knitting taught in the Public Schools, was referred by the Grammar School Committee to this Board, and after being read, was referred to the Standing Committee, who subsequently reported that it was unnecessary to take any action on the subject, as these branches of domestic education were already attended to in the Primary Schools.

The efforts of those who desired to supersede the labors of the Primary School Committee, by the appointment of a Superintendent, not having accomplished their object through the intervention of the Grammar Board, appear to have brought the subject before the Common Council. Upon learning this, the Primary Board unanimously adopted the following preamble and vote, viz.:

Whereas, the subject of the organization of the Primary School Board, and other matters relating thereto, have been referred to a Committee of the City Council; and whereas, the said Committee may desire to communicate with this Board, in an official manner, on the subject matter of their appointment; and whereas, this Board is solicitous to facilitate, in every proper way, the labors of that Committee; therefore,

Voted, That Messrs. Pray, Hartshorn, Bumstead and Otis, be a Committee to confer and communicate in the most ample and free manner, with the aforesaid Committee of the Council, if desired, on all the subjects appertaining to their appointment, and all others which may be brought under consideration in connection with the accountability, proceedings and duties of this Committee.

1840.

The regular quarterly meeting was held, March 3, and the members of the Board having been notified of their appointment, they proceeded to organize their body by the choice of officers and Committees for the current year.

Chairman — RICHARD W. BAYLEY.

Secretary — JOSEPH CURTIS.

Standing Committee — Josiah F. Bumstead, *Chairman;* Frederic A. Sumner, *Secretary;* R. W. Bayley, Francis Brown, Wm. D. Ticknor, Edmund Jackson, J. B. Stebbins, Samuel McBurney, J. W. Bourne, Wm. P. Jarvis.

Committee of Conference — R. W. Bayley, F. A. Sumner, J. F. Bumstead.

The thanks of the Board were presented to Dr. GEORGE W. OTIS, Jr., " for the able and satisfactory manner in which he had discharged the duties of Chairman of the Board for several years."

It was also " *Voted,* That the Standing Committee be authorized to make arrangements for furnishing the teachers of the Primary Schools with instruction in vocal music, provided it can be done without expense."

In conformity with this vote, the Standing Committee appointed a Sub-Committee to confer with Mr. Lowell Mason on this subject, and make the necessary arrangements for carrying the same into effect. This Sub-Committee reported, April 28, that the conference with Mr. Mason was favorable to the project; that they had accordingly sent a circular to the teachers, and that two meetings had already been held, which had been attended by about two-thirds of the teachers connected with the Primary Schools.

By a vote of the Board, September 1, " the Standing Committee was directed to confer with the Mayor on the subject of providing each of the Primary Schools with a Blackboard; and if necessary, to petition the City Council for an appropriation to accomplish the same."

The same Committee were also authorized to apply to the Common Council for the use of their room in the City Hall, for the future meetings of the Primary Board. This request was granted, and the next meeting, September 15, was held in that place.

A petition of sundry inhabitants of Section 1, East Boston, for the establishment of a new school in that section, having been sent to the Standing Committee; and there appearing to be good reasons for another school, they recommended to the whole Board that a new school be established agreeably to the tenor of the petition.

In October, the teacher in school No. 2, East Boston, having left the care of her school to a substitute, who was reported as unqualified, the Standing Committee appointed their Secretary to investigate the circumstances; and upon his report the teacher and substitute were both discharged, and another teacher elected.

1841.

At a meeting of the Grammar Board, January 12, the members of the Primary School Committee were appointed, and at their regular quarterly meeting, March 2, the Board was organized as follows:

Chairman — RICHARD H. BAYLEY.

Secretary — JOSEPH CURTIS.

Standing Committee — J. F. Bumstead, *Chairman;* F. A. Sumner, *Secretary;* R. W. Bayley, W. D. Ticknor, S. McBurney, W. P. Jarvis, Alvan Simonds, A. D. Parker, Samuel Wheeler, George Bemis.

The Committee of Conference were all reëlected.

Mr. LEWIS G. PRAY having sent in his resignation to the Board at this meeting, the following preamble and resolutions were adopted as a just tribute to his devoted services, for the interest of the Primary Schools, for nearly twenty years:

Whereas, this Board is notified of the resignation of LEWIS G. PRAY, Esq., who has so long and so faithfully discharged his duties in the several departments of this Board,

Resolved, That in view of his past services, the Board cannot part with Mr. Pray without expressing to him their strong and deep sense of obligation, as well for themselves as for the community at large, for his untiring, benevolent and efficient exertions in the cause which this Board has for its object to forward.

Resolved, That while we wish to make no invidious distinctions, we know of no one to whom the Primary School system in this city is more largely indebted for its present advancement and completeness than to Mr. Pray; and that, in losing him, the Primary Schools have lost a long-tried and faithful friend.

Resolved, That the Secretary forward to Mr. Pray a copy of these resolutions, and transcribe the same on the record book of the Board.

The Grammar School Committee having extended the June vacation of their schools, a special meeting of the Primary Board was held, May 21, to consider the expediency of making their vacations correspond with those granted to the Grammar Schools. After considerable discussion, it was decided that any increase in the vacations of the Primary Schools was inexpedient, and the whole subject was indefinitely postponed.

At a special meeting, June 15, a Committee reported in favor of giving the reports of the Standing Committee a more permanent form; and Messrs. Bayley, Bumstead, Ingraham, Marvin and Flint, were appointed "a Committee to collect and put into substantial binding, all the reports of the Standing Committees, (and of the District Committees,) and all other reports and papers connected with the Board, which, in their judgment, it is desirable thus to preserve." The same Committee were "instructed to request from the City Government a suitable place of deposit for the safe keeping of the various records, reports, &c., belonging to the Board, which are not of immediate use."

The Semi-Annual Report of the Standing Committee, compiled from the reports of the teachers, and of the District Committees, was prepared and read by Mr. JAMES B. Dow, at the quarterly meeting, September 7. Mr. Dow also offered a resolution, that the teachers be permitted to use the spelling book prepared by Mr. Bumstead, entitled, "Spelling and Thinking Combined," as a substitute for "Lee's Spelling Book," which was referred to the Committee on School Books, who reported, at an adjourned meeting, September 21, in favor of its adoption in the First and Second Classes, and that it be introduced into the schools immediately after the ensuing semi-annual examination.

This report was accepted, and the recommendations

adopted. At this meeting a vote was adopted, by which the schools at East Boston was constituted a separate district, and were authorized to be organized under the name of District 11. Up to this time the schools at East Boston had been under the special charge of the Standing Committee, by whom the teachers and Local Committees were chosen.

At the opening of the quarterly meeting, December 7, the Chairman announced the decease of Mr. JOSEPH CURTIS, late Secretary of the Board, and paid a feeling tribute to his worth; and on motion of Mr. Marvin, the following votes were unanimously adopted:

Voted, That this Board deeply sympathize with the bereaved family of our late Secretary, Mr. Joseph Curtis, and would cheerfully and unanimously express our feelings of regret that we have been deprived of his services, which we were happy to testify, were always promptly, unremittingly and faithfully rendered.

Voted, That the above be communicated to the family of Mr. Curtis, by the Secretary.

The Board then elected Mr. ALVAN SIMONDS as Secretary.

1842.

The Board was appointed January 11, and on the 1st of March was organized as follows:

Chairman — R. W. BAYLEY.

Secretary — ALVAN SIMONDS.

Standing Committee — J. F. Bumstead, *Chairman*; F. A. Sumner, *Secretary*; R. W. Bayley, S. McBurney, William P. Jarvis, Alvan Simonds. A. D. Parker, James

B. Dow, George Bemis, Joseph W. Ingraham, Otis A. Skinner.

The Committee of Conference were all reëlected.

The Semi-Annual Report of the Standing Committee was made by Mr. Ingraham, June 7, which was recommitted to the Standing Committee for revision and condensation, and subsequently accepted by the Board at an adjourned meeting, June 10. At this adjourned meeting it was "*Voted*, That the thanks of the Board be presented to Mrs. Minot, (lady of William Minot, Esq.,) for her generous and disinterested services in giving a series of lessons on drawing to the teachers of the Primary Schools." This tribute of respect, on the part of the Board, was worthily bestowed upon a lady, who, for two hours a week, for three months, had freely devoted her time and talents to the instruction of the teachers in an interesting branch of education.

By a vote of the Board, September 6, the vacations in the Primary Schools were made to conform with those in the Grammar Schools.

September 20. The Chairman reported, verbally, that the Committee appointed, June 15, 1841, to procure of the city authorities a room for the deposit of the books and papers of the Board, had obtained the room formerly occupied by the Directors of the House of Reformation in the City Hall. Mr. Ingraham, from the same Committee, reported that some progress had been made in collecting the papers and reports from the various districts, and asked for further time, which was granted.

It appears, however, that this duty was never completed; and it is probable that the Committee found it impossible to collect a perfect file of the papers and reports; and after making the collection as complete as they could, they seem to have abandoned the undertaking.

The schools had been gradually increasing in number, and the labors of the Standing Committee as steadily becoming more and more arduous, until it became necessary that some relief should be obtained; as the number of members of the Standing Committee was limited by the number of districts, several attempts had been made to increase the number, but without success.

In August, 1841, the Standing Committee, on motion of Wm. D. Ticknor, appointed a Sub-Committee to consider and report upon some plan of relief. The subject was frequently discussed by the Standing Committee, and finally resulted in a recommendation to the Board to divide the schools into seventeen districts. This was presented to the Board at their meeting, September 20, 1842, by the Chairman of the Standing Committee, and the following votes were passed:

Voted, That Districts Nos. 1, 2, 3, 4, 5 and 8, meet and divide themselves, each into two districts, as nearly equal in the number of schools as possible, and organize themselves by the choice of a Chairman and Secretary of each district, renumbering the schools, and report the same to the Secretary of the Standing Committee, on or before the third Tuesday in October next.

Voted, That the Standing Committee, after receiving these reports, proceed to number the districts, beginning with the north part of the city, and proceeding to the south.

The Standing Committee then made a nomination of six members of their body for the new districts, and Lewis G. Pray, Aaron Ordway, Wm. Dall, Lemuel Capen, Nathan Metcalf, Jr., and Frederic A. Eddy, were chosen.

Mr. Pray, however, declined to accept, and the Standing Committee requested Dr. JOHN ODIN, Jr., to examine District No. 17, and to make the abstract of the several reports for the use of the Board. These duties were performed in a manner so acceptable, that after the adoption of the report by the Board, at the quarterly meeting in December, it was "*Voted*, That the thanks of the Board be presented to Dr. John Odin, Jr., for the able manner in which he has discharged the duty of preparing the semi-annual report."

At the request of the Grammar School Committee, the Board authorized District No. 3 to establish a new school for colored children.

1843.

The members of the Primary Board having been notified of their appointment by the Grammar School Committee, January 10, held their annual meeting for the organization of the Board, March 7, and the following officers were unanimously reëlected:

Chairman — RICHARD W. BAYLEY.

Secretary — ALVAN SIMONDS.

Standing Committee — J. F. Bumstead, *Chairman;* F. A. Sumner, *Secretary;* S. McBurney, Alvan Simonds, James B. Dow, Otis A. Skinner, W. P. Jarvis, A. D. Parker, R. W. Bayley, George Bemis, I. W. Ingraham, Lemuel Capen, John Odin, Jr., Wm. Dall, Nathan Metcalf Jr., Aaron Ordway, Frederic A. Eddy.

The Committee on Conference were also reëlected.

The Chairman reported, that under a vote of the Board, December 6, 1842, the Committee appointed to apply to the City Government for an appropriation to furnish each of the Primary Schools with a clock, had held a consultation with some members of the City Council, and that the Committee deemed it inexpedient for the Board to make the application at the present time.

By an act of the Legislature, passed March 3, 1842, the sum of $15 was appropriated to every school district in the Commonwealth, to be expended in books, for a School District Library; *provided* that there should be raised or appropriated a similar sum in each school district for the same object, by the cities or towns in which the districts were located. But, in the city of Boston and some others of the cities and towns, the schools were not divided into districts, so as to receive any advantage from this appropriation by the State; and to obviate this, the act of March 3, 1842, was amended, by extending the provisions of this act in such a manner as to give as many times fifteen dollars to every such city or town as the number sixty is contained, exclusive of fractions, in the number of children between the ages of four and sixteen years in said city or town, on condition that an equal sum be raised by the town or city.

This amendment was passed March 7, 1843, and on the 14th of the same month, the Primary Board appointed Messrs. Ingraham, Snelling and Bumstead, a Committee to take into consideration this law of the Commonwealth, in relation to school libraries, and authorizing them to communicate with the City Government in relation to this law, in connection with the Primary Schools. It appears, however, that no appropriation was made by the City Council, which was necessary to secure to the schools a participation in this bounty of the State; and we believe that no advantage accrued to our schools from any of the acts passed by the Legislature, for the encouragement of school libraries, although a second amendment was passed March 25, 1845, with special reference to this subject, in connection with the several grades of schools in Boston.

At the quarterly meeting, March 14, a communication was received from His Honor the Mayor, (MARTIN BRIMMER,) stating that one hundred copies of a book entitled, "The School and the Schoolmaster," were at the order of the Board for distribution among the Primary Schools. It being understood that these books were a present from the Mayor, on motion of Mr. B. P. Richardson, the thanks of the Board were tendered to Mr. Brimmer for his liberal and acceptable donation. The Board also "*Voted*, That after having the number of the school and district stamped upon the covers, one copy should be sent by the Secretary to each member of the Board, to be deposited and kept in their several schools; and that the Chairman or Secretary of the Board supply every new school established during the present year with a copy of the "School and Schoolmaster," bound and lettered in the same manner.

The subject of proper books for the several classes, had for a long time earnestly engaged the attention of the Standing and Book Committees, under whose direction several had been specially prepared and successfully introduced into the schools. It was, however, desirable that more order and system should be introduced into the classification and arrangement of *all* the books; and after a careful examination of the various books which had been specially prepared for the use of Primary Schools, the Book Committee, through Dr. HENRY G. CLARK, presented their report to the Board, December 5, from which we select the following remarks, defining the views of the Committee, and their reasons for recommending a change in the books:

In pursuance with their duty, the Committee have been particularly struck with the want of adaptation of several of the books to accomplish the purposes for which they were designed. These your Committee understand to be, to furnish an easy, systematic and certain means for giving to pupils of from four to seven years of age, [by the aid of competent teachers,] such an acquaintance with the printed characters of our language, so that in its simpler combinations they shall be able to read it with a good degree of distinctness, readiness and propriety. We do not understand that the design of *primary* instruction is to teach the principles of natural or moral science, nor do we believe it to be proper or expedient to furnish to these young and immature minds elaborate treatises upon the structure of language, accompanied with a full set of expressional arbitrary signs, a knowledge of which is as difficult to acquire and retain as that of the twenty-six letters of the alphabet.

26

The Committee, after a critical examination of the merits of the books, prepared by six different authors for Primary Schools, conclude their report in favor of those prepared by Mr. Josiah F. Bumstead. Of these books, the Committee say:

But by far the best books which we have examined, are the concluding numbers of a series of " Reading Books for the Primary Schools," prepared by a member of this Board, whose experience, taste and good judgment well qualify him for a task he has so ably accomplished. These books are intended for the use of the First and Second Classes, and are a continuation of the books, some time since introduced into the Third and Fourth. They do not contain, as do some of the other books named in this report, pages of labored disquisition upon the art of reading, spelling and pronouncing the English language, but they do what is much better,— teach by good examples,— practice instead of preach. The lessons are thoroughly digested, and adopted from the best sources. There is a unity and simplicity in the gradations from simple to difficult, which is admirable. The lessons and chapters are judiciously arranged for every-day use, the selections are of the most interesting and excellent character, and the mechanical execution, in paper, printing, and binding, is of the first order, and we believe, for a school-book, entirely *unequalled.*

The fact that these books are written and published in Boston by members of this Board, ought not to be omitted, as it is a sufficient guaranty that they will always remain to a certain extent under our own control, and, without doubt, receive all the alterations and improvements which time and experience may dictate.

For these reasons, the Committee unanimously re-commended the adoption of " Bumstead's Second and

Third Reading Book," in place of those used in the First and Second Classes. This report was accepted, and the recommendation adopted by the Board; and from this time the series of books thus introduced, have been exclusively used in all of our Primary Schools.

That this series of school-books should have retained possession of our schools for so long a period, will not excite surprise, when we consider the fact that the pledges made in their behalf by the Book Committee, on their introduction, have been most honorably fulfilled, and that they have been, to all intents and purposes, under the control of the Board and its Committees. The author, Mr. Bumstead, and the publisher, Mr. T. R. Marvin, to whose public spirit we are also much indebted for their compilation, were members of the Board; and every suggestion which was made by the Standing Committee or members of the Board, in regard to the matter, or in the execution of the mechanical portions, were always cheerfully received, and the improvements as promptly adopted as circumstances and the interests of the schools would allow.

That these books have not been more extensively introduced into similar schools in other places, does not arise, as we believe, from any want of intrinsic merit, but because the plan upon which they are arranged is peculiar, and does not coincide with the views of other School Committees; and also, because they have probably not been pressed upon their attention so assiduously as some others. To this limited circulation of *our* proteges, we enter no protest or complaint, as our firm opinion is, that the advancement of the scholar depends far more upon the teacher than upon the book; and as we will cheerfully yield all due deference to the views of others upon the almost endless variety of school-books, we doubt not that we shall be pardoned for expressing our decided attachment and preference for those which have so long been part and parcel of the Boston Primary Schools.

1844.

The Primary Board having been appointed, January 9, held their annual meeting on Tuesday evening, February 6, and organized themselves for the current year as follows:

Chairman — JOSIAH F. BUMSTEAD.

Secretary — ALVAN SIMONDS.

Standing Committee — John Odin, Jr., *Chairman;* F. A. Sumner, *Secretary;* Amos A. Phelps, Asa Swallow, Eben Jones, Frederic O. Prince, J. F. Bumstead, Alvan Simonds, Andrew Geyer, John C. Park, Lemuel Capen, Daniel T. Coit, W. P. Jarvis, Joseph Moriarty, J. W. Ingraham, George Bemis, Ezra Lincoln, Jr.

Committee of Conference. — It was "*Voted*, That hereafter this Committee consist of the Chairman of the Board, and the Chairman and Secretary of the Standing Committee."

It was then "*Voted* unanimously, That the thanks of the Board be presented to RICHARD W. BAYLEY, Esq., for the faithful and impartial manner in which he had presided over the deliberations of the Board for the past four years; and that a copy of this vote be furnished to our late Chairman, who declined a reëlection."

The Committee of Conference were instructed to confer with the Committee of Conference of the Grammar Board, on the subject of an appropriation for lighting the fires and cleaning the rooms occupied by the Primary Schools, and endeavor, either through the assistance of the Grammar School Committee, or in some other way, to obtain an appropriation from the City Council for that purpose. Rev. John Woart and Hon. John C. Park were added to the Committee to aid them in obtaining the object.

By a vote of the Standing Committee, September 5, 1843, Messrs. Ingraham and Simonds were appointed a Committee on the preparation of a new form of a record book for the teachers. This record book was prepared with great care and labor by Mr. Ingraham, and was adopted by the Board, March 5, who ordered it to be introduced at once into all the Primary Schools. A vote was also passed, expressing to Mr. Ingraham the thanks of the Board, for his disinterested labors in preparing so complete and useful a work for the purpose.

On the report of the Standing Committee, Messrs. R. W. BAYLEY, JOHN WOART, FRANCIS D. STEDMAN, and WILLIAM T. PARKER, were elected to fill the vacancies occasioned by the resignations of Messrs. Swallow, Geyer, Lincoln and Capen.

The Standing Committee, in their Semi-Annual Report, which was prepared by Dr. F. A. SUMNER, proposed several important alterations of the rules, in regard to the examinations of the schools. The plan which they recommended was " to dispense with one examination of the Standing Committee, and substitute an examination by the District Committee, to be made in the same form and manner as that made by the Standing Committee. The visits to the schools to be made by sub-committees, and the whole state and condition of the schools to be embraced in a report, drawn up by some member of the District Committee, and forwarded to the Standing Committee, to make an abstract therefrom, and present to the Board. The Spring examinations to be made by the Standing Committee, and those in the Fall by the Districts."

These recommendations were adopted by the Board; and at a subsequent meeting of the Standing Committee, the proper blanks were prepared for the use of District Committees in their examinations; and it was "*Voted*, That the Chairman of the Standing Committee should prepare the abstract of the Spring examination, and that the Secretary should prepare the abstract from the reports of the District Committees."

The Committee on School-houses were instructed " to consider and report on the best form of seats in the school-rooms; that measures may be taken to secure uniformity of seats in the rooms hereafter to be fitted up."

A communication was received from Districts Nos. 2 and 3, stating that they had agreed on a new division of their districts, by which some of the schools would be changed, and asking for the sanction of the Board.

This arrangement being considered judicious and proper, a vote was passed, authorizing the changes proposed.

In consequence of the repairs being made in the Common Council room, the usual quarterly meeting of the Board, in September, was postponed by a vote of the Standing Committee until October 1, when their action was approved by the Board, and the following vote passed to provide against future contingencies :

Voted, That the Chairman of this Board and the Chairman of the Standing Committee, or either of them, in the absence of the other, and in case of the absence of both of them, then a majority present at any meeting of the Standing Committee, shall have power to postpone any regular meeting of this Board to some other evening in the same month, when, in their opinion, unforeseen circumstances may render it necessary or expedient so to do.

At this time a controversy arose between Hon. Horace Mann and the masters of the Boston Grammar Schools, in consequence of some statements made upon these schools in Mr. Mann's " Seventh Annual Report of the Board of Education, and a Review of this Report by the Masters." In this " Review " some allusions were made to the Primary Schools, which the Standing Committee thought proper to notice in their Semi-Annual Report. The Board, however, not wishing to enter into a controversy, which could only result in acrimony and the formation of a party feeling, without either benefit to the cause of education, or honor to the parties concerned, refused to accept this portion of the report, and it was accordingly recommitted to the Standing Committee for revision ; and the supposed allusions to the Primary School Committee in the " Review," were referred to a Special Committee, to consider and report at a future meeting.

The revised report of the Standing Committee was accepted at a special meeting, November 8, at which Mr. Bayley presented a report from the Special Committee on the remarks of the schoolmasters in their "Review," which, after considerable discussion, and the striking out of certain personal matters, was recommitted to the same Committee, with instructions to print a suitable number of copies for distribution.

The Committee on School-rooms reported in favor of small arm-chairs being used for the seats in the Primary Schools, and recommended that application should be made to the Committee on Public Buildings of the City Council, to supply this kind of seat in the future furnishing of the schools.

1845.

The usual certificate of the appointment of the Primary School Committee having been received, the Board met for organization, February 5, when the following officers and Committees were chosen:

Chairman — JOSIAH F. BUMSTEAD.

Secretary — ALVAN SIMONDS.

Standing Committee — Joseph W. Ingraham, *Chairman ;* Alvan Simonds, *Secretary ;* Amos A. Phelps, John Woart, Charles E. Wiggin, F. A. Sumner, R. W. Bayley, Fred. O. Prince, John Odin, Jr., W. P. Jarvis, Eben Jones, Francis D. Stedman, John Spence, Jr., John C. Park, Henry I. Bowditch, Wm. J. Parker, Josiah F. Bumstead.

Dr. HENRY I. BOWDITCH presented the petition of sundry persons, praying for the abolishing of separate schools for colored children, and that they be admitted into the schools with other pupils ; and moved its reference to a Special Committee, which was refused, and the whole subject laid on the table. This petition was taken from the table, March 4, and referred to Messrs. Bowditch, Ingraham, Bayley, Blake and Tolman, to consider and report upon at the next quarterly meeting. There not being time to act upon the subject at the quarterly meeting, June 4, an adjourned meeting was held June 18, at which Mr. Ingraham submitted a report, signed by a majority of the Committee, adverse to the petition; and Dr. Bowditch read a minority report, and resolutions in accordance with the petition. A long discussion ensued, which was closed by the adoption of the following resolution, by a vote of fifty-five in the affirmative, to twelve in the negative:

Resolved, That it is inexpedient, at the present time, for this Board to act upon the subject of abolishing the separate schools for colored children.

In the Standing Committee, February 25, Dr. F. A. SUMNER was elected Chairman, but declined, and Mr. J. W. INGRAHAM was chosen.

Messrs. Stedman, Bumstead and Ingraham, were appointed a Committee to prepare a memorial to the City Government, asking for an appropriation for making the fires, cleaning the rooms, and removing the snow in winter from the Primary Schools.

At the quarterly meeting of the Board, September 2, the subject of a Superintendent of the Primary Schools was again brought forward, on a motion by Rev. Chas. Brooks; and "Messrs. Brooks, Jones, Dall, Sumner and Humphrey, were appointed a Committee to take into consideration the expediency of the appointment of a Superintendent of the Primary Schools, whose duty it shall be, under the direction of this Board, to devote his whole time in promoting the improvement and extending the usefulness of the Primary Schools."

27

Messrs. Brooks, Park, Cragin and Oliver, were appointed a Committee to report upon the expediency of increasing the salaries of the teachers to $300 per annum; and also, whether the teachers of the "Schools for Special Instruction," ought to receive a larger compensation than the others.

On the 6th of October, Hon. Thomas A. Davis being in declining health, resigned the office of Mayor; the resignation, however, was not accepted by the City Council. As Mr. Davis was unable to perform the duties of the office for some time previous to his death, which occurred November 22, and no provisions for such a contingency having been made in the City Charter, the regular course of business was embarrassed, and the settlement of accounts against the city was necessarily deferred. The payment of the teachers' salaries was thus delayed; and as it was uncertain how long a time this state of things might continue, a special meeting of the Primary Board was called by the Chairman on the evening of November 21, for the purpose of adopting some measures for the payment of the salaries of the teachers of the Primary Schools, who were subjected to much inconvenience from this singular state of affairs.

At this meeting, Messrs. Ingraham, D. Kimball and Bumstead, were appointed a Committee to procure the necessary funds for the immediate payment of the salaries of the teachers due on the 1st of November.

This Committee reported, December 17, by stating that the salaries of one hundred and eight of the teachers, being all that had presented their bills, had been paid from the funds furnished by a number of gentlemen; and they recommended the passage of the following resolution:

Resolved, That the cordial thanks of this Board be presented to James Whiting, George R. Sampson, Charles E. Wiggin, Thomas B. Curtis, J. F. Bumstead, Peleg W. Chandler, Daniel Denney, Martin Brimmer, James C. Dunn, Richard W. Bayley, and Benjamin Seaver, Esquires, for their kindness in advancing the funds necessary to liquidate the demands of our teachers upon the City Treasury.

The report was accepted, and the resolve was passed by the Board.

The special assignment of the meeting was then taken up, which was the consideration of the report of the Committee on the expediency of a Superintendent. The main question being upon the adoption of a "Resolve, That the highest good of the Primary Schools of Boston required that a Superintendent be appointed."

The discussion continued through the evening, and was postponed to an adjourned meeting, December 24, at which, after a further discussion, the vote was taken by yeas and nays, and the resolve rejected, by forty-six nays to eighteen yeas.

1846.

FEBRUARY 6. The Board was organized as follows:
Chairman — JOSIAH F. BUMSTEAD.
Secretary — ALVAN SIMONDS.
Standing Committee — J. W. Ingraham, *Chairman;* Alvan Simonds, *Secretary;* J. F. Bumstead, R. W. Bayley, W. P. Jarvis, William Dall, John Woart, F. O.

Prince, Eben Jones, John Spence, Jr., John C. Park, F. D. Stedman, H. I. Bowditch, Richard Soule, Jr., William Crowell, J. W. Merrill, Dorus Clarke, F. A. Sumner.

The petition of sundry citizens, in relation to special schools for colored children, was taken from last year's files, and referred to Messrs. Crowell, Kimball, Bowditch and Ingraham, to consider and report.

At a meeting, March 3, the Standing Committee reported that they had selected Mr. WILLIAM B. BROOKS to be a member of that Committee, in place of William Dall, resigned. It was also "*Voted*, That the Standing Committee have power to fill vacancies in their body by reporting the fact to the Board."

Mr. D. Kimball, from the Committee on the neglect of members to examine and visit their schools, made a report, recommending that Rule 6, chapter 3, be altered by inserting the following:

Whenever it shall appear by the returns of the teachers, or from any other source satisfactory to the Standing Committee, that any member has neglected to examine the school under his special charge for three consecutive months, his name shall be stricken from the list of members; and it shall be the duty of the Secretary to notify the Chairman or Secretary of the district of such vacancy. Provided, however, that in case of sickness or absence from the city of any member, the charge of his school may be confided to another member or members; notice of which shall be given to the Secretary of the Board, and such substitution shall continue for a period not exceeding six months.

This amendment was laid upon the table, and the Secretary directed to insert it in the notice for the next meeting, June 2, when it was unanimously adopted.

At the quarterly meeting, June 2, several important votes were passed. The subject of Ventilation, and the necessity of some action in regard to it, was introduced by Dr. H. G. Clark; and "Messrs. Clark Brooks and Buck, were appointed a Committee to devise some mode of ventilating the various rooms used for Primary Schools."

Notwithstanding the large number of schools (one hundred and fifty) at this time, there was some difficulty in accommodating all the children in some sections of the city; and occasionally a member of the Committee refused to admit a child to his school, on the ground of its being already crowded, or because he did not consider the residence of the child included within his school limits. The exercise of this discretion, on the part of a Local Committee, to admit or not, was liable to serious objections, inasmuch as the poor and uneducated parents could not understand how to proceed, when their application for a certificate had been rejected by the Committee, to whom they had been sent; and the child might thus be prevented from obtaining an education to which all were justly entitled.

With these views, the Standing Committee appended to their quarterly report a series of alterations to the Rules, by which *all* children were entitled to enter the school *nearest* their residence; and it was made the duty of every member to admit to his school all applicants of suitable age and qualifications; and when the number in his school was such as to prevent the child's admission, the teacher or Committee should take the name and residence of the child, specifying the cause of its non-admission, and transmit the same to the Standing Committee, whose duty it was made to provide a remedy. These amendments were adopted by the Board, and a vote was passed, " requiring the several teachers to report to the Secretary of the Board, on the second Monday of each month, the names and residences of all children belonging to their schools, who may be incorrigibly stubborn, or habitual truants; and as far as they can learn, the names and residences of the parents of any children who may be growing up in idleness and neglect of all school privileges. And the Secretary shall transmit the same to His Honor the Mayor, to take such action upon the several cases as he may deem proper."

On the 15th of June, Rev. Mr. CROWELL presented his report, in behalf of a majority of the Committee, on the petition of sundry citizens, for the abolishing of separate schools for colored pupils; concluding with a resolve adverse to the prayer of the petition. Mr. EDMUND JACKSON submitted a minority report, and a resolve favorable in part to the request of the petitioners. The reports were received, placed on file, and the Committee discharged from further consideration of the subject. The resolutions were then taken up, and the debate continued to an adjourned meeting, June 22, at which Mr. Crowell read the opinion of JOHN PICKERING, Esq., the City Solicitor, respecting the legal power of the Primary School Committee to regulate and classify the children in their schools. The report of Mr. Crowell was able and conclusive in its argument, and the resolve appended to it, "That in the opinion of this Board, the continuance of the separate schools for colored children is not only legal and just, but is best adapted to promote the education of that part of our population," was passed by a vote of fifty-nine yeas to sixteen nays.

Both the majority and minority reports[*] were ordered to be printed and distributed to the members.

At a meeting of the Standing Committee, November 24th, the Chairman reported, that from the returns of the teachers it appeared that twenty-five members of the Board had "neglected to examine *their* schools for three consecutive months," and that these members were liable to be stricken from the list, under the rule adopted by the Board in June. It was, however, deemed advisable to refer this whole subject to a Committee to consider and report. Accordingly, a form of notice to delinquent members was prepared, and adopted December 10; but the City Solicitor being consulted, gave it as his opinion, "That the Primary Board had no right, *at present*, to strike off members from their lists until the time had expired for which they were appointed by the Grammar School Committee." Application was subsequently made to the Grammar Board, and a standing authority given to the Primary Board to discharge members who may neglect to perform their duties. Of the twenty-five gentlemen reported as delinquent, thirteen were excused from sickness, absence from the city, and other causes deemed sufficient by the

[*] City Document, No. 23, 1846.

Committee; three were found to be errors in the teacher's returns; three had previously resigned, but were not reported; and six were referred to the Standing Committee of 1847, as they were not amenable to the present Committee, under the ruling of the City Solicitor.

By a vote of the Board, December 7th, the rule in regard to delinquent members was so far amended as to give discretionary power to the Standing Committee in deciding upon striking the members from the list, or excusing them, as circumstances might render it expedient or proper.

1847.

FEBRUARY 2. For the first time, since the organization of the Board, a majority could not decide upon a Chairman. Mr. Bumstead having declined a reëlection, a Committee was appointed to present a list of names of suitable persons as candidates for Chairman, who reported the names of GEORGE S. HILLARD, CHARLES BROOKS, and EBEN JONES. After two ballotings, in which Mr. Hillard had within two of the necessary number, the meeting was adjourned to Monday evening, February 8, when Mr. Hillard objected to being considered as a candidate. A Committee then proposed the names of Francis Brown, Samuel W. Hall, and William Crowell. Mr. Hall declined being a candidate; and on the fifth ballot Mr. EBEN JONES was elected *Chairman*, ALVAN SIMONDS was then unanimously reëlected *Secretary*.

Standing Committee — Joseph W. Ingraham, *Chairman ;* Alvan Simonds, *Secretary ;* J. F. Bumstead, R. W. Bayley, John Woart, Eben Jones, H. I. Bowditch, R. Soule, Jr., W. Crowell, Amos Smith, Thomas Wilder, W. P. Jarvis, F. O. Prince, J. Spence, Jr., J. W. Merrill, Dorus Clark, Wm. B. Brooks, David Kimball, F. A. Sumner.

The Committee on Ventilation made an elaborate, practical and scientific report upon this subject, and were authorized to have three hundred copies printed for the use of the teachers and Committee of the Primary Schools, after which, " the thanks of the Board were presented to Messrs. Henry G. Clark, Charles Brooks, and Ephraim Buck, Jr., for their time and attention bestowed upon the subject of ventilation, and for their able and interesting report upon this subject, in connection with the Primary Schools."

The same gentlemen were also requested to continue to act as a Committee on Ventilation for the ensuing year, and to take all necessary measures to obtain the means from the City Government to effect the proper ventilation of the Primary School-rooms.

It is gratifying to state that to this appeal the City Council responded by a liberal appropriation, which was expended under the general supervision of this Committee, and that of the City Council on Public Buildings ; but to Dr. HENRY G. CLARK we are principally indebted, for the effective manner in which this most desirable aid to the health and comfort of our schools was accomplished.

The instruction and practice of plain sewing, as an auxiliary in the moral training of the girls in the

28

Primary Schools, had always been regarded by the Committee as highly important, and its necessity had become more and more apparent, as the schools were increased, and were filled up by a class of children from the lowest ranks of society, where home education was unknown, and whose moral as well as intellectual faculties must be developed by our teachers. With a view to increased attention to this subject, the Board appointed Messrs. Charles Brooks, J. W. Ingraham, Joseph M. Wightman, J. V. C. Smith, and Isaac Adams, a Committee to consider the expediency of a more general introduction of plain sewing into the Primary Schools; and upon their report, made at a subsequent meeting of the Board, it was

Ordered, That plain sewing shall be introduced into any of the Primary Schools, whenever the Committee of such school shall deem it expedient.

Ordered, That each teacher shall specify in her semi-annual report the number of pupils who practise plain sewing in her school.

The Standing Committee reported that they had elected Dr. E. D. G. PALMER to the vacancy occasioned by the resignation of Richard W. Bayley; they also reported that the Grammar School Board had assented to their request, to change the age from *seven* to *eight*, for the transfer of children from the Primary to the Grammar Schools.

Under the vote of the City Council, passed in March, 1838, the Primary Board established several schools for the education of children *over* eight years of age. These schools had proved eminently successful; and as the proportion of this class of children had increased so as to require additional accommodation, the Board petitioned the City Council for a modification of the original order, and in December, 1846, the Joint Standing Committee on Public Instruction reported an order, by which the Primary School Committee " were authorized to admit into one or more schools, in each of the districts, any children over seven years of age, not qualified for admission into the Grammar Schools." This order was passed by both branches of the City Council, and officially communicated to the Board at their annual meeting in January, 1847.

Several of the teachers in the Grammar Schools having taken the responsibility of deciding upon the qualifications of pupils from the Primary Schools, and rejecting the certificates given by that Committee, the Standing Committee requested the Grammar Board to take some action in reference to the matter, upon which the following resolution was passed by that Board, February 3, 1847:

Resolved, That the children coming from the Primary to the Grammar Schools, and bringing a certificate of the requisite qualifications from a member of the Primary School Committee, shall not be rejected on account of want of qualifications, unless the rejection shall be sanctioned by the Sub-Committee of the Grammar School, to which application for admission shall be made.

The vacations in the Grammar Schools had been gradually increased by the action of the Committee, until, including Wednesday and Saturday afternoons, the aggregate amounted to nearly one-third of the year. The Primary Board had usually allowed the same vacations in the schools under their care, although they had long felt that so much vacation was a great disadvantage to the children, and very troublesome to the parents. Under these circumstances, when the Grammar Board voted to add two more weeks to the vacation, the Standing Committee felt it their duty to notice the evil effect of this proceeding in their Semi-Annual Report to the Board, March 2, 1847, and recommended the following to their consideration:

Whereas, the Committee have understood that the Grammar Board have by a late order voted to add two weeks to the summer vacation of their schools; and

Whereas, it is desirable that the vacations in the Primary Schools should continue to occur at the same time, and be of the same length, as those in the Grammar Schools; and this Committee are of opinion that the extension of our vacations will be injurious to our schools, and a source of complaint from the parents of the scholars; therefore,

Resolved, That a respectful request be presented to the Grammar School Committee, that they will reconsider their late order extending their summer vacation to five and a-half weeks.

This was unanimously adopted by the Board, and the Standing Committee instructed to confer with the Grammar Board on the subject.

Mr. Ingraham announced the death of Dr. Ephraim Buck, Jr., and paid an appropriate tribute to his worth, and valuable services as a member of the Board, and of the Committee on Ventilation, which was responded to by the Chairman; and Dr. William E. Coale was appointed to fill the vacancy in the Committee on Ventilation.

The order introduced February 8, by Mr. Ingraham, for the reduction of the members of the Board, was considered at the quarterly meeting, March 10th, and after several amendments it was decided to make the experiment under an order in the following form :

Ordered, That whenever the seat of any member of this Board shall be vacated, the District Committee, of which he was a member, be empowered to assign the care of his school to some other member of their Committee, who is willing to assume it, instead of nominating a new member to fill the vacancy; no member being allowed to have the care of more than two schools.

September 7. Messrs. Ingraham, Wilder, Simonds, Jones, Bowditch, and Soule, were appointed "a Committee to confer with the city authorities in relation to the evils of truancy and vagrancy among the young of our city, and adopt such measures in concurrence with said authorities as may be deemed expedient to remedy these evils."

In the report of the Standing Committee, much gratification was expressed at the efforts which were being made to establish a Public Library; and the Board passed the following resolution at their meeting, December 7 :

Resolved, That the Primary School Committee view with feelings of pleasure the efforts of the City Government, aided by liberal-minded men, towards the establishment of a Public Library, designed for the benefit of the citizens generally, and that an object so desirable in itself is worthy of their highest countenance and support; and that they look forward to the time when the hopes of its friends will be fully realized.

1848.

On the 12th of January, the Primary School Committee received their usual appointment from the Grammar Board, and their first meeting for organization was held February 1, when the following officers and Committees were chosen:

President *— Eben Jones.

Secretary — Alvan Simonds.

*Executive** *Committee* — J. W. Ingraham, *Chairman;* Alvan Simonds, *Secretary;* F. A. Sumner, Wm. Crowell, Joseph M. Wightman, Oliver Carter, Richard Soule, Jr., William Butters, John Spence, Jr., W. P. Jarvis, E. D. G. Palmer, Samuel B. Cruft, Samuel F McCleary, Jr., Albert Bowker, David Kimball, John Woart, S. L. Abbott, Eben Jones, Thomas Wilder.

On motion of Mr. William D. Ticknor, it was

Voted, That in view of the increase of schools, and the additional duties of the Secretary of the Board, he be authorized hereafter to present to the city a semi-annual bill for $50, instead of $30, as heretofore, and that the president be requested to approve the same, and present it with this vote to the Committee on Accounts of the City Council.

March 7. A Committee having been appointed for the purpose, the schools at East Boston were divided into three districts, which were designated as Districts

---

* In the Rules of the Board, which were carefully revised by a Committee and adopted by the Board, November 16, 1847, the title of " Chairman " of the Board was changed to that of " President," and the " Standing " Committee changed to the " Executive " Committee.

1, 2 and 3, East Boston; the districts in the other parts of the city remaining as at present numbered.

The following statistics of the Primary Schools for one year will show the labor and duties of the Committee at this time:

	No. schools.	Boys.	Girls.	Total.	Av. attend.	No. exam's.	No. visits.
Jan. 31, 1847,	138	4517	4069	8586	6579	759	2004
July 31, 1847,	146	4831	4589	9420	7220	853	2460
Jan. 31, 1848,	159	5101	4747	9838	7548	841	2311

The Executive Committee made a report on the order referred to them, at the last meeting of the Board, in relation to placing the $25 allowed to the teachers for making fires, care of rooms, &c., at the disposal of the District Committees. The Committee deemed it inexpedient to make any change, but recommended that the attention of the teachers be particularly called to the provisions in the Rules, in relation to the opening and warming of the school-rooms at seasonable hours, and that their particular attention be called to these provisions. The report and recommendations were adopted.

The Executive Committee were requested to consider the expediency of asking an appropriation from the City Government to furnish each of the Primary Schools with a dictionary.

The subject of employing one or more teachers of music for the teachers and pupils of the Primary Schools, was referred to a Committee composed of Messrs. Brooks, Ticknor, Cragin, Humphrey and Coit.

A Committee of five was appointed to report upon the best method of securing to all the pupils in our Primary Schools, that religious and moral instruction which is required by the constitution and laws of the Commonwealth.

Frequent allusions have already been made to the efforts of the Primary School Board, in relation to some improvement in the rooms which were provided for this class of our Public Schools. They had, after years of effort, succeeded in inducing the city to erect a few buildings for this purpose; but the contrast between the accommodations for the Grammar and Primary Schools was very marked. The former were exhibited with pride, and justly regarded as monuments of the prosperity and intelligence of our citizens, while the latter, often crowded into obscure hired rooms, with but few comforts or conveniences for a school, were a constant subject of mortification, whenever the Committee were called upon to show this class of our schools to strangers.

The buildings which were erected by the city for the Primary Schools, were built of wood, and contained but a single room, after the model of the common village school-houses. It had not been, nor was it then, the practice of the City Council to confer with either of the School Committees in relation to the location, size or construction of a school-house; and when, occasionally, a suggestion was made by the Grammar School Committee, it was regarded rather as an interference with the prerogatives of the City Council, the members of which, sometimes, carried the idea of the peculiar fitness of their own members to provide the school-houses, to an extreme not warranted or sustained by the manner in which some of the buildings were constructed.*

Because a large majority of the members of the School Committee were *professional* men, it was no reason why their judgment should be entirely ignored in *all* matters pertaining to the arrangement of the school-houses. The importance of judicious warming and ventilation, — the arrangement of the windows and the seats, so that the room might be properly lighted without injuring the eyes of the pupils, and the manner in which many things could be advantageously introduced to increase the comfort, convenience and health of the children and teachers, can only be thoroughly understood and appreciated by those of our citizens, who, as members of the School Committee, have experienced the evils attendant upon a neglect of these matters. And it is but justice to assert, that, to the perseverance and scientific investigations of these *pro-*

---

*In 1846, an order was introduced in the Common Council by a member, instructing the Committee on Public Buildings to consult with the Committee on School-houses of the School Committee, before purchasing a site, or deciding upon a plan for a school-house, which was voted down by almost a unanimous vote. The Chairman of the Committee on Public Buildings asked with an air of triumph, " What do the School Committee know about buildings? They may know how to take care of the schools and children, but they are not architects, or masons, or carpenters, and know nothing of the erection of buildings, while the Committee on Public Buildings is composed of *practical* men, who know all about the matter." To show the value of the *practical* knowledge of this Committee, we would state that in the erection of the Lyman School-house, at East Boston, under their direction, the ventilating flues were carried up within the walls to the top, and then *covered over tight* with the stone coping ! and in other school-houses, erected under the direction of this same *practical* Committee, the flues were made to terminate in the attic, from which no outlet was provided; and thus, so far as ventilation was concerned, the flues might just as well have been closed by the coping.

fessional members of the School Committee we are principally indebted, for the cheerful, healthy, and attractive schools now enjoyed by our children.

The continued efforts of the Primary Board, and the indefatigable perseverance of Mr. J. W. Ingraham, seem finally to have made some impression on the Government; and during the years 1847 and 1848, three Primary School-houses were built in different parts of the city, — the plans and arrangements of which were, generally, in conformity with the views and desires of the Primary Board. And there is reason to believe, that when the buildings were completed, the Committee of the City Council were satisfied that the views of the Executive Committee were judicious, and justified the adoption of the plans they had submitted.

The third, and probably the best arranged of these buildings, was that erected on Sheafe street, for three schools in District No. 1. This was also the first school-house erected for Primary School instruction in this city, which was set apart for its appropriate uses by a formal dedicatory service. At the request of the Executive Committee, Mr. Ingraham delivered an interesting address upon the progress of the Primary School system, and on the duties of teachers and others connected with the schools. Other addresses were made by Hon. Horace Mann, Secretary of the Massachusetts Board of Education, and gentlemen connected with the City Council, and School Committee, which, with the singing of several hymns and songs by the school children, rendered the occasion exceedingly agreeable and encouraging.

On the 13th of June, the Semi-Annual Report of the

Executive Committee was read to the Board by Mr. INGRAHAM, which was the last report made by him, as his useful life was brought to a close on Monday evening, August 28th, preceded by an illness of less than a week. His long connection with the Primary Schools, and his sudden and unexpected decease, produced a profound impression upon the Committee and teachers with whom, for many years, he had been associated.

In the year 1821, Mr. Ingraham was elected a member of the Primary School Committee, and for more than a quarter of a century he was a most zealous and efficient member.

The wide field of usefulness thus opened, was congenial to his active mind, and he entered upon it with the most lively interest. He was always regular and punctual at the meetings of the Board and Committees, and his labors were of a character and amount scarcely to be credited by those who were not familiar with them. At a special meeting of the Executive Committee, held August 29th, the following resolutions were unanimously adopted:

Resolved, That the Executive Committee have learned, with heartfelt sorrow, the sudden decease of their esteemed Chairman, JOSEPH W. INGRAHAM, in which event they have to deplore the loss of a valuable and indefatigable member of their Committee, and the senior member of the Primary School Board.

Resolved, That his ardent devotion to the cause of popular education, his faithful discharge of the laborious duties of Chairman of this Committee for many years, his unwearied and gratuitous exertions for the best interests of the Primary Schools of this city, entitle him to the grateful remembrance of this community, and of the friends of education generally.

Resolved, That the Executive Committee will attend the funeral of the deceased at Christ Church, on Thursday next, at four o'clock, P. M., and they do hereby invite the members of the Primary and Grammar School Committees to unite with them in this expression of their respect for the memory of their late friend and Chairman.

Resolved, As a testimony of respect for the many virtues of the deceased, the Committee recommend that the several Primary Schools throughout the city be suspended on Thursday afternoon next, that both teachers and children may pay the last sad tribute to departed worth.

Resolved, That a copy of the above resolutions be transmitted by the Secretary to the relatives of the deceased, with whom this Committee deeply sympathize in their sudden bereavement.

The funeral of Mr. Ingraham took place at Christ Church, on Tuesday afternoon, August 31st. Every part of the house was crowded with the friends of the deceased, among whom were the members of the School Committee, the Primary School teachers, members of the City Government, distinguished friends of education, and many of the children of the schools in the vicinity. The body was met at the church door, and conducted up the aisle by the Rev. Drs. CROSWELL and EATON, and the Rev. Mr. WOART. Appropriate music was performed by the choir, and a beautiful and touching eulogy upon the character and life of Mr Ingraham, as a citizen, as a man, and as a Christian, was pronounced by the Rev. Mr. Woart, who was his pastor, and for many years his associate in the Board. Almost the entire congregation followed in procession to the burial ground, on Copp's Hill, where the exercises were concluded by the Rev. Drs. EATON and CROSWELL.

At the quarterly meeting of the Board, September 5, the death of Mr. Ingraham was announced by Mr. Woart, and a series of resolutions were adopted, expressing their sense of the loss the schools had sustained; and the following votes were passed, after which the Board adjourned, as a testimonial of their respect:

Voted, That Messrs. J. V. C. Smith, T. R. Marvin, and W. D. Ticknor, be a Committee to wait upon the Rev. Mr. Woart, and solicit for publication a copy of his just and appropriate observations on the character of the late Joseph Wentworth Ingraham, as delivered at his funeral.

Voted, That the doings of this Board, and of the Executive Committee, in relation to Mr. Ingraham's decease, be printed for the use of the Board, in connection with Mr. Woart's address, under the direction of the same Committee.

The Executive Committee held a meeting on the afternoon of September 5th, at which Mr. JOSEPH M. WIGHTMAN was chosen Chairman, in place of Mr. Ingraham. The Secretary read the semi-annual report, to which a vote was appended, "That the subject of the bad binding of school books, as referred to by several teachers, be specially brought to the notice of the Board in the report." Mr. Wilder having resigned the special charge of the school on the Mill Dam, it was voted to revive the old practice of examination by the members of the Executive Committee, in rotation, two members in each month.

SEPTEMBER 12. An adjourned meeting of the Board was held, at which the quarterly report of the Executive Committee was read by the Secretary; and on motion of Mr. Wales, it was

Voted, That the Primary School-house, lately erected in Sheafe street, upon a plan furnished by our late associate, Joseph W. Ingraham, be hereafter known by the name of the " INGRAHAM PRIMARY SCHOOL."

Voted, That Messrs. Wales, Bumstead, Ober, Dall and Metcalf, be a Committee to communicate the foregoing vote to the City Council, and request their concurrence; and that they cause the name aforesaid to be affixed to said house in the usual manner.

DECEMBER 5. This being the regular quarterly meeting, the Semi-Annual report of the Executive Committee for the preceding six months was presented and read by the Secretary. From this report it appears that on the 1st of November the statistics of the schools were as follows, viz. :

Whole number of schools,	166
Whole number of pupils,	10,273
Pupils admitted during the last six months,	4,791
Pupils sent to Grammar School during the last six months,	962
Pupils now prepared for admission to Grammar School,	631
Average attendance,	7,973
Average absence,	2,178
Per cent. of attendance,	78
Number that attend to sewing,	879
Number of pupils of foreign parentage,	4,977
Number of examinations,	877
Number of visits to the schools,	2,577
Number of pupils over seven years of age,	3,969

The Executive Committee also recommended an alteration of the time of *their* examination, to the first two weeks in February; and that by the District Committees to the first two weeks in August; and the same was adopted at the succeeding meeting.

1849.

The Primary School Committee having been appointed by the Grammar Board, on the 17th of January, the first meeting for organization was held February 2d, and the following officers were chosen:

President — EBEN JONES.

Secretary — ALVAN SIMONDS.

Executive Committee — Joseph M. Wightman, *Chairman;* Alvan Simonds, *Secretary;* William P. Jarvis, Eben Jones, John Woart, John Spence, Jr., E. D. G. Palmer, Albert Bowker, Samuel F. McCleary, Jr., Charles Brooks, Thomas Restieaux, William H. Calrow, David Kimball, Thomas Wilder, Alvah Hobbs, Moses J Gove, William R. Lawrence, Oliver Carter, William A. Butters, Samuel A. Abbott.

On motion of Dr. John Odin, it was

Ordered, That the Committee of Conference be requested to ascertain and report at the next meeting of this Board, what directions are given to the masters of the Grammar Schools in relation to the keeping of long sessions on stormy days, and suggest such action as may create uniformity in this matter in the Public Schools.

A communication was received from the City Auditor, requesting an estimate of the appropriation required for the Primary School department for the next financial year, upon which it was "*Voted*, That so much as refers to the ordinary expenses of the schools be referred to the Executive Committee; and so much as relates to school-houses, be referred to the Committee on School-houses."

MARCH 6. *Quarterly Meeting.*—New schools were authorized to be established in Districts Nos. 5, 16 and 19.

Rev. C. Brooks stated that the Grammar School Board had appointed a Committee to consider the expediency of a new organization of all the Public Schools, and moved that a Committee from the Primary Board should be appointed to confer with them; whereupon, Messrs. T. R. Marvin, Francis Brown, and Benjamin P. Richardson, were appointed a Committee for this purpose.

The Semi-Annual Report of the Executive Committee was then read by the Chairman, (Mr. Wightman,) from which it appeared that on the 31st of January, 1849,

The number of schools was   168
The number of pupils—girls, 4,984; boys, 5,455,   10,439
The number of pupils sent to the Grammar Schools, ...   769
The number of pupils now prepared for Grammar Schools, ...   1,029
The number of pupils attending to sewing,   .   1,089
The number of pupils of foreign parentage,   .   4,996
Per centage of attendance last six months,   .   .76
Number of examinations by the Committee,   .   874
Number of visits to the schools,   .   .   .   2,449

The Chairman also reported that Messrs. Charles Brooks and Thomas Restieaux having declined the office of members of the Executive Committee, they had filled the vacancies by the choice of James B. Dow and Israel P. Procter, which action was confirmed by the Board.

Mr. Wightman, for the Committee of Conference, made a report upon the order passed at the last meeting, in relation to "long sessions on stormy days," stating that the Grammar School Committee had voted that such sessions were "unauthorized and inexpedient," and that probably no farther action was necessary.

The report was accepted, and it was voted that the Local Committees should not permit long sessions to be held in the schools under their charge.

The Committee of Conference with the Grammar Board, were directed to request the restoration of the rule in relation to Intermediate Schools, and the repeal of such provisions as conflict with reciprocal action of the two Boards in the transfer of pupils.

A special meeting of the Board was held May 25th, " to consider the expediency of granting a vacation of *two weeks*, instead of *one week*, in conformity with the action of the Grammar Board towards the schools under their charge."

After considerable discussion, during which it was demonstrated that it was not for the interest of the parents, the children or the schools, to increase the vacations; and that the frequent demand for vacations, by the teachers, ought not to be encouraged, it was voted unanimously that the subject be indefinitely postponed.

30

The Committee on School Books made a report, recommending that the words in the spelling books be visibly divided into syllables, and that the author of the book styled "Spelling and Thinking Combined," be requested to publish an edition of said work, in which the words of more than one syllable should be divided according to the best standard dictionary. Also recommending that the following charts be introduced into *all* the Primary Schools, viz.: "Table for Training the Organs of Speech in Articulation," "Numerical Table," and the "Punctuation Table," which had been partially introduced, with satisfactory evidence of their utility.

The Executive Committee reported the following resolution, which was adopted:

Resolved, That it is inexpedient for the teachers of our Primary Schools to act as agents, or use their influence as teachers, in the distribution among their pupils of periodicals or any other publications, not specially recommended by the Primary School Board.

A special meeting of the Board was called, July 2, the object of which was "to see if the Committee will take any measures for altering the time of commencing the schools in the afternoon, from two to three o'clock, so as to conform with the action of the Grammar Board."

The subject elicited considerable discussion, in which the frequent changes in the legislation of the Grammar Board, in regard to vacations and school hours, were objected to, as being detrimental to the general welfare of the schools; and under the circumstances, it was considered advisable for the Primary Board to defer making any important alterations in the schools under their care, until some settled plan should be adopted by the Grammar Board, after a trial in the schools under their own charge.

The inconvenience of having the Public Schools assemble at different hours, was urged as a reason for the change; but the Board voted to indefinitely postpone the further consideration of the subject.

The quarterly meeting was held September 4th, at which the Semi-Annual Report of the Executive Committee was presented by the Secretary and accepted.

Mr. Wightman presented a petition of Sidney Fisher, and other residents in Wards 10 and 11, requesting a special investigation into the causes of the removal of certain teachers of the Primary Schools in District No. 18, by the Local Committee. While the appointment of a Committee was pending, a motion was made and carried that the whole matter be postponed.

Much interest, however, being felt in the course of the Committee, a special meeting of the Board was called on the evening of October 9, upon the written request of Rev. Otis A. Skinner and eleven others, members of the Committee, "to take into consideration the proceedings of the Committee of schools in District No. 18." After the request for the meeting had been read, Mr. Wightman presented the following preamble and resolves:

Whereas, the 62d section of the Rules of this Board declares that no District Committee shall consist of less than half as many members as there are schools in the district; and

Whereas, the Committee of District No. 18 have neglected to conform to the above-mentioned rule, having had for a long time past but four members for the nine schools in their district; and

Whereas, at a regular meeting of the Executive Committee, held in June last, the Committee of District No. 18 were duly notified of their violation of the rules, and the necessity of complying with them, which notification has been neglected to the present time; and the Committee have continued to exercise the rights and prerogatives of a District Committee, without being legally constituted so to act; and

Whereas, they have assumed powers not delegated nor sanctioned by the letter or spirit of our rules, inasmuch as they have discharged faithful and competent teachers from a number of schools in their district, without reasonable cause, and have elected other teachers in their places, proceeding upon a system of arbitrary acts, tending to injure the character and integrity of the Primary School Board, in the minds of the citizens, and to weaken the confidence of the teachers in the legislative powers of this Board: therefore,

Resolved, That the Committee of District No. 18 have exercised executive powers, without being composed of the number of members required by the rules, or being legally authorized so to act.

Resolved, That their proceedings, in regard to the teachers in their district, while thus legally disqualified by our rules, are not, and cannot, be sanctioned by this Board.

Mr. Wightman proceeded to relate the circumstances of the case, and read several letters that had passed between the Committee and teachers of the district. Mr. Wales responded in defence of the Committee, and made sundry explanations in regard to their action, and submitted a "protest" from them, against any interference in the affairs of the district committed to their charge.

The principles involved in this case, as to the powers of the District Committees, and the right of appeal from their decisions to the Executive Committee and the whole Board, led to a long and interesting discussion, and resulted in passing the first resolution, by a vote of forty-four yeas to fifteen nays; and of the second resolution by a vote of thirty-seven yeas to ten nays.

On motion of Mr. E. Hobart, it was

Voted, That District No. 18, now being without a legally constituted Committee, be placed in charge of the Executive Committee, in connection with the remaining members of the District Committee.

After the passage of this vote the Board adjourned.

At a special meeting, held November 6th, the Joint Committee, in whose care the schools in District No. 18 were placed, made a report by the Chairman of the Executive Committee, (Mr. Wightman,) "recommending five gentlemen to fill the vacancies in said district; and that these gentlemen and the remaining members of the District Committee be organized, according to the rules, as the Committee of District No. 18, and that the schools of that district be then placed in their charge."

The report was accepted, and the following gentlemen elected, viz.: Albert T. Minot, Charles E. Cook, Alexander H. Rice, Joseph H. Allen, George W. McLellan.

It was also "*Voted*, That Mr. George R. Sampson, of District No. 18, be requested to call the first meeting of the present Committee, for organization, under the rules, without delay."

In conformity with this vote, a meeting of the Committee was called, and organized by the choice of a Chairman and Secretary; but as the new members of the Committee would not agree to the action or policy of the original members, in regard to the teachers, the subject was again brought before the Board at their meeting, December 4th, in a report from Mr. Charles Edward Cook, the Chairman of the District Committee, in which a detailed statement of their proceedings was given, from which it appeared " that the three original members of the Committee had resigned; and after a careful investigation of the circumstances, the Committee had deemed it their duty to reinstate the teachers, and restore the schools to the same position as they were in July last."

The report was accepted, and this subject, probably the most exciting which had ever agitated the Board, was brought to a final close, by the election of Joshua B. Fowle, William Willett, Aaron H. Bean, and Theodore P. Hale, to fill the vacancies in the Committee of this district.

1850.

The first meeting of the Primary School Committee, after their appointment by the Grammar Board, was held February 5th.

Joseph Smith, Esq., was chosen Chairman, *pro tem.*, who read the certificate of appointment, and authority to organize themselves and adopt such rules and regulations for the schools as they may deem expedient. ALVAN SIMONDS was chosen Secretary, *pro tem.*, and it was "*Voted*, That the Rules and Regulations of the last year be adopted by this Board until otherwise ordered."

A Committee of one from each district was appointed to nominate a candidate for President, who subsequently recommended FRANCIS BROWN, Esq., for that office, and he was duly elected. ALVAN SIMONDS, Esq., was also re-elected Secretary, by a unanimous vote.

Executive Committee — Joseph M. Wightman, *Chairman;* Alvan Simonds, *Secretary;* John Woart, Dexter W. Wiswell, Samuel F. McCleary, Jr., David Kimball, James F. Clark, Oliver Dimon, Charles Brooks, Thomas S. Wright, George M. Randall, F. F. Raymond, Alexander H. Rice, Charles A. Turner, Francis Brown, Benjamin H. Greene, Theodore D. Cook, Luther Parks, Jr., Thomas Wilder, William H. Calrow, Albert Bowker, Moses J. Gove.

An order was received from the Grammar School Committee, appointing Messrs. J. M. Wightman, Frederic Emerson, and Rollin H. Neale, a Committee, to be joined by this Board, " to consider and report what changes, if any, ought to be made in the present organization of the Grammar and Primary School Committees." Upon which, Messrs. L. S. Cragin, David Kimball, and Alvan Simonds were joined on the part of Primary School Board.

On motion of Mr. O. Dimon, it was *unanimously*

Resolved, That the late Chairman of this Board, Eben Jones, Esq., has rendered services to the Public Schools and the public interest, as a member of this Board, for fourteen years, and as President of it for the past three years, which prompt an expression of our thanks, and occasion our sincere regret that his connection with the Board has necessarily terminated.*

Resolved, That the Secretary transmit to Mr. Jones a copy of the foregoing resolution.

The regular quarterly meeting was held, March 12th, when the Chairman of the Executive Committee submitted the Semi-Annual Report on the condition of the schools for the six months previous to January 31st. At this time there were one hundred and seventy-six schools, containing eleven thousand one hundred and thirty-eight pupils. The average per centage of attendance, .76. Eight hundred and fifty-four examinations had been made of the schools by the Committee, and two thousand eight hundred and fifty-eight visits were recorded by the teachers.

In addition to the usual abstract, and in conclusion, the Executive Committee made some suggestions on the subjects of schools and school government, from which we copy the following paragraphs:

The presence of the Local Committees at this Semi-Annual examination has been alluded to in a number of the reports as a very gratifying circumstance; and the Committee would also notice in this connection, that from a careful examination of the returns, it is shown that in those districts and schools in which the Local Committees have devoted the most attention, the schools are higher in character and proficiency than any others; and, as it has been expressed by one of the examiners, " the confident tone of the reader, the upraised head, the fixed, attentive eye and listening ear, are unfailing

* Mr. Jones had removed from the city.

signs that the Local Committee of such a school has been attentive to his duty."

Ventilation is another subject of great importance; and the Executive Committee deem it necessary that some steps should be taken to bring this matter before the proper authorities. If, by the Rules, ventilation is to be required of our teachers, some means should be furnished which does not involve the health and life of the children. In a large number of the schools there is no other method of ventilation than that of opening the windows upon the backs and heads of the children, a method as absurd as it is cruel and dangerous. It may be said by some that this is not necessary; if it is not thus ventilated, the choice between the evils is very little; for without it the fœtid air, produced by the respiration and the exhalation from the persons and clothing of fifty or sixty children, whose poverty may prevent the necessary change for cleanliness, will, in a short time, render the odor and atmosphere of the room intolerable. Such a state of things ought not to exist. The Grammar Schools are almost universally well ventilated; and the contrast between them and our Primary Schools is altogether unreasonable. The children in our schools are of a more tender age, and their little bodies are more susceptible of injury from exposure, or the neglect of proper ventilation; and while we can but rejoice at the fostering care of the city displayed towards the Grammar Schools in this respect, we feel that the Primary Schools have as high, and in some respects a higher claim upon their bounty and attention.

The report was accepted, and the following orders were, on motion of Dr. J. Odin, Jr., adopted:

Ordered, That from and after the passage of this order, the sum of $25, appropriated by the City Council for the care of each school-room, be separated from the amount of the quarterly payment on the teachers' bills.

31

Ordered, That the Executive Committee be directed to take such measures as shall place the amount of $25 for each school, under the control of the several District Committees.

Messrs. Brooks, Dexter and Turner having declined to serve on the Executive Committee, Messrs. James B. Dow, Charles E. Wiggin, and George W. Parmenter, were elected to their places.

DECEMBER 3. The subject of vacations in the Primary not corresponding to those in the Grammar Schools, continued to be agitated in the Board, and was finally submitted to a Committee, who reported the following rule as a substitute for that in relation to the vacations of this Board:

The holidays and vacations of the Primary Schools shall be the same as are granted to the Grammar Schools, either by the rules of the Grammar School Committee, or by order of the Mayor, and also the day of the annual visitation of the Grammar Schools.

Mr. Wightman submitted the following amendment to the rules, which was subsequently adopted:

Any Committee wishing to establish a new school in their district, shall send a request to the Executive Committee at least two weeks before the quarterly meetings; and the Executive Committee shall examine into the expediency of complying with the request, and report at the succeeding quarterly meeting.

The Executive Committee reported in favor of the introduction into the Primary Schools of the Tables for Training the Organs of Speech, the Punctuation and the Numeral Table, and recommended that they be furnished to all those schools not at present supplied.

1851.

The appointment of the Primary School Committee having been made by the Grammar Board, the meeting for organization was held January 27th. BENJAMIN P. RICHARDSON, Esq., was chosen Chairman *pro tem.*, and the Board organized by the election of the following officers:

President — FRANCIS BROWN.

Secretary — ALVAN SIMONDS.

Executive Committee — Joseph M. Wightman, *Chairman;* Alvan Simonds, *Secretary;* Levi Tucker, William H. Learnard, Jr., Chas. E. Wiggin, Samuel F. McCleary, Jr., James B. Dow, Francis Brown, Benjamin H. Greene, Alexander H. Rice, Luther Parks, Jr., A. B. Child, Wm. H. Calrow, Moses J. Gove, David Kimball, Charles Demond, Oliver Ditson, Thomas Wilder, George M. Randall, Albert Bowker, George W. Parmenter, Fred. W. Sawyer.

MARCH 10. The Semi-Annual Report was read by Mr. Wightman, Chairman of Executive Committee.

Whole number of schools, January 31st, . . 189
Whole number of pupils, January 31st, . . 11,788

JUNE 5. A request, signed by Thomas Ranney and others, that the phonetic system of teaching be introduced on trial into two of the Primary Schools, was referred to the Executive Committee.

SEPTEMBER 2. The Semi-Annual Report of the Executive Committee was presented by the Secretary.

Whole number of schools, July 31, .   .   .   189
Whole number of pupils,.   12,110
Whole number attending to sewing,   .   . 1,444
Whole number of foreign parentage,   .   . 6,870
Whole number of examinations by Committees, 1,424

A report was received from the same Committee, upon the subject of phonetic instruction, recommending that the petition of T. Ranney and others be complied with; but not expressing any opinion of the Committee in regard to its value or utility as a system. The report was laid on the table.

The Executive Committee, to whom was referred the subject of introducing the Tables for Training the Organs of Speech, for Punctuation, and for Numeration, into those schools not already supplied, reported the following:

Resolved, That the introduction into some of the Primary Schools of the Table for Training the Organs of Speech, the Punctuation Table, and the Numeral Table, has much conduced to the progress of the children, and facilitated the arduous labors of the teachers; and this Board recommend that they be furnished to those schools not already supplied.

Read, accepted, and the resolve passed.

The same Committee reported adverse to the establishment of a new school in District No. 14; and also that measures must be taken to supply accommodations for School No. 6, East Boston, the room in which the school was located having been burned. School-rooms would also be required for the Primary Schools in the Hancock School-house, as the rooms now occupied were needed for the Grammar School classes.

On motion of Mr. Wightman, it was

Voted, That Messrs. Wightman, Dow and Fowle be a Committee to confer with the Committee on Public Buildings of the City Council, that the ordinance may be so modified that the vote of the Executive Committee may be regarded as sufficient for providing of the necessary rooms and furniture for the temporary accommodation of primary schools.

At the quarterly meeting, December 2, the Executive Committee reported in favor of new schools in Districts Nos. 10 and 11, and adverse to the request of District No. 9.

The Special Committee, to whom the subject of a new school in District No. 14 was referred, reported that they had, under the powers granted to them, made such changes in the schools of Districts Nos. 13 and 14, as would, in their opinion, render a new school unnecessary.

The report of the Committee on the subject of phonetics, referred over from the September meeting, was taken from the table and ordered to be printed, with the other matters relating to the subject, for the use of the Board.

1852.

JANUARY 27. The Committee having been duly appointed by the School Committee, were assembled for organization, and called to order by Mr. L. S. Cragin. Mr. THOMAS WILDER was elected Chairman *pro tem.*, and CHARLES DEMOND, Secretary *pro tem.*

A Committee of one from each district being appointed to nominate candidates for President and

Secretary, reported the names of CHARLES EDWARD COOK for President, and ALVAN SIMONDS for Secretary; both of whom were elected by ballot.

Executive Committee — Joseph M. Wightman, *Chairman;* Charles Demond, *Secretary;* John J. Meston, Thomas Restieaux, W. H. Learnard, Jr., E. D. G. Palmer, Abraham G. Wyman, Thomas B. Hawkes, David Kimball, Alvan Simonds, Frederic W. Sawyer, Wm. H. Dennett, Thomas Wilder, George M. Randall, Benj. H. Greene, Samuel B. Cruft, William S. Thacher, John A. Cummings, Albert Bowker, William H. Calrow, Jackson Richardson, Charles E. Cook.

At the quarterly meeting of the Board, March 2, a communication was received from ALVAN SIMONDS, Esq., who, on account of his health, had been unable to attend to his duties as Secretary, since his election in January, and resigned his office, in the following letter to the President:

BOSTON, *March 2d,* 1852.

CHARLES E. COOK, Esq., *President of the Primary School Committee of Boston:*

At the annual meeting of the Committee on the 27th January last, they were pleased for the twelfth time, unanimously, to elect me as their Secretary. It seems to be my duty now to resign that office, which resignation you will please to communicate to the Board this evening. Since I have held the office, the number of the schools have increased from one hundred to one hundred and ninety-two, and the members of the Committee have nearly doubled in number. The nature of the office has brought me in connection with the various members of the Board very frequently, not only at its meetings, but on numerous sub-committees, as we met in our daily walks, in the schools, and as we sought each other's advice and information, in the discharge of our important duties. This intercourse with them has been uniformly pleasant; and for all their kindness, courtesy and aid, I now desire, through you, to return them my sincere and heartfelt thanks. With the large body of teachers, past and present, I have often met. In May, 1849, it was my privilege, in the discharge of my duties, to do what I believe no other person has ever done; that was, to visit every school in the city, examine every "record book," and spend a few minutes in every school-room. It may not be out of place, therefore, for me to bear testimony also to the general high character of the teachers for moral worth, and for adaptation to the high and noble purposes in which they are engaged.

The more thoroughly any one becomes acquainted with the great work that is daily going on in our Primary Schools, the more he must be convinced of their importance. Here are one hundred and ninety teachers in daily intercourse with eleven thousand pupils. More than half of these children are of foreign origin; and I am persuaded that our Primary Schools are doing more to *Americanize* that class of our population than all other causes combined.

In making up the reports, from time to time, I have been astonished to notice the amount of gratuitous labor performed by very many members of the Committee, indicating a devotion to their duties, and an appreciation of their responsibilities worthy of all praise.

It is to be hoped that any movements made to change the present mode of supervision of these schools, will be made with calm consideration, and that they will be put in practice only upon a clear conviction of having found "a more excellent way." After twenty years' active service upon the Board, it appears to me that in *practice* the present system has done, and is doing so well, that no mere *theory* should take its place. It is fashionable in some quarters to call the Primary School Committee an "*anomaly.*" It may be so; but when such results are produced in the moral and intellectual improvement of such a multitude of immortal beings, even an "anomaly" may be preferable to a succession of doubtful and ever-changing experiments.

With renewed thanks to yourself, and every member of the Board,

I am your obedient servant,

ALVAN SIMONDS.

The resignation of Mr. Simonds was accepted; and on motion of Mr. Cragin, it was

Voted, That the unanimous thanks of this Committee be tendered to Alvan Simonds, Esq., our late Secretary, for the prompt, efficient, thorough, and satisfactory manner in which he has for so many years discharged the duties of that office.

The Board then proceeded to elect a Secretary, which resulted in the choice of CHARLES DEMOND, Esq.

The President read a communication from the Secretary of the Committee on Public Instruction, informing the Board that the Joint Committee from the City Council and the Grammar School Board, had passed the following vote, viz.:

Voted, That the said Committee invite the members of the Primary School Board to appoint a Committee to meet and confer with the Joint Committee, in relation to the subject of changing the organization of the Primary School Board.

On motion of Mr. Minot, the President appointed Messrs. F. Brown, L. S. Cragin, Joseph Smith, David Kimball, John Odin, Jr., Albert T. Minot, and B. P. Richardson, as a Committee of Conference, to which the President was subsequently added.

Mr. Wightman, in behalf of the Executive Committee, reported the vacancies which had occurred in that body, viz.: T. Restieaux, W. H. Dennett, Geo. M. Randall, B. H. Greene, Alvan Simonds, Charles E. Cook, and J. A. Cummings; and recommended to fill their places, Charles E. Wiggin, Oliver Ditson, J. B. Dow, Samuel Tolman, Caleb Gill, Otis Kimball, and Asa B. Snow.

The report was accepted, and the persons recommended declared elected as members of the Executive Committee.

The Semi-Annual Report of the Executive Committee, compiled from the teachers' returns, to January 31, and from the examinations of the Executive Committee, in February, was submitted by the Chairman, from which the following statistics are presented:

Whole number of schools, ... 190
Whole number of pupils, ... 11,868
Whole number of pupils of foreign parentage, 6,605
Average number of examinations of *each* school, 5½
Average number of visits to *each* school, . 18½
Average per centage of attendance, . . .78½

The report gave an abstract of the condition of the schools, and recommended some improvements

32

that were required for the comfort of the larger pupils, and concluding with the following votes, which were unanimously adopted:

Voted, That the Executive Committee apply to the Committee on Public Buildings of the City Council, for suitable chairs and desks, for the use of the larger and advanced scholars in School No. 8, District No. 9, on the Western Avenue.

Voted, That the Executive Committee be requested to take into consideration and report upon the expediency of providing some form, or desk, for the Intermediate and Primary Schools.

Voted, That the entrance to the school-house in Bumstead Court is dangerous to the pupils attending the school; and the Committee on Public Buildings of the City Council are respectfully requested to adopt some measures to remedy the evil.

June 1. *Quarterly Meeting.* — The rules of the Grammar Board, requiring a report annually, in relation to the condition of the Primary Schools, were read; whereupon it was "*Voted*, That the subject be referred to the Executive Committee, with instructions to make that report in behalf of the Primary School Board."

On motion of Mr. Mead, it was

Ordered, That the Executive Committee be requested to take into consideration and report at some subsequent meeting, whether, in their opinion, the interests of the Primary Schools cannot be promoted, by the adoption of some of the suggestions made by the Superintendent of the Public Schools, in his late report; or whether some change in the classification of the pupils cannot advantageously be made.

On motion of Mr. Otis Kimball, it was

Ordered, That the Executive Committee consider and report upon the propriety of establishing geographical limits to the several Primary School Districts.

SEPTEMBER 7.   *Quarterly Meeting.* — The Semi-Annual Report of the Executive Committee was read by the Secretary, by which it appeared that the

Whole number of schools, July 31, 1852, was .	193
Number of pupils, ...	11,970
Number of pupils sent to Grammar School last six months, ...	1,497
Number of pupils prepared for admission, .	1,431
Average attendance to each school, . . .	48
Per centage of attendance to each school, .	.79
Number who attend to sewing, . . .	1,360
Number of foreign parentage, ...	6,788
Number over eight years of age, . . .	3,076
Number under five years of age, . . .	1,836
Number of examinations last six months, . .	1,722
Number of visits last six months, . . .	3,704

Mr. Wightman, in behalf of the Executive Committee, made a report, returning the resolutions referred to them at the last meeting of the Board, in relation to geographical limits, and to the report of the Superintendent of Public Schools, stating their reasons for so doing; and recommended the passage of the following resolution, which was adopted:

Resolved, That in view of the present position and uncertain action of the City Government, in relation to the Primary School system, it is inexpedient for this Board to take any further action upon the orders in relation to the geographical limits of the districts, or the suggestions of the Superintendent of Public Schools, in his late report.

On motion of Dr. John Odin, Jr., the Executive Committee were requested to have printed one thousand copies of an abstract of the Semi-Annual Report, and of the report on the subject of geographical limits.

1853.

FEBRUARY 8. The Primary School Committee having been appointed by the Grammar Board, held their first meeting this evening, and the following officers were elected :

President — CHARLES EDWARD COOK.

Secretary — CHARLES DEMOND.

Executive Committee — Joseph M. Wightman, *Chairman ;* Charles Demond, *Secretary ;* James B. Dow, E. D. G. Palmer, Thomas Wilder, William H. Calrow, Oliver Ditson, Caleb Gill, Abraham G. Wyman, Thomas B. Hawkes, John J. Meston, Jackson Richardson, Philo Sanford, N. C. Stevens, E. W. Blake, James N. Sykes, Stephen Tilton, Jr., William Read, Samuel G. Bowdlear, Isaiah Faxon, Henry L. Dalton, S. J. M. Homer.

On motion of James B. Dow, it was

Voted, That a Committee be appointed to take into consideration the subject whether it is expedient or desirable to make any alteration in the organization of this Board, to render it more efficient in promoting the best welfare of the Primary Schools of this city, and report at a future meeting.

MARCH 14. *Quarterly Meeting.* — The Semi-Annual Report of the Executive Committee was presented by the Chairman, and one thousand copies ordered to be printed. The following orders, appended to the report, were adopted:

Ordered, That a Committee of five be appointed to prepare a revision of the Rules and Regulations of this Board, and to recommend such alterations and amendments as they may deem expedient, and report the same to the Board at the next quarterly meeting.

Ordered, That a Committee of one from each district be appointed to take into consideration and report upon a reorganization of the schools into new districts, so that the number of schools in each district may be more convenient and uniform.

Resolved, That the salaries of the teachers in the Primary Schools should be the same as is paid to the female teachers in the Grammar Schools; and that the Executive Committee be directed to lay this subject before the proper authorities.

December 15. The Committee on the Revision of the Rules submitted their report, which was adopted, and two hundred and fifty copies of the same were ordered to be printed.

The Board also deemed it inexpedient to make any reorganization of the districts.

On the recommendation of the Executive Committee, a new school was established in Porter street, East Boston; and the Secretary was directed to request the Committee on Public Buildings of the City Council, to provide the usual furniture for this school.

1854.

January 31. The first meeting of the members of the Primary School Committee for the current year, was held this evening.

A communication was read from Hon. CHARLES EDWARD COOK, declining to be a candidate for President, after which the Board was organized by the choice of the following officers:

President — ALVAN SIMONDS.

Secretary — CHARLES DEMOND.

Executive Committee — Joseph M. Wightman, *Chairman*; Charles Demond, *Secretary*; James B. Dow, E. D. G. Palmer, William H. Calrow, Oliver Ditson, Caleb Gill, Abraham G. Wyman, Thomas B. Hawkes, Jackson Richardson, Philo Sanford, N. C. Stevens, James N. Sykes, Stephen Tilton, Jr., William Read, Samuel G. Bowdlear, S. J. M. Homer, Elijah Stearns, N. P. Mann, Edmund T. Eastman, H. W. Williams, Thomas F. Caldicott, Charles A. Turner.

On motion of Mr. Wightman, it was

Voted, That the several District Committees be requested, annually, to select either their Chairman or their Secretary to provide articles required by the teachers, in conformity with the order of the City Council, passed May 30, 1853.

Voted, That the Secretary of each district be requested to furnish the Secretary of this Board with the length of time of service of each teacher of the Primary Schools in his district, on or before the fifteenth day of April next.

On motion of Mr. Otis Kimball, it was

Voted, That the thanks of this Board be presented to the Hon. CHARLES EDWARD COOK, for the faithful, courteous, and dignified manner in which he has performed the duties of presiding officer during the past year; and that a copy of this vote, signed by the President, be transmitted to him.

MARCH 14. The Semi-Annual Report of the Executive Committee was presented by Mr. Wightman, and ordered to be printed.

A communication was received from the Grammar Board, announcing a change in the hours of opening the schools under their charge; and the rules of the Primary Schools were amended to conform thereto.

September 12. Mr. Demond, in behalf of the Executive Committee, read the Semi-Annual Report, which was accepted, and ordered to be printed.

By an amendment to the City Charter, which had been adopted by the citizens, the Grammar School Committee was increased to seventy-two members, who were to have direct charge of the Primary Schools, and supersede the organization of the Primary School Committee. As the act in relation to a new Committee would go into operation on the first Monday in January, 1855, the following communication was addressed to the City Solicitor:

Boston, November 2d, 1854.

Hon. George S. Hillard, City Solicitor:

Sir:— The undersigned, officers of the Primary School Committee of Boston, desire to ask your advice and opinion upon certain points relating to the operation of the new City Charter upon that Board.

Under the vote and rule on page second of the pamphlet, herewith transmitted,* the present Primary School Committee were appointed, with the powers and duties therein named; and have proceeded to execute said trust, under the rules adopted in the same pamphlet. They have elected teachers, according to section 9, page 12, most of them, for the school

---

* Rules and Regulations of the Primary Schools.

year, ending with July next, and have given them certificates of appointment.

It has been usual for the Grammar School Committee to appoint the Primary Board near the close of January in each year, and for the previous Committee to have charge of the schools until the next annual appointment, and to receive the returns and make up the Semi-Annual Report to the 31st of January, annually.

By the City Charter, just adopted, to take effect on the *first Monday of January next*, in sections 54, 55 and 56, it is generally supposed that the present Primary School Committee is abolished. We would, therefore, respectfully request of you information on the following points, viz:

First. When do the duties of the present Primary School Committee cease? On the first Monday in January, when the charter takes effect; on the second Monday in January, when the Committee of seventy-two are to organize; or should they continue to act through the month of January, and make up the Semi-Annual Report? And at what time is it proper for them to surrender the one hundred and ninety-seven schools under their charge, with all their records, books and papers, to the School Committee chosen under the new charter?

Second. When does the time of service of the teachers cease, under their present appointment? and can they properly continue and be the *legal* instructors of the schools, after the first or second Monday in January next?

Third. Will it be competent for the persons chosen as School Committee, by virtue of the new charter, under the power given by section 55, to "choose such subordinate officers as they may deem expedient," to appoint any number of persons which they may judge suitable; to aid them in the care and examinations of the Primary Schools, without compensation; somewhat in the same manner as the Primary School Committee have done in past years?

We require an answer to the *first* question, that we may not, on the one hand, seem to desire to hold our offices too long, nor, on the other, to abandon a post of duty at too early a day.

We require an answer to the *second* question for the information of the teachers.

The *third* question is prompted by the deep interest we feel in the Primary Schools, from our long connection with them; and our desire that the new plan in regard to them should be fully understood, and put in operation, from the first, in the best manner, without subjecting them to experiments or want of proper supervision.

We apprehend that some gentlemen, whose services have been found valuable on the Grammar School Committee, will shrink from the service if the whole labor and care of nearly two hundred Primary Schools were added to their labors. We believe, also, that if it be legal and proper to receive the voluntary and unpaid services of many of our active, benevolent citizens, like some of those who have heretofore served for many years on the Primary School Committee, great advantages would result to the schools.

As the quarterly meeting of the Board occurs on the 2d Tuesday in December, if your duties will permit you to favor us with a reply to the foregoing in season for the meeting, it will greatly oblige

Yours respectfully,

ALVAN SIMONDS, *President.*
JOSEPH M. WIGHTMAN, *Ch'n Ex. Com.*
CHARLES DEMOND, *Secretary.*

In his reply, the City Solicitor stated, that in his opinion —

The duties of the Primary School Committee would cease on the organization of the new Grammar Board. That the

33

teachers would continue their term of service under the new organization; and that it would not be proper for the new Board to substantially continue the Primary School Committee, inasmuch as the former had been largely increased, upon the express understanding that the latter body was to be superseded.

This correspondence was submitted to the Board at their meeting, December 5th, by the Chairman of the Executive Committee; and on his motion the following orders were read and laid upon the table:

Ordered, That the Secretary be, and he hereby is, authorized and instructed to address a communication to the School Committee, who are to meet for organization on the second Monday of January next, and inform them, in behalf of this Committee, that the schools, records and papers of which the Primary School Committee have had charge, are subject to the order and direction of said School Committee.

Ordered, That the Secretaries of the several districts are hereby requested to forward to the Secretary of the Board, the records of their several districts, on or before the second Monday of January next.

On motion of Mr. Marvin, it was

Voted, That the Executive Committee be requested to draw up a brief history of the Primary School Committee, from their organization to the present time.

After which, the Board adjourned to meet on the evening of the first Tuesday in January next ensuing.

1855.

FINAL MEETING OF THE BOARD.

JANUARY 2. In conformity with the vote passed at the preceding meeting, Mr. Wightman, in behalf of the Executive Committee, presented a historical sketch of the Primary School Board, from its first establishment, which was recommitted to Messrs. Simonds, Demond, and Wightman, with a request that one thousand copies of the same be printed for the use of the Board, if the Committee deem it expedient.

The orders in relation to the records read at the last meeting, were taken from the table and passed.

The business of the meeting having been thus accomplished, Mr. Wightman submitted the following resolution :

Resolved, That the thanks of this Board be presented to Alvan Simonds, Esq., for the very acceptable manner in which he has performed the duties of President of the Board.

The President responded thus :

Gentlemen of the Primary School Committee: — Accept my warmest thanks for the vote just passed — for the kindness ever manifested towards me, and especially for your friendly coöperation and sympathy during the past year, when called to preside in your meetings, and that you have thrown the kind mantle of charity over my inexperience and shortcomings.

Our duties, as members of the Primary School Committee, are now closing. Our appointment, received one year since, is about to expire. Many of us have been honored with reäppointments from year to year. For one, it has been my privilege, by reëlection from time to time, to have been a member of this body for twenty-one successive years.

I can recognize among the members the names of Bumstead, Marvin, Cragin, and Brown, who are my seniors in office. It is because the Grammar School Committee (themselves subject to annual changes) have been pleased to avail themselves of the continued services of gentlemen upon this Board, that the impression had obtained in many minds, that this was a perpetual self-appointing Committee. As a matter of fact, our existence has been (as legally defined) only like that of a sub-committee, and expired annually. Towards the selection of no officer or officers in this city has a more rigid scrutiny been observed. We have had no money at our disposal, we have asked or desired no pecuniary reward; no suppers, no excursions, as a body, or as sub-committees, at the public expense, have been ours.

By the new city charter the number of the Grammar School Committee is increased, and the whole care of the Primary Schools is transferred to their hands. We take leave of the pleasures, the cares, the labors and the responsibilities of the office, without any regret, except that we have been no more faithful in improving the opportunities afforded us for doing good. Whatever the private views of some members may be, as to the utility of the change, it becomes not me to prophesy evil, nor prejudge unfavorably the operations of the new system. We love the cause of primary instruction too well; our experience leads us to see and feel its importance too deeply, for any wish even to find a place in our hearts, except an earnest hope and expectation of its increased prosperity. Our desires are that these schools may have a more vigilant and effective supervision, and a more enlarged success under the new arrangements where they are now to be placed. We recognize many names among those to have charge of them of enlarged experience, and whose delight it is to do good. By their devotion of the time needed for the examination and supervision of these schools, we may safely hope that under the new organization even brighter days are in reserve for them.

Allow me to congratulate you, my friends, and all our fellow-citizens, on the success which has attended our schools, and on the good accomplished by them. A devoted attention to their wants and interests has led you to adopt a course of study, a system of supervision and of examinations of these schools, which have been most beneficial in their results, and which have stood the test of experience. Great improvements have also been made in school buildings — in the ventilation of the school-rooms — in providing comfortable seats, and such physical exercises within and without the schools as secure health and prevent weariness. A thorough examination of candidates for teachers, and great care in their selection, have been well repaid by a knowledge of their fitness and their success. The frequent visits to every school, and the monthly examinations by the Local Committees, have aided and cheered the teacher — have encouraged and instructed the pupils.

The system of thorough examinations semi-annually, by the District Committee collectively, or by the Executive Committee, when the schools of each district were brought together; when the faults or excellences of each school were powerfully though silently presented to the notice of each instructor, by contrasts, has admirably contributed to raise the character of the schools. The semi-annual gatherings of the teachers to hear the reports of the defects or excellences found in the schools, have been attended with favorable results. You have bestowed much time and labor to the care of the schools. As evidence of this, I may point to the abstract of the teachers' reports in July last, for the preceding six months. They record in that time one thousand eight hundred and sixty-four examinations, or an average of more than nine to a school, and three thousand six hundred and thirty-five visits, or more than eighteen to each of the one hundred and ninety-seven schools.

This constant watchfulness, the aid and encouragement thus afforded to the teachers and pupils, has done much towards making our schools what they are, and cannot be dispensed with without essential injury. Nothing so much inspires and encourages the teacher, as the kind aid and advice of those who seek the welfare of the young. The good effect upon the children, of a friendly visit, and a few words of advice and of encouragement, is truly wonderful. It is but half known to those who have seen it, and, therefore, have realized it the most. There are those among you who have found and have given pleasure in frequent visits to these schools; in addressing a few words to these ever-listening little ones, on their studies, their manners, or their morals.

Desires for good, and a conviction of the misery to which evil courses lead, have thus been excited in these little minds, which will have an effect upon them through their whole lives. Winning orators, wise men, great statesmen, may employ hours in eloquent and powerful speeches in halls of legislation, and produce little practical effects, for they address minds already made up or bound down by party or sectional ties; but one who has the privilege of addressing the impressible minds in a Primary School wields a power for good not found in the Legislature or in the Congress of our nation. A trust so weighty, a privilege so exalted, has been yours. That it has been often well used, many can testify.

The moral power of these schools is very great. They have done and are doing more, I almost believe, than all other causes combined to *Americanize* our foreign population.

While in our Grammar Schools the use of the Bible is almost, if not wholly, confined to the reading of it by the teachers in the pupils' presence, in the Primary Schools it is a part of the regular reading lessons for the upper classes.

The Ten Commandments and the Lord's Prayer are so taught and imprinted on the memory as rarely to be forgotten. The worship of the true God, and of him only, the evil nature and tendencies of the sins forbidden in the Decalogue, and the pleasantness of the path of truth and virtue as there recommended, are thus deeply impressed on the minds of the young.

Pain, pleasure and hope mingle in this parting hour. Pain, in severing our pleasant connections in the Board, and in reflecting on opportunities for doing good which we may have neglected; pleasure, in the belief that we may have usefully served our beloved city and the young, in this humble capacity, and in the good accomplished; hope, in the future prosperity and continued usefulness of these schools, and that there shall rise up from them, those who will uphold and maintain all the best interests of Boston, and will finally meet us, and the faithful teachers, and our beloved associates of precious memory who have gone before us, in the better " City of our God " above.

The thanks of the Board were also voted to the Chairman of the Executive Committee, for the interesting report he had submitted, and for the manner in which he had discharged the duties of the office. A similar vote of thanks was tendered to the Secretary, who responded in a brief address.

Many very interesting reminiscences and remarks were made by a number of the oldest members, among whom were Messrs. Marvin, Bumstead, Wilder, Marsh, Sleeper, Norcross, Weltch, Howland, Cragin, and Greene, all of whom expressed their deep interest in the schools, and their intention to continue to visit them as citizens, and unofficially to aid and coöperate with the new organization of the School Committee in sustaining and improving these educational nurseries of our city.

Mr. Dale, Chairman in District No. 15, stated, "that on Wednesday morning the Committee propose to meet the First and Second Classes of all the schools in the district, eight in number, and that farewell speeches will then be made; the Committee will present each scholar with a Bible and dictionary."

Mr. Wightman offered the following resolve, prefacing it with a few remarks, complimentary to the daily press:

Resolved, That the thanks of the Primary School Committee are due to the reporters and conductors of the public press, for their very full, elaborate and accurate reports of the proceedings of this Board.

The resolution was adopted by a unanimous vote; and at ten o'clock, P. M., the Boston Primary School Committee adjourned *sine die.*

REVIEW.

In reviewing these annals of the Primary Schools, from their commencement to the close of their existence, as a separate organization, there is a strong feeling of gratification that so noble a mission, in the cause of popular education, should have been so successful in accomplishing the objects for which it was originally established.

Its eminent conservatism, — its entire freedom from political bias in the selection of members, — the personal responsibility of each member to a faithful discharge of his duties, — its careful watchfulness over the schools under their control, — its strict adherence to the powers conferred by the City Government, never exceeding, in a single instance, the authority with which it was invested, — and its acknowledged success for thirty-six successive years, renders an explanation of the causes, which resulted in its dissolution, important to a correct history, and an act of justice to the earnest and disinterested devotion of those citizens who have served upon the Board.

We have already alluded to the proceedings of the Grammar Board, on the suggestions of the Secretary of the State Board of Education, (Hon. HORACE MANN,) in

1838, as the first overt act of opposition to the organization of the Primary Board; and although other causes, undoubtedly, had an influence, it is to the resistance then made, to the course of the Secretary and his friends, that we may attribute much of the subsequent agitation, and endeavor to bring the Primary Schools under the exclusive control of the Grammar Board.

The doctrine of "centralization," initiated by Mr. Mann, had its advocates, not only in the Grammar School Committee, but in the City Council, who were impressed with the idea that economy, progress, and complete success in the administration of our schools, were to be attained by making our whole educational system a "unit;" and placing it under the supervision of a "Superintendent of Public Schools."

The natural conservatism of our citizens, in regard to public matters, is proverbial; and the entire change proposed, in the organization of the Boston schools, excited considerable feeling, which became more or less partisan in its character, until it appears to have culminated in 1845, in an open issue between the Boston schoolmasters and Mr. Mann. Impatient of criticism, and submitting to no opposition, the Secretary, in this controversy, exhibited his usual zeal in defence of his opinions, and aided by the prestige of his official station, and the active coöperation of his friends, the masters were silenced; and means were adopted by which a large majority of those subsequently elected to the School Committee, were in favor of Mr. Mann and his peculiar views. From this time *annual* attempts were made to establish the office of "Superintendent;" but as this required the concurrent action of both branches of the City Council and of the Grammar Board, the measure was defeated in one branch or the other until April, 1851.

In the meantime it was evident that the Primary Board, being the exponent of the principle of " diffusion," instead of " centralization " of power, presented a serious barrier to the success of the new system ; and accordingly a regular crusade was commenced upon it, as an organization, in the inaugural address of the Mayor, (Hon. John P. Bigelow,) in January, 1850, in which he makes the following exposition of the grounds of opposition to the Primary Board:

I have reason to believe that the Public Schools, in general, were never in a more satisfactory state than at the present time; and that the Committees having them in charge, during the past year, have faithfully and efficiently performed their duties. But I cannot overlook the fact that one of these Committees (that having direction of the Primary Schools) is constituted in a way which is entirely anomalous to the genius of our institutions — although the members themselves are deservedly held in grateful respect by the people for their services.

This Board, which consists of about one hundred and seventy individuals, (one to each school) having charge of more than half the public pupils, and of the expenditure of a very great amount of the public moneys, is not chosen by the people, nor by the City Government. Its vacancies, as they occur, are filled by the remaining members, in the manner of close corporations, — the people, over whose affairs they exercise such an important control, having no voice in the matter whatsoever. The principle is utterly wrong, and of course, sooner or later, will be productive of practical evil. The body itself, as the schools have increased in number, has already become inconveniently large for mutual consultation, and advantageous coöperation. There is no good reason why so important a Board, (which is not even recognized in our charter,) should not derive its power from, and be responsible to, the people, in the same manner as the Committee having charge of the Grammar Schools, — and I recommend the adoption of such measures as shall remedy the defect.

This was followed by a report of the Committee on Public Instruction, in October, substantially reiterating the same views; but as the efforts to establish the office of Superintendent had not been successful, further action, in relation to the Primary Board, was suspended, until a report on the whole subject of the reörganization of the school system could be prepared.

The office having been established, and a Superintendent of Public Schools elected, in 1851, the Primary Board was again brought to the attention of the City Council, in January, 1852, by the Mayor, (Hon. Benjamin Seaver,) who addressed a special communication to the President of the Common Council, on "The Present Organization of the Grammar and Primary School Committees." This communication was referred to the Committee on Public Instruction, who, in April, submitted a very elaborate report, by their Chairman, (Sampson Reed, Esq.,*) in which, after glancing at the early history of the schools, and the establishment of the Primary Board, the following grounds were urged against the continuance of the latter: *First,* because of its questionable legality; *second,* because, as a deliberative or executive body, it had become too numerous for the purposes entrusted to its care; *third,* because of

* City Document No. 22, 1852.

the mode in which its members were elected and vacancies filled; and *fourth,* because its continuance perpetuated a want of unity in our school system.

The arguments adduced in support of these propositions were ably presented in the report, and have been so frequently referred to in various reports of the Grammar School Committee, as to render it unnecessary to present them at this time.

If, therefore, to the several grounds of opposition, as enumerated in the report of the Committee on Public Instruction, we add the declaration of the Mayor, that "the constitution of this Committee is anomalous to the genius of our institutions," and the charge, that "they have the expenditure of a very large amount of the public moneys, without being chosen by the people or by the City Government," — we shall have a full exposition of the reasons, which, in various forms and at sundry times, were urged as good and sufficient for the dissolution of the Primary Board.

A general response to all these statements and arguments might be, that, admitting all these propositions and charges to be true, — in what manner had the public interest, our schools, or the cause of education, suffered from the "anomalous" character or the exercise of these powers, by the Primary School Committee? The several documents, in relation to the subject, answer the question.

Mayor Bigelow says of the Committee, "The members themselves are deservedly held in grateful respect by the people for their services;" and the Committee on Public Instruction, of the same year, add —

Your Committee cannot, however, in justice to those of our fellow-citizens, by whose public spirit and devotion, the one hundred and seventy-eight Primary Schools of our city are regulated and controlled, dismiss the subject without adding their testimony to that of His Honor the Mayor, in favor of the zeal and efficiency evinced by the Primary School Board. Though elected by a wrong system, these gentlemen have performed the arduous duties of their station in an able manner, and to their enlightened action is the present satisfactory condition of the schools mainly attributable.

Those schools indicate how successfully the action of talented and devoted agents can overcome radical defects in the system by which those agents were placed in power.

These opinions are confirmed by the report of the same Committee, in 1852,* as follows:

Little was it probably thought, at the commencement of these schools, that this humble beginning would grow into the great system which now exists, underlying our whole school system as its ground work, and affording the means of education, not only to the poor and neglected, but to all classes of society, however intelligent or wealthy. There are now no less than forty-five Primary School-houses, many of them elegant structures. There are one hundred and ninety Primary Schools. The number of pupils instructed in them is eleven thousand eight hundred and sixty-eight! and the expenditure for their support the last year, was $97,648 47 for current expenses; and $51,010 69 for school-houses, making a total of $130,659 16. The statement of these facts is in itself a well merited compliment to those gentlemen who first interested themselves in this cause, and to those who have from time to time devoted themselves with so much zeal and usefulness in its service. And it may be proper to premise, before

* City Document No. 22.

proceeding further, that all our remarks are made with entire respect to those individuals who have comprised the Primary Sohool Board in times past, or who at present comprise it, and apply, not to the persons, but to the system. The catalogue of the names of the gentlemen who have served on that Committee, contains those which would do honor to any city, — those who, from their quiet, unobtrusive labors in this department of duty, for a long series of years, should be held by their fellow-citizens in lasting remembrance.

At an adjourned meeting of the School Committee, January 16, 1855, Rev. Dr. LOTHROP, in behalf of the Committee, to which was referred the communication of the Secretary of the late Primary School Committee, reported that they had discharged the duty assigned them, and added :

When first instituted in 1818, the Primary School Committee consisted of thirty-six members; twenty-five Primary Schools were established, and about one thousand children were in attendance. At the time that it became extinct, the Committee consisted of one hundred and ninety-six members, and bequeathed to the care of our Committee one hundred and ninety-seven schools, at which over twelve thousand pupils attended. In view of these facts, however satisfactory may be the various reasons that prevailed with the public mind to produce the change which has been adopted, all will agree that the plan which has now been abandoned had many excellences; that under it this department of public instruction has been constantly enlarged to meet the wants of the increasing population of the city; and that the gentlemen who, from time to time, have served on this Committee, many of them for many years, have generally been men of integrity, honor, and public spirit, who have aimed at a strict and faithful discharge of the duties of their trust, and who are entitled to the gratitude of the community for the services they have rendered.

The following resolution accompanied the report:

Resolved, That in receiving the records and papers of the late Primary School Committee, this Board, in behalf of the citizens of Boston, by whom they have been entrusted with the guardianship of the great interests of public instruction, desire to place upon their records an expression of the just appreciation which they entertain of the value and fidelity of the services of those gentlemen who, from time to time, have been members of said Primary School Committee, and zealously discharged its duties.

The report was accepted, and the resolution was adopted.

These universal expressions of respect and confidence, in regard to the members, and the unreserved testimony in favor of the manner in which the affairs of the Primary Schools had been conducted, prove conclusively that no *injury*, but great *benefits*, had resulted from this "anomalous" organization.

With this disposition of the general question, we will now proceed to examine the grounds on which the "system" was condemned.

First. It was "anomalous to the genius of our institutions."

The "genius of our institutions" may be defined as "the voice of the people, legally expressed;" and the establishment of the Primary School Committee, by the people assembled in town meeting at Faneuil Hall, was an act preëminently in conformity with this aphorism. Established by competent authority, its public position was always recognized by the City Government, and remained unchallenged from 1822 till 1850.

Second. They had "the expenditure of a very great amount of the public moneys," without being "chosen by the people, or by the City Government."

The Primary Board have never possessed nor exercised the power to expend the "public moneys." The salaries of their teachers were fixed by vote of the City Council, and paid by the City Treasurer; the schoolhouses were planned and built, — school-rooms were hired, — the furniture and fuel were supplied, by the sole order of the City Council, — the incidental repairs and alterations were made by the Committee and Superintendent of Public Buildings, entirely independent of the Primary Board or its Committees. With the exception of about one hundred dollars, for the delivery of notices and the expenses incurred by the Secretary, and two dollars to each school for rewards, neither the Board nor its members ever had the control or expenditure of a dollar of the " public moneys."

Third. They assumed powers "not vested in them by law," and illegally increased their number of members. A complete refutation of this is contained in the Memorial of the Board and the proceedings of the City Government in 1823.*

Fourth. "As a deliberative or executive body, it had become too numerous for the purposes entrusted to its care."

As this appears to be merely an opinion, without any reasons or proof being given to sustain it, it is only

* See page 72–76..

necessary to state, that *we* are not aware of any difficulty being felt or experienced from the number of members. On the contrary, the large number of our citizens who, by this means, were brought into immediate contact with the schools, became thoroughly acquainted with our system of public education; and by participating in the labor, care and responsibility of its management, felt a higher degree of interest in its success, disseminated a knowledge of its details and operation, and by this means strengthened and elevated our Public Schools in the estimation of the people at large; and to this cause may be attributed much of that preëminence which has characterized the Boston Public Schools. The reasons for the large number of members, as presented in the Memorial of the Board to the City Council, in 1823, were as valid in 1850 as at that time.

Fifth. " The objectionable mode in which the members were elected and vacancies filled, in the manner of close corporations."

The City Solicitor, in reply to questions by the Grammar Board, in 1849, declared that the Grammar School Committee, " being originally authorized by the town, might properly appoint the Primary School Committee to take particular charge of the Primary Schools, as a department or sub-division of the general system of Public Schools."

This was the practice during the entire existence of the Primary Board; and as a sub-committee, they were subject to appointment every year, under the following rules of the Grammar Board:

In January or February, annually, this Board shall nominate and appoint a suitable number of gentlemen, whose duty shall be to provide instruction for children between four and eight years of age, by means of the *Primary Schools*, and shall authorize the Committee of these schools to organize their body and regulate their proceedings as they may deem most convenient, and to remove such members thereof, as, in their opinion, do not attend to their duties, and to fill all vacancies which may occur in the same, and they shall report to this Board, at its quarterly meeting in May, as follows:

1st. The plan of their organization, including the names of the officers and Committees, the rules and regulations which govern their Board, and the classification adopted in the schools.

2d. The number of schools under their charge, their location, together with the number and names of the teachers.

3d. The number of scholars, male and female, and the studies required.

4th. A schedule of the Primary School-rooms owned by the city, the number of the same hired by the city, the number vacant of the same, owned by the city, the number new of the same, which will be required during the year, and the districts in which they must be provided.

And this Board will respectfully receive such other communications as from time to time they may please to make on the subject of those schools.

With these facts before us, it is difficult to discover the analogy between the Primary Board and " a close corporation."

To judge whether the mode of filling the vacancies, *ad interim*, by the Primary Board, was justly liable to censure, it is proper to state the process. Whenever a new school was established, or a vacancy occurred, by resignation or otherwise, the Committee of the district in which the school was located, proceeded to select a gentleman whose known interest in the schools and social position qualified him for the office. This was done by ballot, and in all cases preference was given to those whose business or residence was in the vicinity of the school. This was of much importance, as all matters pertaining to the teacher or school were under the special care of the Local Committee. It was also a great convenience to the citizens, inasmuch as all the children were admitted and transferred by certificate of the Committee, which they were obliged to obtain from him. After the ballot was taken, and the party selected had signified his willingness to serve, his name, with the number of the school and district with which he was to be connected, was issued in a printed notice to all the members, and his admission was subjected to ballot at the quarterly meeting of the whole Board. A person, therefore, was subject to *two* elections, by different bodies, before he could be even nominated for appointment by the Grammar Board, as a member of the Primary School Committee. A "mode" of proceeding far more critical than is usually attempted in the selection of candidates for the Grammar School Committee. The power to remove any member for neglect of duty, vested in the Executive Committee, had a tendency to maintain the standard of supervision to a healthy point. This and an entire absence of all political bias in the selection of members, were elements of great value in a system of universal education, but which could only be attained by some other "mode" than that of popular nominations at the ward rooms.

The *Sixth* and last objection we have to notice, is, "that its continuance perpetuated a want of unity in our school system."

The union of the Primary and Grammar Schools, under one Committee, was but one step towards the object in view. Other elementary changes were contemplated, some of which had been already introduced. Among these projected improvements, was the congregating of large numbers of children and teachers under one roof, subject to the control of a single head, rendering the duties of the master those of a subordinate superintendent, rather than an instructor. The reduction in the number of the Committee, and consequent increase of care and responsibility on each of the members, rendered the appointment of a Superintendent necessary and imperative, to aid in the discharge of the onerous duties incumbent on the Committee. The natural tendency of all this was to concentrate the vast interests of our schools in the hands of a few; and through the agency of the Superintendent, to bring the Boston schools more directly under the influence of the Massachusetts Board of Education, — a body created by the State Legislature as a great central power, to give impulse and direction to the method of conducting the education of the young in all the Public Schools throughout the Commonwealth.

To render the Boston schools subordinate to this system of centralization, was the real development of the idea of "unity in our school system."

That the Primary Board, in principle and practice, was in direct antagonism to this system, is true. Its origin and organization were essentially popular and democratic. Its object was to extend the blessings of education to the children of poverty and ignorance, and by this means to qualify the children of the poor emigrant for intelligent citizenship. Opposed by the constituted authorities, the object was approved and the schools established, by the people. And it was the peculiar province of this organization to *diffuse* the control and administration of our schools among as large a number of the citizens as practicable.

Whether the change, by which a new, untried and experimental system has been substituted, will prove to have been judicious, or be so beneficial as was confidently predicted by its friends, *time* only can determine. Through that inexorable ordeal the Primary School system has passed, with honor and success. That equal, if not greater success, may attend our schools, under their present organization, or in whatever manner they may be organized and governed, and that they may continue to be a source of pride and hope, is our own, and will always be the desire of every good citizen and friend of popular education.

In closing our labors by this review of the opinions and action of those gentlemen, through whose influence and exertions the Primary School Committee was abolished, we desire to disclaim attributing to them or their coadjutors, any other than high and honorable motives in their opposition; and we believe that the correction of the historical errors in their representations, upon which it is evident much of their opposition has been based, will be received by them in a kindly spirit; and as an act of justice to a body, that, however "anomalous" and peculiar it might be in its constitution, was, nevertheless, a Boston institution of acknowledged excellence, efficiency, and success, and one whose entire record is unsullied by a single act that we would wish to blot.

APPENDIX.

Annual Report of the School of Industry, No. 1.

FOR THE NORTHERN DISTRICT.

BOSTON, NOVEMBER, 1819.

THE Managers of the *School of Industry* again have the pleasure of presenting their acknowledgments to the friends and benefactors of this Institution for the encouragement and support they have thus far liberally bestowed. And with gratitude for favors conferred, they would offer the general sentiment of the Ladies to dissolve the Association, for the present; convinced as they are, necessity does not immediately urge the duty, and fearful of taxing private individuals unnecessarily — as the number of children is very small, compared with the many who have attended the past years; the smaller class having been sent to the Primary Schools, lately provided by the town, which prevents in a degree, our longer continuance to our own satisfaction. Some few of the oldest have been placed in good families, where they will be made useful members of society, and blessings in the world.

Seven years have now elapsed since the commencement of this institution, and the purest motives of our hearts have been exercised in its progress; and the success that has generally attended our efforts, has been a sufficient stimulus to the performance of one of the most interesting duties of life, and it is with sensations of regret we this day dissolve a connection that has ever contributed to our happiness, formed as it was, at a period when most needed, and when every day presented a scene of ignorance and vice, melancholy to behold; children almost constantly in the streets, exciting the pity of strangers, and sympathy of friends, exposed as they were to the present evil world, without employment, and perhaps no virtuous example, to guide their steps aright, acquiring habits of indolence and wickedness, not easily effaced. Here they have been early taught the first lessons of knowledge,

the most simple branches of learning, and their diligence and industry have
been frequently commendable; and we trust some good impressions have
been made, some seeds of virtue will be permitted to thrive; as their opening minds expand, they will naturally appreciate the advantages given them,
and be ready to bless the friends who have thus kindly prepared them for
virtue and goodness.

Much praise is due to the young ladies for the interest they have displayed
in the welfare of the children; their attention to the reading, and constant
attendance, entitle them to our warmest thanks.

Since the formation of this society, several others have been established on
a similar plan with our own, and this, we are happy to think, was the first of
the kind instituted in Boston.

After examining the Treasurer's accounts, it is hoped the benefactors will
be perfectly satisfied with the statement given, and appropriation of the
funds. The *medals* presented as rewards of merit to the children, it is proposed, should be distributed for the same purpose, to the Primary Schools in
the three neighboring wards.

May the time spent here cheer the recollection as hours well spent, and
each member be rewarded with an approving conscience, and the smiles of
Heaven.

At a meeting of the Managers at the school room, on the 2d day of Nov.,
1819 — the above report, together with the abstract of the Treasurer's
accounts, was directed to be read, and copies distributed.

Voted, That this meeting be adjourned to the 29th November, and in the
mean time, Joseph Austin, Esq., and Dr. Robert Fennelly be requested to
examine and settle the Treasurer's accounts.

The following abstract was presented by the Treasurer. Expenses of
School of Industry from the first year to the present, viz.:

Paid for stock,	$284 57
Wood,	191 07
Clothes,	39 95
Shoes,	251 56
Hose,	7 33
Mrs. Wheelwright,	364 00
Miss Trench, as assistant,	39 00
Miss Hill, do.	46 50
Col. Bager's rent,	640 00
Miscellaneous, viz., books, furniture, &c.,	49 14
Repairs,	7 54

Writing School, ... 7 55
Advertising, ... 3 00
Counterfeit bills, ... 5 00
____
$1,936 21
By amount of subscription, and donations from Nov.
1812, to Nov., 1819, ... 1,420 92
Amount of sales and work, ... 587 34
____
$2,008 26
Balance, ... $72 05

Three hundred children have been admitted into the school.

Boston, *Nov. 26th*, 1819. — We have at the request of the Managers of the School of Industry, examined the accounts of the Treasurer, and find them correct, leaving a balance of 72 dollars 5 cents.

Signed,

JOSEPH AUSTIN,
ROBERT FENELLY.

At a meeting of the Managers of the School of Industry, Nov. 29th, 1819, it was agreed that the balance in the hands of the Treasurer be appropriated towards the schooling of poor children, (not otherwise provided for.) That Mrs. Wheelwright be authorized to take such children as any of the subscribers may approve, and present her bill quarterly for payment, until the whole remaining money shall be expended, after deducting ten dollars now presented her, and the necessary expenses for printing, &c.

The managers of the School of Industry having been in the practice of distinguishing the most attentive scholars, by the wearing of a medal on each monthly day of examination, and finding that the hopes of such a distinction excited a spirit of industry among the children, and as that institution is now dissolved, the Committee of the Primary Schools, in Ward Nos. 1 and 2, are requested to accept the said medals to be used for the same purpose in the schools which they superintend.

SARAH AUSTIN, *Secretary.*

[FORM OF CERTIFICATE.]

TO MRS. WHEELWRIGHT.

Admit   into your School for one quarter from the   day of   1820, and write on the back of this that she has attended one quarter, and I will give an order on Mrs. Webster the Treasurer, for the payment of your bill, (at ten cents a week,) for one dollar and thirty cents.

COPY OF THE FIRST

RULES AND REGULATIONS

ADOPTED BY THE

PRIMARY SCHOOL COMMITTEE.

BOSTON, JULY, 1820.

AT a meeting of the Primary School Committee, held July 27th, 1820, the following Rules and Regulations were adopted for the government of this Board, and the several schools under their jurisdiction.

Attest,   P. MACKINTOSH, JR., Sec'y.

RULES AND REGULATIONS.

ORGANIZATION.

The officers of this Board shall consist of a Chairman, Secretary, Treasurer, and a Standing Committee.

SECTION I.

OF THE WHOLE BOARD.

A representation of seven wards shall be a quorum at any meeting for the transaction of business.

The quarterly meetings of this Board shall be holden on the third Tuesdays in August, November, February and May.

All nominations to fill vacancies at this Board, shall be made at a meeting previous to that when the election shall be made.

The elections of the permanent officers and the Standing Committee, and also the filling of all vacancies of members, shall be made by written ballots.

In order to secure the due attendance of members, the Secretary, in issuing notifications for the meetings, shall note in writing on the notification of any member absent from the last meeting the fact of such absence, and that his attendance is desired, unless he intend to resign his seat.

SECTION II.

The Chairman of the Board shall preside at all meetings, and be respected and obeyed accordingly.

SECTION III.

DUTIES OF THE SECRETARY.

The Secretary shall keep a faithful record of all the doings of the Board he shall notify the members of all meetings; he shall note their absence from the last meeting, agreeably to the last clause of the first section ; and perform all other duties which by custom appertain to his office.

SECTION IV.

DUTIES OF THE TREASURER.

The treasurer shall keep a fair and accurate account of the moneyed concerns of the Board. He is authorized to receive from the Town Treasurer all moneys granted for the support of the Primary Schools ; and pay the instructors of the schools, quarterly, their bills being first approved by the Committee of the ward or district to which they belong. His accounts shall be audited, or inspected, whenever the Board may appoint a Committee for that purpose. At the close of the year he shall make a transcript or an abstract of his accounts as audited, to be laid before the Board.

SECTION V.

OF THE STANDING COMMITTEE.

The Standing Committee shall consist of seven members, to be appointed by this Board, whose duty it shall be to meet on the second Tuesday of each month, to consider of every subject relating to the Primary Schools, and the same to visit semi-annually, and report at every quarterly meeting, recommending any improvements necessary to obtain the general objects of this Board.

SECTION VI.

WARD OR DISTRICT COMMITTEES.

The Ward Committees are constituted of the three gentlemen appointed by the School Committee from each ward. When two or more wards are joined, they shall be termed a district, and the Committee a District Committee.

Each school shall be opened and directed by the Committee of the ward or district in which it is placed, consulting, if it stand near another ward, the Committee of that ward. To the same shall belong the duty of locating the schools, of engaging competent mistresses, and the same to remove, on proof of any sufficient cause, and of controlling all matters relating to the establishment. They shall visit, examine, and inquire into the state of the school or schools under their charge, at least once a month, and oftener, if convenient. They shall meet at least ten days previous to the quarterly meetings, to prepare, from the returns of the several schoolmistresses, A REPORT to be made forthwith to the Standing Committee, together with said returns, with such observations as they may deem proper to make.

Previous to the removal of a child to the Grammar School, such child shall pass an examination to the satisfaction of one or more of the respective Ward or District Committees, who, to each child appearing sufficiently qualified for entrance at the upper school, shall grant a certificate in the following form :

The bearer A. B., child of C. D., having been instructed at the **Primary** School, kept by E. F., and being   years of age, is thought qualified for admission at the English Grammar School under your direction, to which he is recommended by

G. H., Committee of Ward No.
To I. K., Master of the English Grammar School.

It shall be the duty of the several Ward or District Committees to keep a record of their proceedings relative to the schools under their management.

When notified by the Standing Committee of an intended semi-annual visitation, each Ward or District Committee shall detach one or more, to introduce the Standing Committee to their schools, and assist at the examination.

SECTION VII.

OF THE INSTRUCTORS AND THE SCHOOLS.

The schoolmistresses are to be appointed, and the schools located, by the Committees of the respective wards or districts, who have the management of them under the direction of the whole Board.

Each schoolmistress shall stand precisely on equal terms in point of compensation; and the compensation allowed them is in full for tuition, school rent, fuel, and all other expenses.

All the schools shall be as nearly equal in point of numbers as may be — it being desirable that none have more than fifty, nor less than forty, as constant attendants.

No pupil shall be received into the Primary Schools without a ticket of admittance from one of the Ward or District Committees.

The instructors employed by this Board are expressly prohibited from receiving pay for any private pupils instructed by them at their schools.

The pupils in each of the schools shall be arranged into four classes, **viz.** :

Those in the Testament shall be of the 1st class.

Those in easy reading, of the 2d class.

Those who spell two or more syllables, of the 3d class.

Those learning their monosyllables, of the 4th class.

The books shall be the same in every school for each pupil, (*hereafter* admitted, viz. :)

The 1st class shall use the Testament.

The 2d class shall use Bingham's Child's Companion.

The 3d and 4th classes shall use Kelly's Child's Instructer.

Rewards of merit bestowed on the scholars shall consist of reward tickets, small moral books, or class medals, as the Committee of the ward or district may determine. If medals are allowed, they are to be worn by the best scholars, for the time being, under the direction of the schoolmistress. To defray the expense of these rewards, one dollar for each school shall annually be appropriated.

It shall be the duty of the mistress, besides the usual business of teaching, to keep an account of the absence or negligence of any children, and make report to the Ward Committee, whose duty thereupon shall be to visit the parents, and endeavor to secure regular attention. She shall also be required to pay particular regard to the neatness and cleanliness of the children.

On the monthly visitations of the Ward or District Committees, and the semi-annual visitation of the Standing Committee, it shall be the duty of the instructors, respectively, to exhibit the progress and improvements made by the children under their care, in conformity to the desires of the visiting Committee.

The schoolmistresses shall be excused from keeping school on the following days, viz. :

Every Thursday and Saturday afternoons throughout the year; the afternoons preceding Fasts and Thanksgivings; the first Monday in June; Election Week; the 4th day of July; Commencement Week, and Christmas Day; but no other day, except by a special vote of the Ward or District Committee.

No scholar shall be removed to the Grammar Schools by the schoolmistresses, without first being examined and furnished with a certificate of recommendation, if he or she deserve it, by one of the Ward or District Committee.

Returns from each of the schools shall be made quarterly, on the last days of July, October, January, and April, by the instructors, to the District or Ward Committees — stating the ages, the number of male and female pupils; the progress of each, and whatever else may be designated by the blanks furnished by the Board.

In order early to impress on the minds of our youth, the importance of religious duties, and their entire dependence on their Maker, the instructors are desired to open their schools in the morning with a short prayer, and close with the same service in the afternoon.

Whenever, by sickness or otherwise, an instructor is compelled to vacate her station for a season, it shall be her duty to inform the Ward or District Committee, who will either appoint a mistress *pro tem.*, or approve one selected by the mistress.

PRIMARY SCHOOL COMMITTEE,

FOR THE YEAR ENDING JUNE, 1821.

Ward No. 1—Three Schools.
Rev. Henry Ware,
George Darracott,
Isaac Harris.

No. 2—Four Schools.
Samuel Hichborn, Jr.,
Lewis Leland,
Thomas Fracker.

No. 3.—Four Schools.
Thomas Wells,
Dr. Horace Bean,
Nathan Webb.

No. 4—Two Schools.
James Davis,
Samuel Howe,
Reuben Richards, Jr.

No. 5—Two Schools.
Moses Grant,
Dr. George C. Shattuck,
Samuel T. Armstrong.

Nos. 6 and 7—Five Schools.
Rev. Paul Dean,
Peter Mackintosh, Jr.,
Andrew Green.

No. 7.
William Thurston,
Samuel Coverly,
Rev. Sereno E. Dwight.

Nos. 8 and 9—Five Schools.
Dr. Samuel Clarke,
Francis Welch,
Isaac Mansfield.

No. 9.
James Savage,
William Brown,
Pliny Cutler.

Nos. 10 and 11—Five Schools.
Thomas L. Winthrop,
Samuel Norwood,
Lewis Tappan.

No. 11.
Elisha Ticknor,
Thomas Jackson,
Samuel Dorr.

No. 12—Five Schools.
William Dall,
Thomas B. Wait,
William Jackson.

Thomas L. Winthrop, Esq., *Chairman.*
Peter Mackintosh, Jr., *Secretary.*
William Brown, Esq., *Treasurer.*

STANDING COMMITTEE.

Thomas B. Wait,
James Savage,
Peter Mackintosh, Jr.,
Moses Grant,
Isaac Harris,
Thomas Wells,
Lewis Tappan.

AT a meeting of the Primary School Committee, held February 20th, 1821, the following System of Instruction was adopted, to be pursued in all the Primary Schools.

Attest, **P. MACKINTOSH, JR.,** *Secretary.*

COURSE AND MODE OF INSTRUCTION TO BE PURSUED IN THE PRIMARY SCHOOLS.

The fourth or youngest class shall stand up with due ceremony, at as great a distance from the instructor as possible, and read, with a distinct and audible tone of voice, in words of one syllable. No one of this class shall be advanced to the third or higher class, who cannot read deliberately and correctly in words of one and two syllables.

No one of the third class shall be advanced to the second class who cannot spell with ease and propriety words of three, four and five syllables, and read all the reading lessons in Kelly's spelling book.

No one of the second class shall be advanced to the first class who has not learned perfectly by heart, and recited, as far as practicable, all the reading lessons in Kelly's spelling book; the Commandments and Lord's Prayer; all the stops and marks, and their uses in reading; and in Bingham's spelling book, the use of the common abbreviations, such as A. M., D. D., L.L. D., &c.; the use of numbers, and letters used for numbers, in reading; the catalogue of words of similar sound, but different in spelling and signification; the catalogue of vulgarisms, such as chimney, not chimbly, vinegar, not winegar, &c.

No one of the first class shall be recommended by the Examining Committee to be received into the English Grammar schools, unless he or she can spell correctly, read fluently in the New Testament, and has learned the several branches taught in the second class; and also the use and nature of the pauses; and is of good behavior. And each of the scholars, before being recommended, shall be able to read deliberately and audibly, so as to be heard in any part of the Grammar Schools.

Thus a foundation will be laid in the Primary Schools for farther and greater improvements in the English Grammar Schools than has heretofore been known; and of course the scholars from the Primary Schools will be qualified to enter the Grammar Schools on an advanced standing.

The Committee particularly recommend, that the instructors shall employ the girls occasionally, (especially those of the first class,) in sewing and knitting, so far as the same shall not interfere with their progress in learning.

N. B.—The books to be used in the schools are the same as prescribed in the Rules and Regulations, viz.:

The 4th and 3d classes, Kelly's Child's Instructer.

The 2d class, Child's Instructer continued, and Bingham's Child's Companion.
The 1st class, Instructer and Companion continued, and the New Testament.
No other kind of books are allowed to be introduced, or used as substitutes for any of the above-cited, unless by order of the Board

At a quarterly meeting of the Primary School Committee, August 15, 1820, the following Rule was adopted:

No child shall be admitted into a school, unless provided with the necessary books.

Also, at an adjourned quarterly meeting, November 20, 1820, the following Rules were adopted:

Teachers will note the absence or tardiness of their scholars daily, and insert the result in their quarterly returns, opposite the names of the scholars, and under the head of " Remarks."

Teachers are not allowed to permit visitors to tarry in their schools, nor to be themselves employed in needle or other work during school hours.

The instructors are requested, in making their quarterly returns, to insert the Christian names of the scholars, and to arrange them by classes, placing the girls first in order.

Attest,

PETER MACKINTOSH, Jr., Secretary.

37

CATALOGUE

OF THE

GOVERNMENT AND MEMBERS

OF THE

PRIMARY SCHOOL COMMITTEE

IN CHRONOLOGICAL ORDER OF THEIR SERVICE,

FROM ITS

INSTITUTION, JUNE 22, 1818, TO ITS DISCONTINUANCE
IN JANUARY, 1855.

CATALOGUE.

CHAIRMEN OF THE BOARD.

Thomas L. Winthrop, 1818—1821; resigned June, 1822.
James Savage, June, 1822, 1823; resigned June, 1824.
Moses Grant, June, 1824—1833.
Lewis G. Pray, January, 1834, 1835.
George W. Otis, Jr., 1836—1839.
Richard W. Bayley, 1840—1843.
Josiah F. Bumstead, 1844—1846.
Eben Jones, 1847—1849.
Francis Brown, 1850, 1851.
Charles Edward Cook, 1852, 1853.
Alvan Simonds, 1854.

SECRETARIES OF THE BOARD.

James Savage, 1818, 1819; resigned June, 1820.
Peter Mackintosh, Jr., June, 1820—22.
Charles Ewer, June, 1823.
William T. Andrews, June, 1824—1828.
Frederic T. Gray, January, 1829—1832.
Edward G. Davis, 1833, 1834.
Gustavus Horton, 1835; resigned May, 1836.
Joseph Curtis, May, 1836—1841.
Alvan Simonds, 1842—1851; resigned March, 1852.
Charles Demond, March, 1852—1854.

CHAIRMEN OF THE STANDING COMMITTEE.

Elisha Ticknor, 1819, 1820; died July, 1821.
James Savage, July, 1821—1823; resigned June, 1824.
Thomas Wells, August, 1824—1829.
Francis Parkman, 1830—1833.
Charles Walker, 1834

George W. Otis, 1835.
Samuel Tenney, 1836, 1837.
Richard W. Bayley, 1838, 1839.
Josiah F. Bumstead, 1840—1843.
Frederic A. Sumner, 1844.
Joseph W. Ingraham, 1845—1847 ; died August, 1848
Joseph M. Wightman, September, 1848—1854.

SECRETARIES OF THE STANDING COMMITTEE.

Peter Mackintosh, Jr., 1819.
Moses Grant, 1820—1829.
Lewis G. Pray, 1830—1832.
Charles Walker, 1833.
George W. Otis, Jr., 1834.
Frederic A. Sumner, 1835—1843.
Alvan Simonds, 1844—1851.
Charles Demond, 1852—1854.

TREASURER OF THE BOARD.

William Brown, 1819—1823 ; office abolished, 1824.

PRIMARY SCHOOL COMMITTEE.

The figures indicate the date of appointment, and the number of years of service.

Austin, Benjamin 1818, 1819
Armstrong, Samuel T. 1820
Adams, Zabdiel B...... 1821—1825
Adan, John R. 1824
Andrews, William T.... 1824—1828
Austin, Richard........ 1833—1838
Appleton, John 1833
Andrews, Henry R. .... 1836—1855
Adams, Thomas 1838, 1839
Allen, James M. 1842, 1843
Abrahams, Benjamin 1843
Atkins, John .... 1844—1847
Allen, Charles J. F. .... 1844—1855
Abbott, Samuel L. ..... 1846—1853
Adams, Isaac .... 1846—1849
Atkins, Ebenezer ...... 1847—1855
Atwood, Charles II. .... 1847—1855
Alvord, John W. ...... 1847—1853
Allen, Samuel C. 1848
Allen, Joseph II............. 1850
Allen, James B. 1850
Allen, Nathaniel G. 1851, 1852
Appleton, William, Jr. .. 1852, 1853
Allen, Frederic D. ..... 1852—1854
Alley, James B. 1853, 1854
Adams, Colman S. 1853, 1854

Burditt, James W. 1818
Baldwin, Rev. Thomas ... 1818, 1819
Bell, Shubael................ 1818
Brown, William........ 1818—1826
Bellows, John 1818, 1819
Bean, Horace 1819, 1820
Bordman, Thomas S. 1819
Baker, John 1821
Bradlee, Samuel .... 1821—1823
Blanchard, Joshua P. ... 1824—1831
Bemis, Charles 1824
Bent, Adam .... 1824—1831
Baker, John........... 1824, 1825

Barry, William, Jr. 1825
Bowdoin, James 1825, 1826
Betton, Ninian C. ...... 1826—1828
Bumstead, Josiah F..... 1826—1855
Bliss, Alexander 1826
Blaney, William 1827, 1828
Barrett, N. A. .... 1827—1831
Bigelow, John P. ...... 1827—1837
Bradshaw, Andrew...... 1827, 1828
Butts, John R. 1828
Barnes, Seth II. .... 1829—1832
Blaisdell, Rev. Silas 1830
Bulfinch, George S. ..... 1830—1832
Blagden, Rev. George W. 1831
Brown, Francis .... 1831—1854
Brown, William C. 1832
Brown, John S. 1833
Bayley, Richard W. .... 1834—1848
Barnard, Rev. C. F. .... 1834—1836
Bourne, I. W. .... 1835—1841
Bullard, Francis .... 1835—1847
Brigham, William 1836
Brown, William.... 1836, 1837, 1850
Brown, Benjamin 1836
Battles, Jason D. ...... 1837—1839
Bayley, Thomas J. 1837, 1838
Bowditch, Henry I. .... 1837—1850
Barry, Charles C. ...... 1837—1850
Bedlington, Timothy.... 1838—1841
Bemis, George .... 1840—1844
Burroughs, Henry...... 1842—1849
Brooks, William B. .... 1842—1848
Buck, Ephraim, Jr. ... 1842—1848
Bell, Theodore II....... 1842—1854
Boardman, Charles ..... 1844—1846
Brooks, Rev. Charles ... 1844—1851
Bond, George W. 1844, 1845
Breed, Horace A........ 1844, 1845
Beal, Thacher .... 1844—1855
Burnham, Choate ...... 1844—1846

Blake, John H........ 1845—1848
Blake, E. W.......... 1846—1855
Bond, Charles R. 1846
Blanchard, William E... 1846—1853
Bigelow, John .... 1847—1854
Bowker, Albert .... 1847—1854
Butters, William A. .... 1847—1850
Brevoort, Henry 1849, 1850
Banvard, Rev. Joseph 1849
Brainard, Edward H......... 1850
Baker, Judah............... 1850
Bean, Aaron H. 1850
Bowdlear, Samuel G. .... 1852—1854
Bartlett, Ezra 1853, 1854
Beecher, Rev. Edward... 1853, 1854
Boynton, E., Jr. 1853, 1854
Barrows, Horace G.......... 1854
Buckingham, Charles E. 1854
Bosworth, Rev. G. W. 1854

Coverly, Samuel .... 1818—1820
Chapman, Henry 1818, 1819
Child, David W............. 1818
Chandler, Gardner L. ... 1818, 1819
Clarke, Samuel 1819, 1820
Cotton, John 1821
Chandler, Abiel....... 1823—1829
Capen, Rev. L. 1823—1831; 1842, 1843
Cartwright, C. W............. 1824
Curtis, Jos. 1826—1829 ; 1834—1841
Child, David Lee ...... 1826—1828
Clark, Joseph............. 1828—1832
Coit, Daniel T. .... 1829—1854
Croswell, Rev. William.. 1829—1831
Clark, James .... 1829—1832
Cobb, Elijah .... 1830—1842
Choate, Charles....... 1831—1834
Center, John .... 1832—1835
Coburn, Caleb .... 1832—1835
Cragin, Lorenzo S. ..... 1832—1855
Codman, Edward ..... 1833—1835
Cutler, Samuel L.............. 1834
Chessman, Samuel...... 1835—1838
Chapin, A. B. 1836
Clark, Henry G........ 1837—1855
Clark, Moses 1837
Clapp, Henry, Jr....... 1838—1840
Crehore, Daniel S. ...... 1839—1841
Cotting, Benjamin E..... 1840, 1841
Coolidge, William D. .... 1843—1847
Cushman, Freeman L. ... 1842, 1843
Calrow, William H. . .. 1844—1855
Cumings, Bradley N. 1844, 1845
Crosby, Loammi .... 1844—1855
Crosby, Frederic....... 1844—1849

Clarke, Rev. Dorus .... 1844—1847
Child, Asaph B........ 1844—1851
Carter, Oliver .... 1844—1855
Coale, William E....... 1845—1847
Crane, Horatio N............ 1846
Crowell, Rev. William .. 1846—1848
Cotton, Nath. D........ 1847, 1848
Cruft, Rev. S. B........ 1847—1855
Cook, Rev. Theo. D. ... 1848—1851
Cole, Morrill .... 1848—1852
Clarke, Rev. James F........ 1849
Chase, Thomas F............ 1849
Cheney, J. H. .... 1849—1852
Cook, Charles E. ...... 1850—1852
Cummings, J. A. 1850
Cushing, Andrew ...... 1851—1854
Chesbrough, E. S....... 1851—1853
Clark, Leister M. ...... 1851—1854
Cutter, A. E............... 1851
Clement, J. S. .... 1852—1854
Curtis, George A. 1853, 1854
Cudworth, Rev. W. H.... 1853, 1854
Clark, Rev. R. W. ..... 1853—1854
Chase, Henry S........ 1853—1854
Clinch, Rev. J. H. 1853, 1854
Cragin, Lorenzo S., Jr. 1854
Caldicott, Rev. T. F. 1854
Clark, Calvin W. 1854
Crowell, Seth K.............. 1854

Dean, Rev. Paul .... 1818—1821
Dorr, John................ 1818
Dall, William .... 1818—1820
Davis, James 1819, 1820
Darracott, George 1820
Dwight, Rev. S. E....... 1820, 1821
Dow, Samuel................ 1820
Domett, George .... 1823—1826
Davis, Samuel .... 1823—1831
Dupee, Israel T. .... 1825—1828
Dorr, William B. 1825, 1826
Dane, John 1826
Dwight, Rev. Louis..... 1826—1833
Davis, Edward G....... 1827—1835
Drake, Jeremy .... 1827—1834
Dyer, Henry .... 1830—1836
Durgin, Clement........ 1833, 1834
Dow, James B. .... 1834—1855
Dunham, J., Jr. 1836, 1837
Dall, Joseph........... 1837—1839
Dix, John H................ 1839
Daniel, Josiah N. 1839, 1840
Dana, Francis.......... 1839, 1840
Daniel, Chester............. 1840
Dupee, Horace, Jr...... 1841—1855

Dale, William J......... 1841, 1842
Dingley, John T. .... 1841—1855
Ditson, Oliver .... 1841—1855
*Dall, William......... 1842—1855
Ditson, Thomas......... 1842, 1843
Day, Albert 1843
Dodge, Charles H. ..... 1844—1846
Davenport, Henry ..... 1844—1846
Dimon, Oliver .... 1846—1850
Davenport, W. W........... 1846
Demond, Thomas D.... 1847—1853
Dyke, William......... 1849—1855
Dutton, Ormond .... 1850—1854
Demond, Charles....... 1850—1854
Dennett, William H..... 1850—1854
Dalton, Henry L....... 1852—1854
Damon, Samuel G. ..... 1852—1854
Dearing, T. H................ 1852
Duncklee, B. W. 1853, 1854
Dutton, George D. 1853, 1854
Damon, Calvin 1853, 1854
Deblois, George L....... 1853, 1854
Danforth, John C. 1853, 1854
Davis, Thomas 1854
Denison, J. N. 1854

Elliot, John .... 1821—1823
Ewer, Charles .... 1821—1823
Edson, Rev. Theo. 1823
Eustis, William T. 1825
Emerson, Geo. B. ...... 1826—1834
Ellis, Samuel 1827, 1828
Elliot, George A. ...... 1832—1835
Esterbrook, James 1835
Emmons, J. L. 1835—1837; 1840, 1841
Everett, Otis .... 1835—1837
Eustis, William 1839
Eayrs, J. H. 1839
Ellis, Rowland .... 1840—1848
Eaton, William .... 1841—1855
Eddy, Frederic A. 1842, 1843
Emmons, Charles G..... 1842—1846
Ellis, Jonathan 1849
Eaton, Charles T.............. 1850
Evans, Jonas 1850
Eastman, Edmund T.... 1852—1854
Elliot, Charles W............. 1854
Ellis, Rev. Rufus............. 1854
Ellis, Calvin 1854

Fennelly, Robert 1818, 1819
Fracher, Thomas....... 1819—1823
Fowle, William B. 1821
Fowle, Henry, Jr....... 1821—1829
Farrington, Thomas 1821

French, Benjamin...... 1821—1823
Fairbanks, Gerry ...... 1821—1839
Fenno, John, Jr........ 1822—1829
Farrie, John, Jr. ...... 1822—1825
Fairbanks, Stephen .... 1824—1826
Fairchild, Rev. J. H. ... 1827—1836
Fisher, John D. 1831, 1832
Freeman, William...... 1832—1835
French, Charles 1833
Foster, William E. ..... 1834—1836
Flint, John............ 1834—1842
Field, Elisha .... 1836—1850
Fowle, Samuel 1836
Ford, John V.......... 1840—1842
Fuller, Henry W.............. 1842
Fowle, Joshua B...1842, 1843; 1850
Fowle, Henry D. .... 1844—1855
Faxon, Isaiah.......... 1847—1855
Fowle, James.......... 1847—1855
Frothingham, Geo. W.... 1851, 1852
Fogg, J. S. H........... 1853, 1854
Fox, James A........... 1853, 1854
Farwell, Lyman 1853
Forbes, Gustavus............. 1844

Gore, Samuel................ 1818
Grant, Moses.......... 1818—1833
Green, Andrew.............. 1820
Guild, Benjamin .... 1821—1825
Greele, Samuel .... 1821—1823
Green, Ellis B.......... 1823, 1824
Gould, Benjamin A..... 1823—1828
Gay, Frederic A........ 1824, 1825
Gray, John C................ 1824
Gray, Rev. F. T.. 1825—1832; 1836
Gulliver, John .... 1826—1839
Greene, Benjamin H.... 1827—1855
Gore, Christopher ...... 1828—1841
Gould, Frederic........ 1829—1831
Gray, Thomas, Jr....... 1829—1834
Gay, Martin........... 1830—1838
Geyer, Andrew .... 1833—1843
Gould, Augustus A. .... 1833—1840
Gavett, William R. .... 1838—1840
Greely, Philip, Jr. 1840
Gove, Moses J. .... 1848—1852
Guild, William H............. 1849
Goddard, Thomas A. ... 1849—1855
Gill, Caleb .... 1849—1855
Goddard, Elias W...... 1849—1853
Gregerson, James B........... 1850
Greene, Moses C. ...... 1851—1854
Gaffield, Thomas .... 1851—1854
Giles, Alfred E. .... 1851—1853
Glover, E. V. 1851, 1852

38   * Son of the member in 1818.

Gardner, T. O................ 1853
Gordon, James M. 1854
Gay, George H................ 1854
Goddard, Daniel F....... . 1854

Hichborn, Samuel...... 1818—1820
House, Samuel......... 1818—1820
Harris, Isaac 1820
Hood, Charles......... 1821—1824
Henchman, Daniel..... 1821—1848
Haven, J. A................. 1823
Hale, Enoch, Jr. ...... 1823—1825
Halleck, Gerard 1824, 1825
Hobart, Enoch .... 1824—1842
Howe, Samuel......... 1825—1835
Head, Francis C. 1825
Hatch, Henry .... 1825—1838
Hunting, Bela .... 1825—1831
Hall, Whitney .... 1826—1828
Hewes, John 1826
Holland, Samuel M........... 1826
Hunting, Thomas ...... 1827—1837
Hutchinson, Thomas L......... 1828
Hartshorn, Eliphalet P.. 1828—1851
Hayward, James H........... 1829
Hunt, Freeman ... 1831, 1833, 1834
Horton, Gustavus ...... 1832—1839
Hall, S. W. 1833—1838; 1846—1848
Holbrook, Josiah............. 1833
Haynes, Guy C......... 1836—1847
Hosmer, Zelotes.............. 1836
Howe, Cranston......... 1836—1851
Howe, William .... 1838—1850
Howes, Willis .... 1838—1841
Haynes, Edward, Jr. 1839, 1840
Holman, Oliver......... 1840, 1841
Hooper, Henry N....... 1842, 1843
Howard, Edward 1842, 1843
Hawkes, Thomas B. ... 1842—1855
Hobart, E. Aug......... 1843—1849
Homer, Henry .... 1842—1854
Humphrey, Francis J. ... 1842—1851
Harris, William......... 1844, 1845
Horton, David W....... 1844—1846
Harris, James W....... 1844—1846
Howes, Osborn........ 1846—1850
Hubbard, George ...... 1847—1853
Hutchinson, J. B....... 1847—1850
Hobbs, Alvah. .... 1847—1853
Hovey, James G......... 1848, 1849
Horton, David R............. 1848
Hackett, Hiram 1849
Heyward, Charles T.......... 1850
Howard, William P. 1849
Hunt, W. L. B. 1850

Hale, Theodore P. 1850
Hart, Nathan O........ 1851—1855
Homer, S. J. M. ...... 1851—1855
Hammond, Thomas .... 1851—1855
Hamblen, David .... 1851—1855
Horton, Henry 1851
Howland, Edwin....... 1852—1854
Hall, Daniel .... 1852—1854
Hinckley, John W. 1853, 1854
Harlow, Ivory........... 1853, 1854
Hapgood, Warren 1853, 1854
Hickey, Thomas H. 1853, 1854
Herrick, J. E. 1853, 1854
Hodges, R. M. 1853, 1854
Homans, Charles D. 1853, 1854

Ingraham, Joseph W. ... 1826—1848
Irwin, Rev. John 1853, 1854

Jackson, William 1820
Jackson, Thomas............. 1820
Jones, William .... 1824—1828
Jones, Ezekiel 1825
Jackson, Francis ...... 1826—1835
James, John W......... 1827—1831
Jackson, J. B. S......... 1834, 1835
Jackson, Edmund ...... 1835—1851
Jenkins, Solon .... 1835—1855
Jones, Eben .... 1836—1849
Jenkins, William C. .... 1836—1842
Josselyn, Lewis 1837
Jarvis, William P. ...... 1838—1850
Jenney, Stephen ...... 1848—1855
Jewell, Harvey .... 1851—1854

Knapp, William .... 1827—1828
Kent, Jacob H............... 1831
Kimball, David`. .1835; 1843—1853
Kittredge, Josiah 1837
Kimball, Joshua B. ..... 1841—1843
Kemp, Nathaniel P. .... 1844—1850
Kingman, George ..... 1851—1854
Kneeland, Samuel, Jr......... 1851
Kimball, Peter 1851, 1852
Kimball, Otis .... 1851—1853

Leland, Lewis .... 1818—1820
Lincoln, Charles .... 1823—1826
Lewis, Joseph .... 1823—1832
Lane, George .... 1823—1826
Loring, Charles G............ 1823
Lowell, John, Jr........ 1825—1828
Loring, John J. 1828
Lane, Jonas H. 1830, 1831
Lowell, Charles R...... 1832—1834

Loring, Ellis G......... 1832—1834
Lincoln, Beza .... 1832—1838
Lothrop, John P............. 1835
Lodge, Giles H........ 1837—1840
Leach, E. W........... 1839—1841
Leavitt, Joseph M. 1840, 1841
Leavitt, Benson ..... 1841—1843
Learnard, William H. .. 1842—1851
Lincoln, Noah, Jr....... 1842, 1843
Lincoln, Ezra, Jr....... 1843—1845
Lovis, Ambrose .... 1842—1847
Little, Eben H........ 1844—1855
Learnard, Wm. H., Jr... 1849—1855
Lincoln, Albert L. 1850
Livermore, L. J............. 1850
Lovejoy, William B. 1851
Lovett, S. Ingersol 1851
Lincoln, Henry W..... 1851—1854
Loud, Andrew J....... 1851—1854
Lothrop, Joshua B............ 1851
Little, Albert 1851
Leonard, Marcus B. 1853, 1854
Lovell, Rev. Stephen 1853, 1854

May, Samuel......... 1818—1820
Marshall, Josiah 1818
Mackintosh, Peter, Jr. .. 1819—1823
Mansfield, Isaac........ 1820—1833
Milton, Ephraim .... 1824—1826
Merrill, James C............. 1824
McKean, Joseph W. .... 1827—1831
Motte, Rev. M. I. 1830, 1831
Monroe, Edmund 1830
Mosely, Flavel 1831, 1832
McCleary, John B. ..... 1833—1848
Marvin, Theoph. R...... 1833—1855
Mann, Nehemiah P..... 1833—1855
Mellen, John 1834, 1835
Merrill, Nathan 1835, 1836
Mead, John 1835
Morrill, James 1836
Morse, Samuel F....... 1836—1842
Morris, L. H. 1837, 1838
Moriarty, Joseph....... 1838—1846
Manning, Francis C..... 1838—1840
Montgomery, Hugh .... 1838—1847
McBurney, Rev. Sam'l.. 1839—1847
Messenger, Eben T. .... 1840—1848
Minot, William, Jr............ 1843
Merrill, Joseph W. .... 1844—1847
Makepeace, William 1846
Mead, Charles........ 1846—1855
Morgan, David .... 1847—1853
McCleary, Sam'l F., Jr. .1847—1851
Maynard, Azor........ 1847—1855

Mudge, Alfred .... 1847—1852
Merrill, George.... ... 1847—1849
Melzar, Parker A. ..... 1847—1853
Meston, John J........ 1848—1855
Mears, Granville 1849, 1850
McLellan, George W.......... 1850
Minot, Albert T. 1850
Moore, Edward B..... 1851—1854
Merriam, R. L. .... 1851—1853
Martin, Pearl 1852
Minot, Francis 1853, 1854
Marsh, Lucius B. 1854
Manson, Thomas L. 1854

Norwood, Samuel 1820
Noyes, Daniel ....1824—1826
Norris, Rufus G. 1838, 1839
Newcomb, Harvey 1838, 1839
Norcross, Loring ...... 1839—1855
Newhall, Daniel B. .... 1847—1852
Newcomb, Thomas C.... 1853, 1854
Noyes, George N. 1853, 1854
Nichols, George B............ 1853
Nutter, Charles C. 1854

Osgood, Isaac P....... 1824, 1825
Otis, Geo. W., Jr...... 1827—1842
Ordway, Aaron........ 1837—1844
Oliver, Samuel P. ..... 1840—1855
Odin, John, Jr........ 1841—1853
Ober, John P. .... 1842—1855

Prince, James .... 1818—1820
Phillips, Edward 1819
Page, Thaddeus .... 1821—1824
Prescott, William H..... 1821—1824
Page, Edward 1823
Pray, Lewis G. .... 1823—1842
Pillsbury, Samuel............ 1825
Palfrey, William .... 1826—1836
Parkman, Rev. Francis. 1826—1834
Power, Thomas........ 1827—1831
Pickering, Edward 1830
Prescott, Edward G...... 1831, 1832
Palmer, Ezra, Jr........ 1832, 1833
Perkins, Benjamin 1833, 1834
Perry, Marshall S....... 1833, 1834
Phelps, Abel 1834, 1835
Parker, Aurelius D. .... 1834—1855
Palmer, Julius A. 1835, 1836
Phillips, Wendell ...... 1836—1838
Phillips, George W............ 1837
Preston, John P. ...... 1839—1841
Parkman, William ..... 1839—1841
Pratt, E. F 1840, 1841

Prince, Frederic O. .... 1841—1848
Parker, William T...... 1842—1846
Park, John C.......... 1843—1847
Phelps, Amos A........ 1844, 1845
Parmenter, George W... 1844—1854
Putnam, J. Phelps...... 1844—1846
Patton, William W...... 1844, 1845
Palmer, E. D. G. ...... 1846—1855
Phelps, Charles A. .... 1846—1849
Parcher, Sewall F. ..... 1847—1850
Perkins, Samuel S.......1847, 1848
Perkins, James .... 1848—1852
Paige, David 1848
Parks, Luther, Jr....... 1849—1851
Putnam, John 1849
Procter, Israel P............. 1849
Parkman, Francis 1849
Prescott, Jeremiah 1849
Preston, Jonathan 1850
Plummer, Avery, Jr. ... 1852—1854
Phipps, J. M. .... 1852—1854
Pingrey, S. H........... 1853, 1854
Porter, Edward F....... 1853, 1854
Pinkerton, J. M.............. 1853
Piper, James S......... 1853, 1854
Pond, Joseph A.............. 1854

Rich, Benjamin.............. 1818
Richards, Reuben ...... 1820—1827
Robinson, Simon W.......... 1825
Reed, Sampson .... 1826—1829
Reed, Hodges .... 1826—1829
Russell, William 1826
Robbins, Dr. Chandler .. 1827—1833
Rogers, George ....1827—1846
Robinson, Horatio..... 1828—1831
Russell, Aaron .... 1829—1832
Rand, Rev. Asa........1831—1833
Reynolds, Brewster..... 1835—1837
Richardson, Joseph...... 1836, 1837
Rogers, Henry B....... 1836—1838
Restieaux, Thomas ..... 1837—1855
Richardson, A. J. ...... 1837—1841
Richardson, Benj. P..... 1837—1854
Robbins, Joseph .... 1842—1853
Rich, Obadiah......... 1844—1851
Raymond, Freeborn F. . 1846—1852
Randall, Rev. Geo. M. . 1847—1852
Richardson, John D..... 1847—1855
Robinson, George W. 1848
Reed, Edward.............. 1850
Rice, Alexander H. 1850, 1851
Rankin, Ira P. 1851, 1852
Robbins, Charles........ 1851, 1852
Rand, George C......... 1851—1853

Richardson, Jackson.... 1851—1854
Read, William .... 1853—1854
Richardson, Charles..... 1853, 1854

Snelling, Nath'l G. 1818, .1819; 1824
Savage, James .... 1818—1824
Shurtleff, Benjamin .... 1818—1819
Shattuck, George C. 1819, 1820
Sharp, Rev. Daniel...... 1818, 1819
Snow, Caleb H........ 1821—1823
Spooner, William J. .... 1821—1830
Stevens, Benjamin 1823
Sumner, Bradford............ 1824
Stoddard, Charles ...... 1825—1833
Streeter, Rev. Seb. 1826—1828; 1850
Snelling, George H. .... 1826—1834
Sampson, George A..... 1827—1835
Scudder, Charles ..... 1827—1829
Spooner, John P. ...... 1829—1831
Storer, D. Humphrey .. 1830—1832
Stevens, John 1831
Stimpson, John 1832, 1833
Stebbins, John B. ..... 1832—1842
Savage, George .... 1832—1834
Sumner, Frederic A. ... 1833—1850
Smith, Benjamin 1834
Simpkins, Samuel G. ... 1834—1847
Simonds, Alvan........ 1834—1855
Sweet, Aaron.......... 1837—1841
Stevens, Ebenezer 1837
Sewall, Samuel E............ 1838
Safford, Henry .... 1838—1846
Sargent, Rev. J. T. 1838, 1839
Stedman, Francis D.... 1838—1847
Sayward, James H....... 1838, 1839
Snow, Asa 1839
Sutherland, George, Jr........ 1839
Stearns, Elijah .... 1839—1855
Sargent, Howard 1841
Simonds, Artemas 1840, 1841
Snelling, Enoch H...... 1840—1855
Swallow, Asa.......... 1841—1844
Skinner, Rev. Otis A. .. 1842—1855
Stoddard, Lewis T. 1842, 1843
Stimpson, Frederic H. .. 1842—1849
Stimpson, Charles ..... 1842—1850
Smith, Thomas P........ 1842, 1843
Story, Charles W...... 1843, 1844
Sylvester, Adam............. 1843
Sturtevant, George .... 1844—1853
Spence, John, Jr. ...... 1844—1851
Sanborn, Greenleaf C... 1844—1852
Soule, Richard, Jr. ..... 1846—1848
Smith, Rev. Amos 1846, 1847
Smith, J. V. C........ 1847—1855

Sanford, Philo.....1847; 1853, 1854
Smith, Joseph......... 1847—1853
Stevens, Seriah........ 1847—1852
Sampson, George R. ... 1847—1849
Schmidt, Frederic 1847, 1848
Sawyer, Frederic W.... 1848—1853
Stevens, John A. 1848
Stevens. Benjamin F......... 1850
Stone, Sawyer S. 1850
Stevens, N. C. .... 1850—1855
Snow, Asa B. .... 1850—1852
Sanford, Miles.............. 1850
Sherman, Charles J. F. . 1851—1854
Sweetser, Frederic ..... 1851—1853
Southard, Zibeon ...... 1851—1854
Scudder, Henry A. ... 1851—1854
Sykes, Rev. James H. .. 1852—1854
Stockwell, Stephen N... .1853, 1854
Smith, William E. 1853, 1854
Stackpole, S. A. 1853, 1854
Stephenson, George A. 1853
Shaw, Benjamin S. 1854
Sleeper, Jacob 1854
Smith, Franklin W. 1854

Ticknor, Elisha .... 1818—1822
Thurston, William ..... 1818—1822
Tappan, Lewis .... 1820—1825
Ticknor, George .... 1821—1824
Ticknor, Benjamin 1824, 1825
Taylor, William........ 1821—1838
Tuckerman, Rev. Joseph 1827—1828
Thompson, John .... 1827—1834
Tenney, Samuel .... 1829—1838
Twombly, A. H...1829; 1833—1835
Tilden, Calvin 1831
Thompson, Thomas H... 1832—1838
Ticknor, William D..... 1836—1850
Teed, E. L. 1838
Tolman, James .... 1839—1847
Thompson, Newell A. .. 1842—1847
Tucker, Stephen....... 1844—1850
Turner, Alfred T....... 1847—1852
Thacher, William S. .... 1847—1853
Taylor, Gustavus............. 1848
Tucker, Levi.......... 1849—1851
Townsend, William E... 1848—1855
Tolman, Samuel .... 1848—1855
Turner, Charles A. .... 1849—1855
Thurston, Horace 1849
Thayer, David .... 1851—1854
Thorndike, William H. .. 1851, 1852
Tyler, Charles C. 1853, 1854
Tilton, Stephen, Jr. 1853, 1854
Thaxter, McBean 1853, 1854

Upham, William B..... 1842—1849

Vose, Thomas .... 1833—1836
Vinton, George 1836, 1837

Ware, Rev. Henry ..... 1818—1820
Webster, Redford 1818
Winchell, Rev. J. M. 1818, 1819
Winthrop, Thomas L. .. 1818—1822
Wells, Benjamin T........... 1818
Webb, Nathan .... 1818—1820
West, Benjamin 1818, 1819
Wait, Thomas B........ 1818—1822
Wells, Thomas .... 1820—1830
Wisner, Rev. B. B. .... 1821—1828
Williams, Moses........ 1821—1825
Ware, John............ 1824, 1825
Willis, Horatio M. 1824
Washburn, Calvin...... 1824—1829
Ward, Richard .... 1824—1826
Wiley, Thomas .... 1825—1832
Watts, Francis O....... 1825—1841
Wigglesworth, Edward . 1826—1829
Walker, Charles .... 1828—1835
Whiton, James M. ..... 1832—1842
Williams, Albert....... 1832—1834
Wright, Winslow 1832
Wright, Edmund, Jr......... 1832
Walley, Samuel H., Jr. . 1832—1839
Wait, William S. 1832, 1833
Wells, Rev. E. M. P. 1834, 1835
Whiting, Calvin.............. 1835
Washburn, J. M. 1836, 1837
Wyman, Abraham G.... 1836—1855
Wheeler, A. B. .... 1836—1843
Weston, E., Jr. 1836-1839; 1842, '43
Weeks, William A. .... 1837—1839
Whipple, James K. .... 1837—1841
Wales, Samuel, Jr. 1837; 1847—1849
Wheeler, Samuel ...... 1837—1842
Whitney, Warren J..... 1839—1844
Wait, Richard G. 1840, 1841
Wiley, Henry G........ 1840—1843
Wilder, Volney .... 1840—1847
Wakefield, Enoch H..... 1842, 1843
White, John, Jr. .... 1842—1847
Washburn, Henry S. .. 1842—1847
Watson, Abram A. .... 1842—1855
Wright, Albert J....... 1842—1855
Woart, Rev. John ..... 1844—1851
Wiggin, Charles E...... 1844—1855
Wood, Alexander ...... 1846—1851
Wiswell, D. W......... 1846—1855
Wightman, Joseph M. .. 1846—1855
Wilder, Thomas .... 1846—1855

Williams, Moses B. 1846
White, Joseph F. . . . . . . 1847—1855
Whiting, James. 1847
Wright, Thomas S. . . . . . 1848—1850
Wellington, Hiram 1850
Winkley, Rev. S. H. . . . . 1850—1852
Whipple, Samuel K. 1850
Willett, William 1850

Warren, John A. 1851
Weltch, Samuel 1853, 1854
Wadsworth, Samuel 1853, 1854
Williams, George F. 1853, 1854
Williams, Henry W. 1853, 1854
Winkley, Swain 1854

Young, Joshua 1851, 1852

PRIMARY SCHOOLS.

ANNUAL EXPENDITURES.

Financial Years.	Salaries and Incidental Expenses.	For School-houses.*	No. of Schools.	No. of Pupils.	Total Expenditures.
June 1, 1818, to June, 1819	$3,750 00	....	18	815	$3,750 00
1819—1820	8,000 00	....	20	1,118	8,000 00
1820—1821	8,000 00	....	34	1,666	8,000 00
1821—1822	8,375 00	....	35	1,896	8,375 00
1822—1823	9,028 15	....	37	1,909	9,028 15
1823—1824	10,510 00	....	42	2,142	10,510 00
1824—1825	11,710 00	....	44	2,463	11,710 00
1825—1826	12,581 56	....	48	2,686	12,581 56
1826—1827	13,207 78	....	53	2,938	13,207 78
1827—1828	14,045 91	....	56	3,236	14,045 91
1828—1829	14,286 71	....	57	3,354	14,286 71
1829—1830	14,373 46	....	59	3,583	14,373 46
1830—1831	14,933 46	....	60	3,700	14,933 46
1831—1832	16,491 88	....	62	3,819	16,491 88
1832—1833	16,859 16	....	63	3,927	16,859 16
1833—1834	17,364 70	....	66	3,959	17,364 70
1834—1835	17,833 11	12,380 00	69	4,479	30,213 11
1835—1836	19,403 32	9,646 99	72	4,338	29,050 31
1836—1837	23,976 23	4,831 95	76	4,369	28,818 18
1837—1838	26,787 00	12,623 32	80	5,092	38,710 32
1838—1839	27,824 10	11,872 53	87	5,103	39,696 63
1839—1840	29,905 35	15,609 35	91	5,439	45,514 70
1840—1841	31,388 00	2,452 62	93	5,846	33,840 62
1841—1842	32,924 55	12,457 25	97	6,657	45,381 80
1842—1843	36,200 83	10,210 18	106	7,206	46,411 01
1843—1844	38,814 17	9,926 14	114	7,572	48,740 31
1844—1845	40,197 96	12,502 27	122	7,595	52,700 23
1845—1846	42,028 53	16,570 86	146	8,870	58,599 39
1846—1847	61,887 13	24,592 02	163	9,838	86,479 15
1847—1848	70,127 99	39,290 46	166	10,273	109,418 45
1848—1849	77,166 22	35,923 72	173	10,875	113,089 94
1849—1850	80,146 92	17,756 86	176	11,138	97,903 78
1850—1851	79,648 47	51,010 69	178	11,376	130,659 16
1851—1852	80,746 78	56,221 16	189	11,788	136,967 94
1852—1853	84,739 79	35,823 09	190	11,868	120,562 88
1853—1854	81,881 43	22,121 66	194	11,980	104,003 09
1854—1855	98,764 34	24,163 35	197	12,172	122,927 69
Total	$1,275,911 00	$337,986 47	......	......	$1,613,897 47

*No appropriations were made for School-houses till 1834.

COMPARATIVE TABLE OF THE INTERMEDIATE SCHOOLS, FOR THE HALF YEAR ENDING JANUARY 31, 1854.

District.	No. of the School.	Admitted last six months.	Left last six months.	Now belonging.	Grammar School.			
					Sent to	Fitted for.	Whole No. sent.	Per cent. of School.
East Boston.								
No. 1	4	60	53	60	13	14	27	45
2	4	65	49	68	16	26	42	63
3	2	39	35	61	12	16	28	46
City.								
2	6	50	48	60	15	7	22	36
	9	46	33	63	7	12	19	30
3	7	24	29	76	1	8	9	11
4	7	59	56	56	12	14	26	47
	8	58	50	64	8	14	22	34
5	5	42	36	73	11	9	20	27
	8	29	21	62	8	12	20	32
6	4	67	60	68	25	10	35	51
7	3	51	58	50	20	12	32	64
8 colored	7	20	17	43	5	6	11	25
9	6	46	45	61	15	13	28	46
10	6 (boys)	90	84	61	44	....	44	72
	11 (girls)	55	60	59	35	....	35	60
	14	58	60	63	27	....	27	42
11	6 (boys)	19	20	34	7	10	17	50
	7 (girls)	23	21	44	14	8	22	50
12	5 (boys)	46	37	60	9	7	16	26
13	10	43	25	55	7	10	17	30
14	5 (boys)	25	20	47	9	8	17	38
	8 (girls)	55	46	61	11	10	21	34
15	4 (girls)	29	42	55	19	11	30	54
	6 (boys)	20	22	50	15	15	30	60
16	5	42	48	54	21	12	33	61
	11	64	55	63	17	18	35	55
17	7	57	40	75	17	12	29	38
18	7	47	26	59	5	11	16	27
	9	35	42	60	12	13	25	41
19	0	....	....	....	....	....	....	....
20	5	48	17	58	12	7	19	32
	7	32	20	63	6	4	10	14
Totals	32	1444	1276	1986	455	329	784	....

32 Schools.   1986 Pupils.   Admitted, 1444 } 2720 changes in six months!!
Discharged, 1276 }

*** In nine of the Schools in the above table, but one sex is admitted.

FORM OF TABLE *appended to each Semi-Annual Report of the Primary School Committee.*
TABLE *for the half year ending July 31, 1854.*

Number of the District.	Number of Schools.	No. in Schools at last Report.	Admitted last six months.	Left last six months.	Sent to Grammar Schools.	Now fitted for Gram. Sch'ls.	Now belonging to the Schools.			Average attendance.	Average absence.	Per centage of attendance.	No. who attend to Sew'g.	Of Foreign Parentage.	No. who are 8 y's old & over.	No. who are under 5 years.	No. of Examinations.	No. of Visits.
							Girls.	Boys.	Total.									
East Boston.																		
1	9	551	380	326	64	83	302	290	592	48	13	75	140	331	151	146	55	40
2	7	363	180	225	61	49	142	183	325	36	10	77	....	151	62	62	88	68
3	6	361	188	142	44	63	207	201	408	47	15	76	29	268	111	61	33	86
City.																		
2	9	516	240	220	63	63	251	285	536	47	9	82	100	315	150	83	64	197
3	9	562	169	147	55	51	271	313	584	47	15	76	108	380	167	87	46	116
4	8	506	207	192	57	70	241	293	534	54	11	83	32	414	188	96	59	62
5	8	567	216	283	70	67	278	281	559	52	16	75	84	463	178	89	100	200
6	10	569	240	252	67	66	255	287	542	42	10	76	24	179	111	76	124	206
7	7	405	148	160	52	54	180	217	397	43	10	77	90	255	75	64	89	88
8	7	421	133	157	58	62	199	217	416	46	14	78	136	104	44	61	52	78
9	9	521	149	184	71	69	220	267	487	41	11	78	88	170	108	68	71	130
10	15	943	491	444	155	91	454	536	990	56	8	86.5	184	982	304	126	127	369
11	8	409	168	146	48	47	185	245	430	43	8	82.5	95	353	121	69	50	155
12	8	407	253	195	46	46	197	268	465	49	9	84	13	378	136	72	90	237
13	9	529	184	173	56	69	255	284	539	47	10	81	32	104	105	76	169	230
14	8	457	159	161	41	51	220	236	456	43	12	77	189	215	125	75	44	275
15	8	476	224	191	61	64	229	253	482	43	12	77	38	191	137	68	102	141
16	12	739	398	340	111	101	382	408	790	50	12	80	38	608	185	142	140	120
17	12	722	281	213	90	93	386	408	787	47	12	78	113	333	155	136	130	227
18	9	598	252	220	55	52	297	332	629	53	11	82	193	317	170	99	64	184
19	9	601	250	226	68	60	304	320	624	54	12	81	8	399	152	79	90	187
20	10	589	235	226	53	58	291	309	600	46	13	78	30	500	217	68	97	239
Totals	197	11804	4945	4763	1446	1429	5746	6426	12172	1034	253	1723	1762	7410	3152	1903	1864	3635
Average ...	....	.....	....	....	....	....	....	....	64	47	11½	80	....	....	....	....	9	18¼